GRANNY D

Villard / New York

GRANNY D

Walking Across America
in My Ninetieth Year

Foreword by Bill Moyers

Doris Haddock
with Dennis Burke

917.3049
Had

VILLARD BOOKS is a registered trademark of Random House, Inc.
Colophon is a trademark of Random House, Inc.

Library of Congress Cataloging-in-Publication Data
Haddock, Doris.
Granny D: walking across America in my ninetieth year /
Doris Haddock with Dennis Burke.
p.   cm
ISBN 0-375-50539-3
1. Haddock, Doris—Journeys.   2. Campaign funds—United States.
3. Women political activists—United States—Biography.   4. Political
activists—United States—Biography.   I. Burke, Dennis.   II. Title.

CT275.H235 A3 2001
917.304'929—dc21   00-050259

Villard Books website address: www.villard.com

Printed in the United States of America on acid-free paper

2 4 6 8 9 7 5 3

First Edition

BOOK DESIGN BY MERCEDES EVERETT

Dear friends along the road:
Thank you for the part you played in
making my trek possible.
If this book were a thank-you letter,
it would require ten volumes
to mention every kindness.
And a special thanks to Bonnie Riley,
who said, "Well, Doris, what are you going to
do about it?"

—Doris

Acknowledgments

I would like to thank the thousands of people who posted messages to the public website GrannyD.com, whose comments greatly encouraged Doris on her hardest days, and whose lively thoughts have improved these pages. My greatest thanks must be reserved for Doris, who sat down for two hours each evening to write down her day's adventures. This she did after her younger walking companions had long since collapsed in total exhaustion for the night. Those notes became this book. Her resolution to write every night, and her walking itself, which she continued despite any pain or turn of weather, were lessons in character and patriotism for all of us who met her and fell in love.

—*Dennis Burke*

Foreword

by Bill Moyers

The soul of a citizen shines through these pages.

Doris Haddock set out to walk across America to protest the betrayal of democracy by money in politics. That mission she accomplished; no one can doubt the source of her intense, disciplined outrage. But understatement is the gift of this book, and there are so many interwoven stories and anecdotes about life, love, and friendship, you almost forget that this is the tale of a ninety-year-old woman who walked ten miles every day for a cause she believed in. Because she never dwells on the pain or discomfort, you sometimes fail to appreciate the wonder of what she did. Not only did she walk with blistered feet and bruised muscles, she did so in some of the harshest environments in our land.

To be sure, the novelty of a nonagenarian innocently protesting corruption by walking at a snail's pace across this nation lights up all sorts of meters for newspaper editors and broadcast producers. For most of us, it is this simplified "Granny D" that we have gotten to know—secondhand, filtered through the media.

But then you pick up her book, read her speeches, and see the trials through which she passed. This is no "innocent" grandmother naively protesting a cause because she misses the good old days. Granny D is a seasoned activist, an eloquent speaker and writer, and an acute observer of the world around us. "Who I am is an old reformer," she told a recent gathering of business executives.

"I have been involved in reform fights through most of my adult life, but I have saved the most important for last—the fight to establish true political democracy in this country."

About her trip she had her doubts. "Chasing my hat again through cacti, the idea of walking across the United States at my age seemed a less than perfect idea. I was being foolish; the country is too big for an old New Hampshire woman with arthritis and emphysema and parched lips and a splintered hat." But since her activist days in the 1960s, she had watched American politics change. Back then, "we were able to appeal to the sense of fair play of U.S. senators and representatives. They listened to our appeal and made a decision they thought best. They did not have to consult with their campaign contributors, nor did they care that we had not given money to them." It was not a perfect world, "but the back-room scandals we heard about then, where cash was traded for votes, are now the front-room norm. There is no room for regular citizens and there is no shame." With other members of the "Tuesday Morning Academy"—a women's group in New Hampshire—she had probed the issue of money and politics for several years. Now she decided to walk and talk about "how our democracy is being purchased from under us."

At first the national media paid little attention, dismissing her as an eccentric and her journey as a stunt. But no sooner had she started collecting petition signatures on a Pacific beach, before heading east toward the Mojave desert, than ordinary people perked up and paid attention, moved by what this cheerful, straight-talking Yankee was saying.

It was the simple truth:

If money is speech, then those with more money have more speech, and that idea is antithetical to a democracy that cherishes political fairness. It makes us no longer equal citizens.

A flood of special interest money has carried away our representatives, and all that is left of them—at least for those of us who do not write $100,000 checks—are the shadows of their cardboard cutouts.

It is said that democracy is not something we have, but something we do. But right now, we cannot do it because we cannot speak. We are shouted down by the bullhorns of big money. It is money with no manners for democracy, and it must be escorted from the room.

The hundreds of thousands of our dead, buried in rows upon rows in our national cemeteries, sacrificed their lives for the democracy of a free people, not for what we have today. It is up to each of us to see that these boys and girls did not die in vain. That's just how serious this message is.

On and on she walked and talked—through the blowing sands of Arizona, past the reddish hills of New Mexico, up the seven-mile steep incline through a southernmost pass of the Rocky Mountains toward the vast plains of West Texas. Like tom-toms, local newspapers and radio stations signaled her advance. Cars began honking, thumbs went up. Children from their playground monkey bars chanted: "Gran-ny! Gran-ny!" Frat boys knelt around her on a street corner in Tucson and, singing, made her a Sweetheart of Sigma Chi. Swarthy tattooed bikers on their Harley-Davidsons offered her protection on the highways. Strangers took her in, providing food, shelter, and encouragement. "I had found so many new friends along the road," she writes, "and they had entrusted me with so much of their hearts, that I was not feeling the least bit alone anymore." She was even greeted in Parker, Arizona, by the Marine Corps Marching Band! How to explain it all? "When you fully dedicate yourself to a good mission," she writes, "the floodgates of heaven open up for you. If you can make a creative crack in the crust of the world's deadly abstractions, the divine will rush up, bringing great bounty with it."

That bounty still did not include the national media. ABC's *Good Morning, America* scheduled a segment with her but scrubbed it at the last minute in favor of a feature on wedding dresses. Fox Network News said they wanted to report on her arrival in Tombstone, then canceled. The mayor, city council, and a group of citizens turned out anyway, in Old West garb, but

Doris Haddock had been reminded what it is to be "a soft-news story in a hard-news world."

Nonetheless, her message, anything but soft, took hold in increasing numbers of hearts and minds. People lined up to listen, ask questions, and volunteer their own stories of political abandonment. They told of hitting the wall that connects HMOs and drug companies, "all in cahoots with crooked politicians." They talked of corporations using their overpowering capital and political influence to annihilate small businesses, "turning our towns into their colonies." They described writing urgent petitions to their representatives in Washington only to receive form letters in return. At night, Granny D filled her journal with their stories.

Then, one day, early in her Texas walking, *The New York Times* came calling. Of the visit she writes, "You rather feel like a teenager whose parents have just come home early—you check your buttons and hope everything is in its proper place." In a Mexican restaurant she bared her heart to reporter Frank Bruni, "telling him my sappy notions of what self-government must be if we are to be a free people. He nodded, raised his eyebrows from time to time, glanced out the window, and otherwise finished his enchilada as I finished mine." The story he wrote took her seriously, and almost overnight the other news organizations—"and the Washington crowd"—could scoff no more. "I read about Granny D in *The New York Times* today," wrote a woman from Sacramento. "She's awesome. I've pasted the article in front of my office door to let others know about it." From Albuquerque: "I am confined to my bed but my thoughts and prayers go to Granny D." From Somerville, New Jersey: "More power to you, Granny D. You really are an inspiration to all of us young'ns— I'm 72—to clean up the worst Congress and White House money can buy." From Vass, North Carolina: "Granny, I am a 70-year-old crippled with arthritis, but in my mind I am marching along with you. I sent a note to my senators and congressmen with the comment that you speak for all of us."

The Reform Party invited her to speak at its national convention. She delivered a memorable speech covered at length by

National Public Radio and carried in full by C-SPAN. Now the crowds grew larger along the road. Strangers flew from distant parts to walk with her. The media flocked alongside—"a woman reporter from Tokyo, Australian cameramen filming for the Discovery Travel Channel, German television, *The Boston Globe*, and *The Christian Science Monitor* . . . Just up ahead, *Good Morning, America*, Diane Rehm, *ABC World News Tonight*, NBC *Nightly Magazine*, *George* magazine." There was "a nightmarish quality to much of this," she writes. "I had a clear idea that Doris Haddock must not get too wrapped up in this Granny D person. I was just me, taking steps across America instead of taking steps around my garden."

In Little Rock, she stopped at Central High School, scene of one of the first great struggles for school integration, and spoke at the First Missionary Baptist Church, where Martin Luther King, Jr., once preached; at first the congregation eyed her suspiciously, but they ended up on their feet, cheering. In the Mississippi Delta, a black police chief sat her down in his office to talk about young people. In Memphis, she traced King's last march and made a speech worthy of him, with the audience weeping and clapping. In Louisville, she entered the lion's den—the office of the most ardent apologist for legalized bribery in the United States Senate, Mitch McConnell—and "with a grandmother's love" asked him to change his ways (he hasn't). In Cumberland, Maryland, near the log cabin that was Washington's headquarters during the Whiskey Rebellion, she celebrated her ninetieth anniversary with a large crowd escorting her through town, carrying flags and singing "This Land Is Your Land."

And in Washington, D.C., after a Scottish bagpiper led her past the Lincoln and Washington memorials, down K Street's Lobbyist Row to the Capitol, Granny D made one more speech.

> Along my three thousand miles through the heart of America, did I meet anyone who thought that their voice as an equal citizen now counts for much in the corrupt halls of Washington? No, I did not. Did I meet anyone who felt anger or pain over this? I did indeed, and I watched them shake with rage

sometimes when they spoke, and I saw tears well up in their eyes. The people I met along my way have given me messages to deliver here. The messages are many, written with old and young hands of every color, and yet the messages are the same. They are this: "Shame on you, senators and congressmen, who have turned the headquarters of a great and self-governing people into a bawdyhouse. The time for this shame is ending. The American people see it and have decided against it. Our brooms are ballots, and we come a-sweeping."

After that speech Granny D went home to New Hampshire. Three months later she returned to Washington and got herself arrested—for reading the Declaration of Independence in a calm voice in the rotunda of the Capitol, "to make the point that we must declare our independence from campaign corruption."

Did America hear? Judging by the returns of the 2000 election, we might say no. It was by far the most expensive election in our history, a quantum leap of nearly 50 percent from the scandalously costly election of 1996. Incumbents returned to Congress on enormous waves of cash provided by people who have now lined up for their payback through tax breaks, loopholes, subsidies, and other favors. Both presidential candidates owed their success to Big Money; Governor George W. Bush collected more than $100 million for his primary campaign alone. Hundreds of millions of dollars were spent on the presidential and congressional races by outside groups who do not disclose their donors or spending, leaving us in the dark as to the identities of those who now own the Congress and regulatory agencies.

So did Doris Haddock walk across America for nothing? Not at all. John McCain and Bill Bradley were looking over her shoulder, reading her speeches, and watching how she succeeded in making campaign finance reform an emotional and patriotic issue with many Americans. When Albert Gore finally signed on to campaign finance reform, his speech cited McCain, Bradley—and Doris Haddock. When the Democrats met in Los Angeles in the summer of 2000, Granny D attended the "Shadow Convention" that gathered outside the arena to challenge, among other things, the power of Big Money over politics. One morning she sat down with friends and allies to have a cup of coffee in the old Figureoa Hotel. Just outside the door thousands of people were protesting, and a common theme running through all the messages was campaign finance reform. A leading activist turned to Granny D and told her that much of the new energy in the movement would not have happened without her walk across the country. She had brought together right and left, white and black, old and young. "It is clear to me," she writes in this book, " that people feel oppressed by Big Money politicians, and they take glee in any chance for a small rebellion." Now, "the fight between the human scale and giant scale, left unresolved by the Progressive Era, is returning for some kind of epic confrontation. Campaign finance reform is a part of it."

So it must be. The rich have every right to buy more cars, more homes, more clothes, more vacations, and more gizmos than anyone else; they do not have the right to buy more democracy. Either we end the arms race of money in politics, or our children and grandchildren will grow up in a society where their civic worth is determined by their net worth; democracy will fade into fiction. What can we do? Sometimes, says Doris Haddock, "all you can do is put your body in front of a problem and stand there as a witness to it." Lacking political leaders of sufficient mettle "to repair the problem," she says, "we shall have to repair it somehow ourselves, in the streets."

When that day comes, the tracks to follow will be the footprints of Doris Haddock. Granny D.

Contents

Acknowledgments   vii

Foreword by Bill Moyers   ix

Book I

Desert Overture   3

My Crazy Idea   6

Getting in Shape   11

Holiday Farewell   14

On the Beach   15

A Man Magnet   21

The Mojave   22

The Colorado River   31

Salome, but Not Dancing   34

Dusting Myself Off   42

A Senator in Hiding   46

The Reservation   48

Fraternity Boys and Bikers in Tucson   57

Tombstone   64

Tail Winds in New Mexico   67

Skinny-dipping and Remembering Dundee   69

Under the Crescent Moon   76

Nick   78

Book II

Coming Alive   83

Wild Texas   85

Grass for Snow   88

The Big Enchilada   93

A Land Waiting for Rain   95

Cloudsplitters   99

The Long X Ranch   104

The Grasshopper Queens   108

Purple Glass   114
Center of the World   118
A Texas Do-Si-Do   121
Roadside Biology   125
Through the Looking Glass   128
Our Traveling Circus   133
The Jeffersonian Hi   136
Thunder and Rain   141

Book III

Beyond Hope   149
Dividing Lines   156
Little Rock   170
I Mistreat Ken   172
Money in Politics Is Not a Bloodless Issue   175
The Greasy Limpopo   178
The Boys   181
I Am a Person   183
Growing Up   194
Into the Hard World   199
Meaningful Things   202
Pretty Old for a Damsel   204
Get Up and Walk   205
Sneaking into Washington   207
Kentucky   209
Please Come to Boston   215
Across the Ohio   217
Alaska   220
A Familiar Old Face Returns   225
Along the C&O   237
A Few Days to Washington   241
The Evening and Next Day   251
Back Home and Onward   254

Epilogue   259
Appendix:
    Selected Speeches of Doris Haddock   262

BOOK I

Desert Overture

To begin a day's walk in California's Mojave Desert is like stepping into a child's drawing: Odd, Dr. Seuss–style cacti interrupt a dot pattern of endlessly repeating gray bushes; the sky is crayoned a solid, royal blue with a brilliant sun; layers of purple hills extend in endless vistas to the next valley and next again. There are no sounds but the mesquite-scented breezes whishing lightly across the brittlebush and the occasional flinch of some tiny, prehistoric creature under dry sticks a few paces ahead.

After I had walked a hundred miles of the Mojave through pleasant days and bitter cold nights, the winds began to rise. Dust blew across the highway and whipped around, more than once sending me staggering. It grabbed my straw hat repeatedly and sent it wheeling across the highway. It was my late friend Elizabeth's poor old garden hat, and it was not to last much longer— nor were my old bones, I thought.

Even at its harshest, the desert is a meditation, where the mechanisms of politics and oppression seem distant and otherworldly. One can consider things more creatively at such a distance. And old age is no shame in the desert: Save for my walking companion, I saw no creature less wrinkled than myself.

I am here: That is the sole fact from which, in the desert, all distractions fall away. The desert teases with the idea that spiritual enlightenment, elsewhere requiring a lifetime of discipline, might happen almost effortlessly here. This tease is not malicious, I think, but the natural warp of things in the neighborhood of great truths. Indeed, most of our great spiritual stories begin in the desert, where there is less to misdirect our attention from the fact of our mortality and our immortality.

I begin my story in the desert not to mimic the great stories of our culture, but because it is where my adventure began. I pray that I may be able to describe, in ways that will be useful or interesting to you, what I learned along my way. If you are not much interested in campaign finance reform—the reason for my protest walk—do not worry: I will not pester you too much about it as we journey together between these covers. You will not need imaginary earplugs I hope, just a good imaginary hat.

*   *   *

I was still something of a desperado in those first months of the walk—roaming over the dry and blank space remaining at the end of a life. Or was it the lull between acts? Who can ever know at such times? There is an urge to just walk into the desert, away from the road, and be done with it. There is also an urge to have some ice cream with chocolate sauce. Life is what we patch together between those competing desires.

So I walked and remembered my late husband, Jim, who had died six years earlier, though the open place that he left in my heart was still fresh. And I walked and remembered my best friend, Elizabeth, who had died just the year before after a long and difficult illness—as had Jim. I replayed over and over our times together as I trudged along. If my eyes were moist when I thought about the long days and nights of their deaths, the desert wind would dry them. I had been quite depressed since their deaths, and this was finally my chance to walk out my memories and my grief. The landscape was right for it. The deteriorations of a lifetime are shown in fast motion in the desert: The Mojave wind and cacti and my sweat were making a mess of Elizabeth's old hat now, and the desert sun had faded its band before my eyes.

My thin and otherwise quiet walking companion, thirty-two-year-old Doug Vance, was clanging sharply in the wind—his dangling canteens and belt-loop supplies spinning like mad wind bells. He took hold of my arm at times to steady me, though he was no Plymouth Rock himself. The gusts slapped around the CAMPAIGN FINANCE REFORM sign on his backpack and sent his bamboo Chinese hat flying back to choke him with its chin string. Passing trucks added to the hot whirlwinds of grit and roadside litter. We had been lucky with the wind and temperature through most of the Mojave, but the final miles approaching the Colorado River and Arizona were very difficult. I had the presence of mind to realize, Dear God, I'm indeed out here doing this!

Seconds later, chasing my hat again through cacti, the idea of walking across the United States at my age seemed a less than perfect idea. I was being foolish: The country is too big for an old New Hampshire woman with a bad back and arthritis and emphysema and parched lips and a splintered hat. These were not so much my own thoughts but doubts planted in me by others. I was trying to resist them, but the harshness of the desert was eroding my own propped-up notion of my abilities. I would remind myself that I had endlessly tramped the mountains of New Hampshire as a young woman and I was still strong enough to cross-country ski and hike with a heavy pack. Anyway, it would be better to die out here, spending myself in a meaningful pursuit, than at home in my old chair—this I repeated to myself a thousand times. So many people, even in my own family, had said I wouldn't get fifty miles. I would just think of that and let myself get a little angry. That would give me a boost.

Approaching the hills along the Colorado River, the mountains of Arizona visible through the dust storm ahead, I realized that I had indeed crossed all of California. That was something. I had come 260 miles from Pasadena. And Sunday, across the river, would be my eighty-ninth birthday—if I lived to see the end of this blowing dust and sand.

In that dust ahead was an old, blue-green van that would be our water oasis and evening camp through the desert.

After mile number eight each day, I would cross the highway and go to the van for a cold drink and a little nap before my final two miles. Curling up in the tight space, I would fall asleep to old memories of the great, overcrowded Volkswagen trip to Alaska in 1960 to stop hydrogen bomb tests that would have destroyed a native village. I also remembered camping trips with my sister when we were Girl Scouts in 1920, and great hikes taken later as a young bride and mother on the mountain trails of New England.

While I waited to cross the Mojave highway for my eight-mile rest, motorists, when there were any, would speed by and give me a curious stare. I must have looked like the old woman of the desert. I remember staring into the eyes of one elderly woman passenger as she looked me over. She must have been wondering about me as I have wondered about other people seen walking along remote highways.

My Crazy Idea

Mother, what are you thinking about?" my son, Jim, said as we were driving toward Florida a year earlier. It was February 1998. I was looking in the side mirror at an old man beside the road— we had just sped past him. My son was headed for a three-week camping trip in the Everglades and had agreed to drop me off at my sister Vivian's house in Pompano Beach. I had just returned from my best friend Elizabeth's funeral.

The old man on the road, wearing a black watch cap and a full-length mackintosh, leaned against his cane and blew his nose with his bare fingers. He was miles and miles from any town or house, carrying only a paper bag. "What's with the old man, do you suppose—way out here?" I said.

"Looks like he's on the road again, Mother," Jim replied.

We talked for a few miles about Jack Kerouac's life and sang a few bars of Willie Nelson's song. That sounds cheery, but I was quite melancholy.

This old man mesmerized me. His image resonated with

something very deep. Now that Elizabeth and my husband no longer needed me, I had been worrying about how I might use what remained of my own time. As we drove further, there seemed to be some connection with this man on the road and that slow-boiling question.

I had been on the road with my husband nearly forty years earlier when we worked to stop the Alaska bombs. This old man was perhaps some ghost of those days, still out there like a part of me. He was calling, as might my Jim be calling. That is rather what it felt like.

Something else had also been eating at me: In the 1960s during the Alaska project, we were able to appeal to the sense of fair play of U.S. senators and representatives. They listened to our appeal and made a decision they thought best. They did not have to consult with their campaign contributors, nor did they care that we had not given money to them. I felt a real sense of belonging as an American back then, in the early sixties. There was a sense that we were adults who respected each other and listened to each other. I don't mean to overidealize it, for politics is often a dirty business underneath. But the backroom scandals we heard about back then, where cash was traded for votes, are now the front room norm. There is no room for regular citizens in that front room, and there is no shame.

I had been watching the change. During my husband's final years, in the early nineties, I had worked hard and successfully to bring some modest respite services to the families in our area who were caring for Alzheimer's patients. The logic of these programs was obvious, yet our only way of getting funding was to raise money privately, which we did. From what I was hearing in the community, and from my own experience fighting the interstate highway system, which had threatened to destroy our little town of Dublin, New Hampshire, congressmen were no longer interested in what some person or village might need if they were not major campaign donors. For the first time in my life I felt politically powerless—something no American should ever feel. It was like living in some other country.

My women friends in our Tuesday Morning Academy, which

is a little study group in New Hampshire, had looked at the campaign finance situation in detail over the previous few years. We had become quite knowledgeable about it, just as we had studied many other issues.

Our group had its origin in 1984, when the Extension Service canceled an adult study class for lack of students. Nineteen of us—mostly retired—were nevertheless set on the idea of learning something new, so we accepted the leadership of Bonnie Riley, a retired teacher whose passions are poetry, drama, and history. She is tall, blue-eyed, and as dignified as a queen, with her light hair fixed in a French twist. She loves dance and in fact studied as a dancer under Isadora Duncan's sister in prewar Germany. She taught school in Africa and has had many fine adventures. Now, as a volunteer, she teaches Shakespeare two days a week to the men in a New Hampshire prison, who love her above all other human beings. Her father was a brilliant man—a Pittsburgh steelworker who labored among the sparks of the Bessemer process by day and poured out the scintillating ideas of our civilization before his daughter by night. Those sparks remain in her eyes, and she passes her father's love of learning on to her friends and students.

At her invitation, we began meeting at her house in Francestown. We continue there today after fifteen years—occasionally picking up a new student and burying an old. Bonnie decides what we will study next, as she has a good radar for issues and knows well our interests and gaps. A new subject always begins with a provocative book on a good topic. We studied China in great detail for a full year and then the Middle East. We never stop with just the book: We find related books and articles and we each make reports. Our Tuesday meetings begin around 8:30 A.M. with some ballet exercises to get the blood moving and our brains in gear. We hold our class in her living room until noon.

We are good followers because Bonnie is a good leader—we trust her because her commitment to us is unselfish, skillful, and generous. It is easy to be a good follower when you have unselfish and competent leaders.

When Bonnie's husband leaves town from time to time for a conference, we ladies have a night out. During one of these evenings—on the same day when the newspaper reported the Senate's failure to pass Senators John McCain and Russ Feingold's campaign finance reform bill—I said, "I am terribly distressed about what is happening to our government. It seems to me that the rich are taking over and that you can't get elected unless you have a million dollars!"

Bonnie, the wonderful leader, said, "Well, Doris, what are you going to do about it?"

"Me? For heaven's sake, what can I do?"

"Well, what *can* you do?"

So I thought it over and remembered what Jim and I did during the Alaska campaign in the sixties. At the next meeting of the Tuesday Academy, I had a plan ready.

"We can make up a petition and send it out to all our relatives and friends throughout the whole fifty states. When we get them back, we will send them to our senators and ask for a meeting to discuss what should be done. What do you think, girls?"

I was still naive enough to think that today's senators and congressmen care what people think and would even look at our petition. Times had changed more than I realized, and politics had become far more "hardball." But we hadn't fully learned that lesson yet, so the ladies agreed to my plan. It took us two years, but we organized tens of thousands of petitions demanding campaign finance reform. We each sent them to our two senators and waited for replies.

What I got back from one of my senators was a form letter quite like the letters senators in other states were sending to others of us, saying that spending money was a form of political speech protected by the Constitution. My other senator didn't respond at all, and when I contacted him he said he never received the petitions. I sent him fresh copies of all of them. Again no response.

I had spent many rainy afternoons standing in parking lots around New Hampshire to talk about campaign reform and get those signatures. The form letter response and total refusal to look seriously at reform sickened me and embarrassed me in front of my friends. I was an old Yankee accustomed to calling up her congressman and getting things moving. To not have proper representation! It was deeply disturbing. That wonderful feeling of belonging, of being a valued participant, was jerked away. I fully understood: I was no longer a village elder at the council fire. Those places were reserved for wealthy campaign contributors. I was a woman scorned.

This was part of the despair I was suffering as I traveled with my son down to Florida. I was in quite a deep pit of it.

A few minutes after I saw the old man on the road, it occurred to me that I should go on the road for my reform issue. A silly idea, but how else might I better spend my remaining days? Think of the adventure it would be! How my late husband, that dear old reformer, would surely cheer me from the other side! It would be a memorial walk dedicated to my love for him and for Elizabeth.

I looked at my son as he drove us along—tough in his Greek fisherman's hat and his scruffy brown and gray beard. I knew I was about to change our lives when I spoke.

"I would like to walk all the way across the United States for campaign finance reform," I said to him. I explained that I would talk to people along the way about how our democracy is being bought out from under us. I would round up some votes for reform in Congress. Perhaps I could help create a modest groundswell to demand action.

Poor Jim. Here is a sixty-four-year-old man driving with his wheezing, eighty-eight-year-old, arthritic mother, and she says something like that. If you would like to know what a remarkable man Jim is, listen to his response.

First of all, of course, he said, "Oh, boy." That was a natural reaction, along with the quick, severe stare through his eyebrows. But he didn't dismiss me. He thought about it for a few miles. He knows who I am, what I have done in life. He understands that people don't change much as they age—the book cover gets tattered, but our defining stories remain unchanged and our personalities only intensify. Of course, we might become a little batty, and a son must consider every possibility. So he silently drove and thought.

If you care to look at him for a moment while he drives, let me tell you that he is not very tall but stocky and strong-looking. He could be a dock worker. He has had just enough troubles in life to make him extremely loyal to his friends and very sensitive to their needs. He used to run a school for the developmentally disabled—he built it from a church basement group of 15 children to a major school of 125 students. It was honored as a national model by Eunice Shriver. So he is quite good at looking for the special genius in each person and focusing on that instead of the negatives. He is fearless in doing the right thing, even when it costs him dearly, as it sometimes has. He shares his own problems very openly, so that he can help others find the help they need.

He snacks continuously as he drives, as you can see in your imagination. A large jar of peanuts will do, if you are trying to think up something for him to have. He can drive a car sideways down an icy road just to give you a more interesting view and a good scare. He can fix or build most anything. His wife, Libby, is the love of his life, and they taunt each other most good-humoredly. Jim is about five-eight, quite like my father, down to the blue eyes and sandy hair. And like his grandfather, he is reserved with a gentle manner, always looking a bit amused at what is going on around him—seeing everything but keeping it to himself. When he speaks, it is usually with a sense of humor and kindness. So, you see, he is a good fellow, and I had placed my new dream in good hands.

Getting in Shape

Jim dropped me off at my sister Vivian's, telling her my idea. Vivian began to cry. My poor sister has watched me get into all sorts of trouble. She stopped sobbing and repaired her eyes and her composure to address me. I squared myself in the chair to hear it.

"Well, I don't approve, you know, but we could lay out about a two-mile course around our park, so you could practice."

She clearly had decided to make the best of things. So had Jim. Before he left for the Everglades, he sat me down and said that he would help me with my adventure if I would master several challenges.

First, I must be able to hike ten miles—day in and day out—with a twenty-five-pound backpack. Second, I must be able to sleep on the hard ground in a sleeping bag without crying about it. Third, I must be willing and able to thumb a ride, for there might come a time, Jim said, when I would wake up and want to get home from the middle of nowhere. Finally, he said, I would need a detailed plan for crossing the country, mapped out, with people identified all along the way who would help me.

When you get to a certain age, your children become like your parents. Jim was trying to be a very fine parent in his constructive approach.

Mr. Plan-Ahead called two weeks later when he ran out of supplies and emerged from the Everglades to go shopping. Over the phone—a twinge of New Hampshire amusement in his voice—he asked how my project was coming along. I was able to report that I was walking every day and was now, in fact, doing ten miles.

In the space of that brief conversation his attitude changed. The amusement vanished. Remarkably, he suggested that I hitchhike up to visit my friends in Frostproof, 180 miles north in central Florida. I agreed to do so and asked him to pick me up there in a week on his way back to New Hampshire. I'm sure he worried about me as he suggested this, but we have always tried to respect each other's serious intentions. During that phone call, he had decided to become my coach in earnest.

As it happened, my friends, the Foxes of Frostproof, would not hear of my hitchhiking anywhere. Out of friendship, I let them talk me into taking the bus to their home. But during my visit there, Mary Alice told me about the life and travels of Mildred Normand, who walked seven times across the United States between 1948 and 1958, speaking along the way about the need for peace in our hearts. Her "walking" name was Peace Pilgrim. Her plan was always to walk until given shelter and to fast until given food—a simple travel plan that immediately appealed to me. She began her trans-America treks by walking in the Rose Bowl Parade in Pasadena and not stopping until she reached the Atlantic.

Back home in Dublin, New Hampshire, which snuggles next to Peterborough, west of Manchester, I began walking my ten miles with a heavy backpack. I am already a little stooped over, which the pack didn't help, but it was manageable. There are lovely roads and hills in my town, and I became something of a constant fixture upon them. Through all of 1998 I walked and walked, probably about eight hundred miles in all, wearing out one good pair of hiking shoes.

I practiced sleeping on the ground, especially in the spring weather. I mapped out my cross-country trek with the help of the auto club. A geology professor revised it for me, routing me away from cold country and steep climbs. In July, I mailed a thousand letters of introduction to police chiefs and churches along my route, plus newspaper offices and radio and television stations.

In the autumn of 1998, after all my hard tramping around my town, and even once walking and hitchhiking sixty miles to hear presidential candidate Bill Bradley speak (it was a good speech, but perhaps only about ten miles' worth), I felt that I was ready. I told my son that it was now or never.

Most good sons would, at this point, think up some additional Herculean labors or sit down and say that this would not do, and Mother must realize that she is eighty-eight and the world is a dangerous place. But Jim is Jim, and he made airline arrangements to Los Angeles, where I might begin.

Holiday Farewell

Before we left the East Coast, I celebrated Christmas in New York City with my three grandsons—Joseph, Larry, and Raphael—and my great grandchildren—Beatrix, Justine, and the twins William and James. It was a beautiful gathering, and I hoped I would survive my adventure to see them all the next year.

In case you are interested, grandsons Larry and Raphael are into investment banking of some kind, and Joseph manages websites for companies. He put together a website for my walk.

My daughter, Betty Lorentz, is a psychologist, which has always come in handy in our family. She is married to David, an internal medicine doctor, and they live in Chevy Chase, near Washington, D.C. My son, Jim, has an office machine service business in New Hampshire. Believe it or not, there are whole companies devoted to helping other companies tape their shipping boxes closed, and Jim's company is one of them.

My grandchildren were quite doubtful about my trip. I think there was some joking and wagering about how many days I would last on the road. This was frustrating to me, but not so disheartening as to put me off the trip. It is always hard when one is not taken seriously. Frankly, the skepticism may have helped, as nothing works better for me than a contest. I like to compete, even if it is against people's expectations, and I do not favor losing.

Betty and David sent me a cellular phone to use in case of trouble. When reporters started calling many times each day, the phone bills became quite a shock to David. Thank goodness he has a good heart and a good medical practice.

In the end, the whole family supported the idea. Just the same, I thought I had better adopt a road name to prevent any family embarrassment. A dear young friend, Caitlin Thomas—a surrogate grandchild, really—had always called me Granny D. So that was that.

On the day after Christmas, 1998, I flew to Los Angeles. I had a window seat and watched, for five hours, the expanse of America sliding below me. It seemed that I would have a very long walk home, and the warnings and eye-rolling of my family members seemed more understandable. But all I needed to worry about was each next step, I assured myself.

I spent most of the time in the air worrying whether I had brought the right things and had made sufficient preparations. I had packed all the supplies I thought might be useful, and I had announced my plans to the press. My coverage began in the columns of Mr. Rousimere in *The Keene Sentinel* back home. From there, *USA Today* got wind of my trek. They have a one-paragraph summary of the news from each state—I was New Hampshire one morning. The little article prompted a number of radio interviews from around the country. One of the people who tuned in one day was the eighty-four-year-old secretary of state of West Virginia, Ken Hechler, who started packing his old kit bag and would become an indispensable part of my experience.

I flew alone, with Jim and Libby coming behind me. I was met at the airport by Lisa Pompelli, the beautiful artist daughter of Libby's cousin. In Lisa's home and studio I was surrounded by her exquisite watercolors. I was pulled into her paintings of green vegetables of the cabbage family—so fresh and clean and so very alive. It was the perfect transition from my world of real greenery to Los Angeles, where life exists more in its depiction.

On the Beach

The next day, Jim and Libby arrived. While they went to rent a car, I began my signature-gathering work on the sidewalk along the Santa Monica beach. I wanted to get petitions signed all along my journey, and here was a good place to begin. I knew signatures didn't count for much in Washington anymore, but it was a good way to interact with people and explain the issue. And it was nice, in the end, to have the names of a few thousand people who were willing to add their voices to mine.

In Santa Monica, I took off my shoes and waded into the Pacific surf to have a private, spiritual beginning to my trek. Then I took position on the beach sidewalk. It was early morning, but there were already hundreds of people relaxing and playing in the sun. Young people on bicycles and skateboards whisked by, not even glancing at me or my petition. I mumbled at them, but they had seen old people mumbling on the sidewalk before.

A mother and daughter were doing their stretching exercises nearby, preparing for their morning jog. The mother, a beautiful woman with flowing blond hair, watched my repeated failures. She came over.

"I'm interested in signing, if you'll tell me your definition of campaign finance reform," she said.

I told her that ideas and character ought to count for more in an election than how much money one can raise. I told her that corporations were buying America's public officials wholesale by funding their campaigns. She decided that was good enough and signed. Then she asked if she could give me some advice, and I agreed.

"Well, I'm new here. I just moved here from Massachusetts to be closer to my daughter. We're both flight attendants. So, I didn't know if this was some local problem you were talking about, which I wouldn't get involved in unless I knew more about it. If you would just add the word 'national'—just say 'national campaign finance reform'—I think people would know what you're talking about."

The extra word worked like magic. A few people stopped to sign. The woman from Massachusetts became my barker: "This woman is walking across the United States for national campaign finance reform! Support her amazing effort by signing her petition!"

We worked that sidewalk for two hours, and I collected forty signatures. Lessons learned: You have to be a little aggressive, but not too aggressive. You have to talk to people even if they look away, because they are still listening and deciding. Two people can work well together, especially if one is bragging on the great political effort being made by the other.

Toward the end of my morning at the beach, a woman who had moved to the United States two years earlier from Russia argued with me that the system should not be changed because it is so much better here than in Russia. I certainly agreed that it is. I described how campaign reform would make America even better, but she became angry and argumentative. I explained everything as calmly and clearly as I could, but no dice.

When she left, I noticed that I had attracted a crowd of half a dozen onlookers, all of whom then signed the petition. "You were very patient with her," one person told me. "You sold us."

Jim arrived with the rental car—a red convertible. A little sporty for a latter-day Peace Pilgrim, perhaps, but Jim wisely tries to squeeze a little extra fun out of each day, and the car did look very nice.

I had mailed letters to every chief of police and every house of worship along my path, but had received only a few replies. Peace Pilgrim, my role model, had a religious message, and so she had had natural helpers in the form of houses of worship. My message was political and complex, and I think the pastors must have scanned my letter and wondered what on earth it was about—Who is this? Some poor, demented woman?

Jim could have used that nil response to claim I had not fulfilled one of his conditions. Instead, for the next two days, he drove to Arizona and back with me. He introduced himself every ten miles or so, looking for friendly houses in those areas where there were houses at all. A friendly house has a sense of joy to it. Maybe there are pennants flying, or an American flag, or wooden, wind-spinning yard ornaments and flowers. You can expect that the people there are special and quite friendly, and that was always the case. If they like quirky yard ornaments, they will probably enjoy meeting a quirky pilgrim.

Nearly all the people Jim talked to were quick to say they would put me up when I walked through. I would find out later, on foot, that things come up; people are not always available to

help you the way they hoped they could. Their lives are compli-
cated, with unexpected journeys, troubled relatives arriving, and
sick friends across town who need them.

But we didn't know all that then, thank heavens. Enough
people said yes to give Jim some confidence that I might be all
right. People are quite friendly in the West. Plus, Common Cause
had sent letters to all their California members, asking them to be
on the lookout for me and to help me with food and lodging.

Two members in particular, Ralph and Maria Langley,
showed up on December 30 and took me under their wing.

Then came another: On the final day of 1998, West Virginia's
octogenarian secretary of state suddenly appeared before my ad-
miring eyes. Ken Hechler had flown out to walk with me for a few
days, to start me off right. A tall, lean, charming man, Ken, who
always looks very fit, is full of hat-tipping courtesy and red-
cheeked optimism. He has a deep, stirring voice and a passionate
command of political issues. When he heard about me in the
news, he said he felt instantly compelled to get to know me. He
suggested that we start the trek that very day. And so we did,
along five miles of the Rose Bowl Parade route in Pasadena.

Ken was a former member of the U.S. House of Representatives, a former speech writer for Harry Truman, the author of a
number of books, one of which was made into a famous war
movie, *The Bridge at Remagen.* A lifelong single man, he said his
one great love did not return his affections: his boss's daughter,
Margaret Truman. The fact is, he is a wild bachelor with too many
love interests, even now, to ever settle down.

For Ken, who sees the strip-mining coal companies ravaging
his West Virginia under the protection of corrupt politicians,
campaign finance reform is the key issue in American politics. In
the months ahead, he would be an invaluable problem solver and
friend. He walked with me from Pasadena to Twentynine Palms in
the California desert, which is quite a walk for an old man. He
would rejoin me many times in the months ahead. I was not sure
at first if his passion was for reform or for me, but at my age,
whatever puts a little spring in your step is welcome.

On January 1, I was interviewed by CNN. My trek, it seems,
was starting to catch the eye of the national news media. On Jan-

uary 2, the serious walking began. I put on my backpack in Pasadena and began walking eastward to Washington, D.C.—a very long way indeed.

It felt wonderful. After so many years fettered by age, parenthood, and the burdens of two death watches, I felt free and in the spirit company of my late husband and my late friend.

I suspect that in old age we naturally turn to the issues left unfinished in youth and to old grooves of behavior we cut deep in those energetic years. One never loses one's youth. It is always just hiding under the wrinkles, excited for a chance to be out in the open air again. Ken Hechler and I walked through Los Angeles like a couple of twenty-year-olds, though our reflections in the store windows showed something else again. My advice is to not look too long at that reflection, which is the book of the past. Life is in the moving on.

We walked through endless neighborhoods and towns of ranch-style homes and green lawns. Strip shopping centers with all the same stores repeated themselves with such likeness that I worried we were going around in circles. The hills were dappled with the creeping mold of subdivisions—lit in a phosphorescent orange glow before dawn.

Gradually, the empty lots turned into meadows, the meadows grew larger, horses appeared, and now and then we could see a grassy hill still free of the coming net of look-alike homes and streets. Always, there were ribbons of freeways and the constant rush of traffic, which broadcasts its sound and soot through the valleys. The pollution of Los Angeles is pushed by sea breezes inland until it piles up against the San Bernardino Mountains and is sometimes pushed higher by colliding desert air coming from the Mojave Desert. In the pass between the San Bernardino Mountains and Mount San Jacinto, near Palm Springs, there is often a clear divide visible in the air, as if a glass wall has been built between the clean desert air and the pollution of Los Angeles.

Standing about in legions through this pass are countless, ten-story windmills. Like a great, whimsical art project of oversized yard ornaments, they creatively trash the dignity of the desert and convert its air currents into electricity for suburbia.

Always at our side or not far away, in a great Cadillac streaming cigar smoke and looking like George Patton in his tank, Ralph Langley kept an eye on us and made contacts up ahead. He and Maria shuttled us back and forth from overnight accommodations to the highway during the first two weeks of walking.

Already my hip and back were killing me. And my arthritic feet! I worried secretly that I was already falling apart.

Ralph, retired from the carpet business, turned out to be a genius in the department of arranging red carpets from mayors and chambers of commerce. We had receptions, small and large, when we arrived at the towns and reservations along the highway between Los Angeles and the Mojave Desert. He put together a big event in Yucca Valley that included an Indian tribe and a high school band and baton twirlers. An important Associated Press story by Michael Coit came out of that event and ran in papers all over the country.

Newspaper, radio, and television stories were indeed starting to pile up. Reporters wanted to write about the hardships of the quirky old woman. The old quirk, however, wanted them to write about the corruption of our elections. I had to learn how to turn a reporter's question to my preferred topics, which is not easy to do gracefully and respectfully.

While I felt encouraged by the press attention so early in my walk, at some level I thought the whole thing was ridiculous. I mean, how far could I really get? Was I a fraud?

GrannyD.com

To whom it may concern, You are a fraud! Your website is fraudulent. Al Gore, Bill Clinton, Bill Bradley and you are all frauds. Sincerely, An American. slicker@_____

Reply: Dear Mr. Slicker, Thank you for taking time to write to me. Sometimes when I first get up in the morning, I indeed wish that I were a fraud! But my old muscles and bones tell me that I am indeed the real thing. But I know what you mean, and we are certainly lucky to be in a country where we can so strongly disagree about politics and yet all live peaceably together. Yours, Doris Haddock

A Man Magnet

All along the way I had the strange experience of being a magnet to men. That is not a bad thing, especially at age eighty-nine. First there was Ken Hechler, then Ralph. Then, not far out of Los Angeles, a pencil-thin, tan, thirty-two-year-old man, Doug Vance, showed up out of the blue with his backpack and an offer to walk across America with me. Generally munching handfuls of something that looked like birdseed, he walked gracefully, looking like the Carradine boy from *Kung Fu*—Chinese hat and all. Ralph looked him up and down, blew some cigar smoke his way—making him wince—and began grilling him.

"Now, son, why do you have enough time on your hands to be able to walk with an old lady across the U.S. of A.?"

"It will be a good way to think about my life ahead," this thin grasshopper spoke. He thought it was a perfect time for such an adventure, as he had no immediate job plans and would later be locked into a routine, he suspected. A good answer, I thought.

"What do you know about campaign reform? This isn't a picnic, you know. Granny is doing this for a purpose. You will have to sing the same tune, right?"

"Well, what do you want me to know about it?" Doug asked.

He admitted that he was more interested in the physical aspects of the walk than the political message, but he said he agreed with the thrust of my message and would help get the word out. His biggest benefit to me, he said, was his expertise on nutrition and health. Ralph chomped on his cigar and said, "Health food. Well, she's done pretty good so far, hasn't she?" Ralph was convinced that chocolate and hamburgers, with a whiskey chaser, were the proper foods for me, as I enjoy them.

Ralph had a sign shop make a CAMPAIGN FINANCE REFORM sign to hang on Doug's backpack. "Now he won't have to say a word, and he'll still be earning his birdseed," Ralph said to me, aside.

He pressed some money into Doug's hand for road emergencies, but he was never comfortable with Doug. Ralph was like a sergeant in an old war movie who must place his squad's fate in the hands of a suspicious member of the resistance—keeping an eye on him every minute. But Doug became an instant and useful friend to me. An extreme vegetarian, Doug told me all about health foods as we walked. As I enjoy learning new things, I was his attentive student. Plus, I had a long way to go, and I knew he was telling me things that could help me. Chocolate could only get me so far.

The Mojave

After two weeks walking, I was approaching the great Mojave Desert. I had stayed each night with hosts along the road—dear people who dragged in their helpless friends to hear me talk about campaign reform in their living rooms. But now we were running out of houses. Our last bit of civilization was the historic Twentynine Palms Inn. It is a palm-shrouded, rambling headquarters for the artists and freethinkers of the area. The stop sign at the end of the resort's driveway includes an addendum: IT'S YOUR DECISION.

The inn, swimming in greenery, is a true desert oasis, with the ground water only twenty feet below the desert soil.

I don't know how Ralph did that sort of thing—he must have told them that the Messiah was coming—for he always had the towns ahead all dressed up and standing at attention. At the inn, we lunched at a long table filled with local artists and chamber of commerce officials.

"Everyone who moves to Twentynine Palms either is an artist, or they become one—and a good one," said Mr. Terry Waite, a metal sculptor across the table from me. I got the idea that the people who live there seem to love the desert and the town at an almost mystical level. Also in town are fifteen thousand crew-cut Marines from the Air-Ground Combat Center. The servicemen give the town a youthful energy, while the artists provide an off-beat, *Northern Exposure* quality, if you remember that television show.

I was always somewhat surprised at how receptive chambers of commerce were to the message of campaign reform. You would think they would be defenders of the status quo, but they are not. The idea that big-money special interests have too much power in Washington is well understood in every community. Chamber people didn't necessarily think I was going to do much good by walking in protest, but they didn't misunderstand the problem. Local business people no longer have the pull they once did with congressmen and senators. They have been outbid by bigger, multinational businesses.

In Twentynine Palms, Ralph and Maria said good-bye to me. Ken Hechler had recently headed back to West Virginia. Dennis Burke, the fifty-year-old director of Arizona Good Government Association and a fourth-generation man of the desert, arrived to help Doug and me through the harsh landscapes ahead. He had heard about me in an e-mail and had called to see if I would need help crossing the desert. Ralph told him to come quickly. Dennis borrowed a camper van and headed our way. In the van, we could take refuge from the afternoon sun and the cold nights, doing all our walking in the mornings. I would not have to tote my backpack and all my water, which would make things much easier.

Doug and I began through the desert the next morning, with Dennis skipping the van ahead of us every few miles.

A young, very tan, and nearly naked, bicycle-riding man named Pancho stopped to welcome us to the desert. He had matted, dreadlock hair and a wild look to his eyes.

"You look pretty old," he said. "It gets pretty cold out here—below freezing sometimes, like last night. Someone old like you could freeze to death. Last night was cold. You gotta butane heater in there? That's good." He looked out to the horizon and allowed a silence.

"You got no houses or motels or stores—not a tweedly-

(DENNIS BURKE)

Crossing the Mojave Desert with Doug Vance in California.

darned thing—for the next hundred miles, but it's sure beautiful, isn't it?" He said there was a burned-out old building forty miles ahead at Rice—the only building in the town of Rice. He said he wished he could turn it into a coffee shop someday.

"That's my dream, anyway," he said. Another man, older with a long white beard, was also on the road somewhere, Pancho said. I would glimpse the old man once, crouched asleep in a culvert. At the time, it didn't seem right to knock on his culvert for a visit, so I walked on.

Time hardly bothers with the desert. The roads in the rocky soil where George Patton trained his tank corps are still visible, and there are bits of thick, broken steel and smashed jerricans out in the brush. At night you can imagine the squeaky tanks in the distance, driven endlessly by the boys who went to North Africa and Europe to defend democracy and who never came back. The stars are unbelievable.

My, how far the horizon! Passing cars were few. We often walked in the utter silence of that great place, with an occasional lizard scampering out from the roadside brush. Military jets, two by two, sometimes zoomed low through the valley on their way to or from gunnery practice on the Goldwater range, one hundred or so miles southeast of us—a short hop for them.

In the mornings we would rise before the sun, have a bowl of cereal, rub on the sunblock, and be on our way. Every few miles I would stop and sit in the open doorway of the van to catch my breath and have some water.

Doug was a walking encyclopedia on all things healthful. We talked about vitamins and minerals and fats and grains and kelp and the horrors of eating what I might call real food. I happen to like a good, greasy burger, as I said, but Doug was insistent that I must change my ways if I were to make it all the way to Washington. I was trying to learn. Every now and then, I had to remind him that I had gotten pretty far in life on hamburgers, but he was always right in reminding me that I was not taking a walk around the neighborhood this time.

As we walked, he also told me about his personal life, and we passed a good deal of advice back and forth. He was still looking for his groove in life, as are many people today. I couldn't help thinking that he should own a little health food store where he could lecture his customers sternly and they would pay handsomely for it.

"Doris, I think you should ask Dennis to get goat's milk for your cereal," he said after walking a mile in silence.

"You do, do you?" That's always a useful thing to say to someone rather than kicking him.

He would explain patiently why such a thing would be better chemistry for me. I would pass the suggestion to Dennis. He would often not be able to find that particular thing in town, which was a shame.

Doug's genius for health extended to a real talent for massage, and he helped my poor feet make it through those hard miles with regular rubbing, soaking, and taping. I was also wheezing like an old steam train, especially toward the end of the day's walk. That was from smoking cigarettes, even though I had quit ages ago.

Dead battery. Flat tire. Radiator leak. These were constant pains, but they were also opportunities to make new friends in the desert. I must say that it was a small source of satisfaction to me that I kept going while the van couldn't quite handle it some days.

A truck with a large house trailer stopped to help one day—Karlene and Jim. He, a retired Marine, is a one-man orchestra. They live in a trailer full of painted drums, dusty accordions, and crumpled horns, and make a living by entertaining at RV parks. She has no teeth and cannot read, but they have a fine life together. Jim, quite handy, got us back on our way.

The beauty of the days and nights made it easy to be philosophical about our vehicle problems and my pains—lovely sunsets and sunrises. We camped one evening at a desert crossroads where other travelers, mostly truckers, were camped for the evening. We had a 360-degree panorama of purple hills with green, gray, and brown bushes all around. It looked like the cheap scenery of an old Western movie, and I tried to grasp that it was real.

To give you a better idea of life on the road, I will tell you about a night at the junction. Let's take Saturday, January 16. I sat under the evening stars on a little camp chair. A large truck pulled over for the night. From the cab jumped a wee doggie—out to do her business, looking for a good spot. She came pitter-patter toward me. Wriggling a plumed tail, she found a good place but was hurried into completion when the burly driver came calling for her.

"Her name is Bear," he told me.

"Bear!" I said, looking at the wee thing, who was now embracing the man's leg with her paws. "I know," he groaned. "I'm her second owner. She was already named that when I got her."

Herb Weinberg, an Arizona reform activist, had come up so that Dennis could get back to Phoenix for a while. Herb, seventy, a tan-faced, silver-haired model of a man, is a retired contractor who talks a mile a minute with very interesting political information and analysis. He has an unmistakable New York accent and attitude, which give his opinions extra force. After dinner, Herb took a walk to go visit the campers next door, where coffee and cake were earlier advertised. When Herb came back, Doug was out under the stars doing tai chi exercises. I was curled in my blanket, wishing I had a smackeral of chocolate.

In the morning, after a few miles walking in the dark, we had a pink sunrise and a back tire stuck in the sand. I collected sticks to put under the wheels, while Doug scooped away sand and shouted at Herb to stop letting the air out of the tire, as we had none to put back in. Herb lost patience and yelled back at Doug. I thought he might have called him a pacifist, but I did not have my hearing aid in, so it could have been almost anything. Doug shouted back that Herb was being autocratic, I believe. The scene resolved happily as Herb drove slowly and Doug pushed with every ounce of his 120 pounds, yelling "Go! Go!" I enjoyed the scene immensely, giggling and coughing.

Herb later scolded me for having such a loose plan. Every day should be planned, with hosts all along the way, he said. Of course, I had tried to make such arrangements, but to no avail. Anyway, this was not a tour vacation. This was an impossibility that could only be rendered possible one mile at a time, one new friend at a time. I had to trust in luck and grit, letting each day be a little leap of faith into the kind heart of America. That, in fact, was my detailed plan.

But in the Mojave, despite the good help from all these kind strangers, my health was sliding. I hacked and hacked through the night, unable to get a good sleep. I had nausea some nights, keeping a little bucket at my side and feeling awful. Doug said to drink more water, eat more birdseed. I should have listened—I was heading for trouble. My back was in pain, despite the steel-ribbed corset I put on every morning for back support. It was so hot to wear it in the desert! My feet were killing me, especially my quite swollen left foot. The acute pain settled down somewhat each morning as I walked. Doug walked slowly to match my limping pace. I was falling apart. My God, this is not going to work. I'm going to look like such a fool to my grandchildren, I thought.

The wind and sand began to blow. Our temperate weather had come to an end. But Arizona was just ahead, across the Colorado River.

Whenever we hiked past the van, which leapfrogged ahead, Dennis, now back with us, was ever on the cell phone with Don Sands of the Parker Lions Club, or John Anthony of Common Cause in Washington. They were making plans for a good arrival in the river town of Parker, just ahead. This was no time for me to disappoint everybody.

"Mayor Sandy Pierce will be there," Dennis would say when we walked past the van. Then, a few miles later as we passed him again, "There's a parade that day. They want you to lead it." Then, "NPR wants to interview you live when you cross the bridge." Then, "Doris, I think *Good Morning America* is coming to see you cross out of the Mojave."

So, heavens, what's a sandstorm or two, or a sore foot? Everyone gets sore feet. Media attention is an important element in moving a reform message forward, and it was happening.

On the night of Tuesday, January 19, we camped near a railway track and prepared a campfire. We cooked a hearty pasta dinner, served with wine on a table made from an old, splintered cable spool we had found among the cacti and rolled to our camp. We hung a Coleman lantern from a telegraph pole guy wire. After dinner, we put on some coffee and sat around talking, sometimes poking the campfire and watching the sparks swirl up to the stars. Dennis pulled a short-wave radio from his pack—we were too far from regular radio stations—and we listened to President Bill Clinton's State of the Union speech on Voice of America. We had a good political discussion during the address.

We talked about what to do in Arizona. One Arizona senator, John McCain, was clearly for campaign finance reform. The other, Jon Kyl, was dead set against it. I asked Dennis to try to get me an appointment with him.

On such evenings Dennis often wanted to know more about me. While the fire burnt down, I told him how I caught my husband, Jim. He was a lifeguard on Nantucket Island, and I was a soon-to-be Emerson College student, swimming back and forth with a purposefully horrible stroke. He told me that I needed swimming lessons. That's how I caught him.

Before we poured our coffee on the campfire, I told Dennis and Doug about my career as a costing expert in a shoe factory, and about my wedding on New Year's Eve, 1930, in Boston's Trinity Church.

What was Jim like? Well, he was a head taller than me, not very handsome. He wore glasses and had all his hair. He grew up in Lakeport, New Hampshire, graduated from Amherst College, and knew history, economics, and literature like a professor. He was rather like Ken Hechler in some ways: energetic, brimming with enthusiasm for good ideas and the right things. He was fun to be with and never boring—always some new project, always full of happy energy. He read everything he could get his hands on and had well-formulated opinions on the important issues. He never stopped learning. He had a younger brother, Bud, who would come to visit often when we were first married, and the two of them would have fine talks together. Jim and our daughter, Betty, had long conversations whenever she came home from Smith College. I was sometimes jealous of their great conversations, as I had dropped out of college in my third year to marry Jim and I always felt a little backward, though I had no business feeling that way.

That was the only kind of jealousy that ever visited our house. I never gave him any reason to worry about my affections, and Jim was a one-woman man. He did admire beauty and did not hesitate to point out a beautiful girl or a beautiful baby or man. He dabbled in painting, and he appreciated the shapes of things, often pointing out the symmetry of something. It was impossible for him not to admire Elizabeth, his closest woman friend after me. They enjoyed horseback rides together at Dundee, the sugar farm where we summered, which only worried me a little.

He was a homebody, seldom going out for an evening with other men. He was a fine athlete, but not a good dancer. I was quite disappointed when, after we were married, I suggested we go to a dance and he said, "Oh, I don't care to dance—that's courting business!" In other rhythmic pursuits he was a dandy.

We had a routine life, eating our three meals together each day. Jim had been brought up on meat, potatoes, and vegetables. I made pies and cakes, and there was always a dessert to end the meal. We shared our happenings of the day and discussed the day's news at our evening meal. We had only one car, so we went to work together, shopped together, went to the movies together. We skied together in the winter and went hiking in the mountains in the summer. Buying books was our one extravagance, though we usually relied on the local library for fiction. We saved our money and put our two children through college with it.

Some people along my walk asked me for the secret of a long and happy marriage. I think it is different for different people. But here is what it was for us: Never let the sun go down on your anger. I don't mean you can solve all your differences by the end of a day, but you can at least get rid of your anger. Call a truce. See the humor in the situation. Make sure you think about how unimportant the issue really is in comparison to the troubles of the whole world. Are you looking at it in perspective? Is it possible to compromise? Can you both give a little? Even if the other person isn't ready, it usually only takes one person to call a truce. Jim and I both tried hard to be kind to each other, especially as the sun went down each evening.

When he died after sixty-two years together, I wanted to die with him. I couldn't think of anything I might enjoy doing without him.

The desert campfire flickered down, and Dennis ran out of questions about Jim. It had been good to talk these things out with someone new, though I quietly cried myself to sleep.

In the morning, the boys nailed an old political sign to a telegraph pole and used a length of rope to bend it into a half-cylinder shower stall. They hung a bag of warm water high on the pole and—my!—true luxury! The north side of the shower was unprotected from view, but there was nothing in that direction except a hundred miles of desert, unoccupied by anything but snakes and perhaps wide-eyed varmints watching from the brush. The fighter jets, seemingly inches apart, that swooped over us from time to time, thankfully did not do so during my shower. I wouldn't have wanted to cause a mid-air accident.

The last miles were ever more windy and dusty. I wore a ban-
dana over my nose to keep the sand out—I looked like Jesse
James and I felt about as mean. My foot was a mess. My back was
a mess. I wheezed like a cheap death scene. The nights were bitter cold. The shoulder of the road was a coarse pea gravel that
provided a disagreeable walking surface. I wasn't at my best, but
the end of the Mojave was just beyond the next hills.

A big, beautiful Hopi man from New Mexico, on his way to
Los Angeles via the back roads, stopped his truck to inquire if we
were all right or if we needed a ride. He said to watch out for bad
men on the road. A highway patrolman did the same thing later,
telling me that elders were sometimes abandoned on these roads.
He said he stopped to make sure I was not one of them. I hoped
he was telling stories.

Dennis needed to get Parker ready for my arrival, and so for
the next few days, he left us in the care of his partner, Maureen
West, a newspaper reporter from Phoenix who was full of questions. Maureen was sorely tested by Doug's late-night habits of
cooking up horrible-smelling concoctions in the confines of our
little vehicle. But she was a good sport. Our girlie treat one
evening was washing our hair in a makeshift shower between the
open doors of the van. We felt so lovely and civilized after so
many miles through hot, blowing sand!

The Colorado River

I walked across the bridge into Arizona at 10 A.M. on Saturday,
January 23, 1999—the great deserts of California finally at my
back.

Parker had indeed been prepared for my arrival. Like a grand
mirage for a woman gone mad in the desert, the Marine Corps
Marching Band—the same gorgeous fellows I had seen in the
Rose Parade—were standing resplendent in red and flashing
brass on the Arizona side of the bridge. As I approached the cen-

ter of the bridge and the Arizona line, they struck up "Happy Birthday." Tears streamed down my cheeks, and I told Maureen that I so hoped my late husband was looking down right then. You can't imagine the emotion of it, after so long and difficult a walk. The band just happened to be in town for the parade, but I was happy to have them to myself for that moment.

The mayor of Parker, Ms. Sandy Pierce, embraced me, gave me the key to the city, and introduced me to the county sheriff, the chief of the Native American community, and other dignitaries, while an *ABC News* video crew orbited us. The welcoming group walked me to a little restaurant called Grandma's Kitchen for birthday cake. I stopped along the way at a phone booth, where Dennis was waiting with an outstretched receiver. It was a live interview with Daniel Zwerdling on National Public Radio's *Weekend Edition.* Dennis and Doug held their jackets up to make a phone booth so that I could hear Daniel's questions over the crowd and traffic noise.

National news wires sent out the story: "Eighty-Nine-Year-Old Woman Walks Across California's Mojave Desert, Arrives in Arizona." Of course, I wouldn't be eighty-nine for another day. But the crossing of the Mojave had earned me some credibility and brought some attention to the reform fight. They could no longer say back in Washington that no one cared about campaign reform.

Later in the morning, I indeed led the town's big annual parade, with Shriners buzzing around in funny little cars, precision parachute jumpers plopping down in front of me, the ABC video crew zooming around, and a crowd of children, retired people, Native Americans, horseback riders, all waving and cheering for each other—what a wonderful, bizarre day! Salvador Dali and Federico Fellini could not have planned it better.

Each winter, the Parker area fills with hundreds of thousands of retirees living in RV camps, up and down the Colorado River. The streets are wide and sparsely developed. The air smells of desert and barbecues and of the wide, warm river. The overwhelming presence of motor homes, motorcycles, Western styling, country music, and gray hair combine to give the area an elder Wild West–Mad Max intensity—as if the whole revved-up town were preparing to invade California at first light tomorrow.

If America's children are looking for their runaway grandparents, here they will find them. From the Mexican line to Las Vegas, they are living in too many vehicles along the river, after escaping hometowns ruined by too many vehicles. But they are having a wonderful time.

Mayor Sandy introduced me all over the sprawling, desert town, taking me to church on Sunday morning, my birthday. She became a great spokeswoman for campaign finance reform in short order. A motel put me up for free, and—my!—the luxury of a real bath and a real bed! Early Monday morning, on the sidewalk in front of the motel, I was interviewed live via satellite by Charles Gibson and Diane Sawyer on *Good Morning America.* Ken Hechler, who had flown into Phoenix the day before and rented a car to come out to walk the first miles of Arizona with me, stood at my side as I was interviewed. I missed a few opportunities to turn the little old lady story to a political reform story, but I was learning by doing. These national news stars did not make it easy, as they didn't take my mission very seriously. They liked my spunk and wanted to ask spunky questions. The local press, especially the newspaper people, understood better what was going on, and they saw the effect this message had on crowds of people—crowds of voters, by the way.

The national morning news programs are shown live back East, but they are delayed in the West until more people are awake. So we were able to go into the motel room and see the *Good Morning America* interview an hour or so later. I knew that the town was abuzz—in fact we had asked the mayor and the president of the chamber, who had allowed me to sit on his Harley-Davidson before the parade, to spread the word that any citizens or children showing up early could be on national television. We got a little crowd of about twenty-five people holding some signs and banners. After watching the show in the motel room, I came out on my motel balcony and saw a crowd of people below, over toward the office. They were looking my way. I thought it only courtesy to wave and then go over and say hello to what I assumed were new fans of campaign finance reform. They were confused by my brief remarks thanking them for coming, as they were there to meet a bus for a golf outing and had no idea what I was talking about. *Sic transit gloria mundi.*

The next morning, my old feet in decent shape, Doug, Ken, and I began the 150-mile walk to Phoenix, though I would not make it in one piece.

GrannyD.com

I'm almost 92 and I support you completely!
  Ruby Fritch, Orlando, FL—Wednesday, January 27, 1999

Could you have picked a dumber thing to walk across America for?
  Williamsport, PA—Wednesday, January 27, 1999

Salome, but Not Dancing

Eastward from Parker, the traffic was fast and the road was narrow and shoulderless. The weather turned breezy and chilly with light rain, and I felt a cold coming on. Doug and I were alone in this stretch. He would drive the van ahead a few miles and then walk back to meet me halfway. Doug had me in his vegetarian grip, and we ate vegetables for breakfast, lunch, and dinner, including a whole watermelon for a lunch. I enjoyed it. But the walking was increasingly horrible, with fresh oil on the narrow shoulder, and rough desert close by.

The Texas populist political commentator Jim Hightower interviewed me on the air as I walked. I had become a regular Friday feature of his show, which went to some two hundred cities. John Anthony in the press office of Common Cause in Washington was on the phone with Dennis about four times a day, scheduling me on other radio talk shows across the nation.

On Thursday night, January 28, with Dennis back, we camped near Vicksburg Junction on Highway 60. After the day's walk and after a long phone call from a French reporter with *Le Monde,* we sat at the counter at the junction café, next to a local man named Max, who was seventy-five. After a while watching him smoke, I told Max he should try to stop it if he wanted to live to a ripe age. He said he had picked up the habit in World War II, when servicemen were given little packs of cigarettes with their rations. He now resented that. He said he had lived long enough anyway, spending most of his time these days watching television in an old mobile home in the desert. We talked about that encounter at camp that evening. You need to have a purpose to your life, and you need friends. Friends often come from your commitments, your passions. If you are all alone, it is usually a sign that you need to commit yourself to your beliefs or at least to a good activity. You need to give yourself away.

The temperature at night dipped below freezing. We slept in the van in sleeping bags, afraid to use the vehicle's old butane heater. Earlier, Doug had made green pea soup and tofu on top of black beans with onions and cauliflower pieces. I had a can of beans. Dennis walked to the junction café and had a hamburger— the rat. Doug put a big pot of water on the butane stove and woke every few hours to heat it up and let it radiate into the cabin. It was still very cold sleeping, even for an old New Hampshire woman.

I awoke with a hacking cough after a restless night of nausea. It wasn't so bad that I couldn't walk, so I insisted that we keep to the schedule. It felt better to walk anyway. I was distracted from my pains by the scenery, which was changing rapidly as we walked. The rolling desert floor was becoming hilly, with rock pillars here and there. Both sides of the road were laced with smoky gray bushes with daisies fluttering atop.

My son, Jim, called every day to see how I was doing. He said Ken was hinting at the idea of buying a used van for us, as Dennis would soon need to return the one he had borrowed. I told him that it was hard to imagine walking without a support vehicle now, and I agreed to it. After all, Ken was like family now, not a corporate sponsor.

About 11 A.M., a video crew from a Phoenix television station caught up with us for a long interview as we walked. Young reporters didn't seem to know much about the campaign finance system, or about politics in general. So I understood that part of my mission would be to wise up a whole group of young reporters along my way. They would then be likely to ask harder questions of politicians.

"So, Mrs. Haddock, Doris, Granny D—what do you like to be called?" The reporter walked beside me while the cameraman walked backward ahead of us, ever in danger of tripping on a stick or a chunk of asphalt.

"Doris would be fine."

"Good. Well, Doris, how do you think walking across the country will change votes in Congress on campaign finance reform?"

"Well, I'm not sure that it will, but walking is the only thing I could think of doing to show that some people care very much about the problem."

"And why do you think campaign reform is necessary?"

"Well, any American ought to be able to run for office without selling his or her soul to the corporations. And, whether or not we ever run for office, we should have representatives who are free to represent us and who are not too beholden to special interest campaign donors. If big money controls our elections, that means we are not a free people, and too many people have died for our freedom for us to let that happen."

Then we would get into the details of different reform proposals, assuming I could get past the questions about how my family feels about my walk, and did I think I would make it all the way.

These miles out of Vicksburg were straight uphill, so I took a five-minute break every mile. My cough seemed to come from very deep down, as though my lungs were filling up. In the early afternoon, three miles from the little desert town of Salome, I took a nap while Dennis hitchhiked ahead to do some advance work. As I walked into Salome later, some of the town's children ran out to meet me and held my hands as I came down the otherwise deserted main street. A party of forty townspeople met me

under a makeshift banner welcoming me, and the town's fire engine came roaring down the street, its siren blaring. After some
petition signing, the town hosted us for cookies and punch in a
community room at their small airport.

I said, "Well, I think you all know why I am walking across
the country, so I will spare you the speech." But Larry, an interesting fellow who had given me a walking stick he made from a
cactus rib, said, "Well, no, Doris. I really have no idea. Why are
you walking?"

So I made a short speech, reminding them that many people
had died or given up their sons and daughters for our freedoms,
and that we mustn't give it away now to the corruption that has
become the normal business of Washington. We then had a good
discussion.

Here we were, common citizens, gathering to hear a small
speech and discuss an issue. I saw in my mind that wonderful
painting by Norman Rockwell—from his "Four Freedoms" series—where a fellow wearing his old flight jacket is standing up
at a town meeting, and his fellow citizens are respectfully listening. Where is that kind of belonging to be found in America
today? Just in an old painting? Well, we had it there for a moment
in Salome, and I realized that I had been having such moments in
living rooms and other gathering places along my way. There
would be many more to come.

After cookies, we were taken out to the little ranch of Jean
and Frank Mangini, about five miles out of town. The Manginis
were among the people my son had magically found on his sweep
through Arizona. Their little ranch is set in a beautiful desert
pass. To keep out the rattlesnakes, they have a low wall around
the ranch house, guarded by a good number of cat sentries. The
cats are sometimes dragged away by coyotes, who I suspect are in
cahoots with the rattlesnakes.

Salome was the home in the 1930s of humorist Dick Wick
Hall, whose columns appeared in *The Saturday Evening Post* and
whose mark is still upon the town. He wrote endlessly about the
desert and about how the creatures—reptile and human—adapted
to the lack of water. There is a big green frog painted on the side of

a main street building to commemorate a favorite Hall story: Dick wrote that he had a seven-year-old frog who hadn't learned how to swim yet for lack of water. Hall dispensed a humorous newspaper, *The Salome Sun,* from his gas station, Laughing Gas, on the main street, before the town was cut off by an interstate highway.

It seems to me that America had a funnier funny bone back in those Will Rogers days. The jokes were often lame, but everybody enjoyed hearing them and masterminding practical jokes upon their friends. Towns along the highways had their well-worn gags and minor, P. T. Barnum mystery attractions—like "The Thing!" still advertised along the road in southern Arizona—designed to pull the legs of visitors and extract an extra dollar and a smile. A good deal of fun died with Eisenhower's interstate highway program, which he copied from the Nazis.

Dick Wick Hall's old green frog had adapted to the desert, but I had not. Salome was where my health finally crashed. On Sunday morning, I awoke for the walk, but was not feeling well at all. During a predawn bowl of cereal, I got into a frightening coughing fit and went back to lie down. I was having a hard time breathing; then I could not breathe at all and was panic-stricken. Doug asked the Manginis to call an ambulance, and he held me up in a hunched-over position where I could finally get some air. He undoubtedly saved my life. Forty long minutes later, I was being rushed to the hospital by darling paramedic boys who had seen me on television and who were joking about the celebrity in their care. They made me smile, and that certainly dispelled any remaining feeling of panic.

I had pneumonia, according to a dear Dr. Julliard, a mother of four who would be my best friend for the next few days.

Dennis called me at the hospital on Sunday evening to tell me that what I had done so far was remarkable and that other people could continue the walk from here, if I was ready to turn over the baton. My breath was still short, but not so short that I couldn't bark at him for such a thought. I told him that I was prepared to die as a part of this journey, if need be. It would be preferable to sitting at home, wishing I had continued. We're all dying, and we might as well be spending ourselves in a good cause.

The hospital staff, quite interested in my mission, became like the pit crew of a very old race car. Nurse Jan told me I must learn to eat three good meals a day, or I'd never make it. In my drowsy moments, I could imagine that she was Doug, on me again about vegetables. I promised to get a little cutting board and keep a pocket full of vegetables with me as I walked—which I never did. A nice fellow, John, insisted that I must take in more water each mile. He said I was seriously dehydrated. David, a nursing school student, talked passionately about the plight of poor people in America, and he knew how connected their fate is to the corruption of politics and, therefore, how my mission was a good one. Russ, who has worked as a desert firefighter, was very interested in my trek because he believes that we cannot do much to protect the environment until we get corporate money out of politics. Even in the space of a hospital ward, one could see how all reform roads lead to campaign finance reform. The things Americans deeply care about are not being addressed by their government, and they know it.

But, oh dear, my hospital roommate was a mess. Poor thing, divorced after forty-six years of an abusive marriage. Nine children. As soon as she got her own Social Security check, she kicked him out. She was trying to quit smoking, was addicted to laxatives, had high blood pressure, and was overweight. But, by heaven, a good soul.

"You know, Doris," she said, "I like the way you don't complain unless the doctor asks you. I'm going to try to do that from now on." She was seventy-one and, like the rest of us, still learning how to live. I agreed with her that she complained a little too much, but we talked about how that can just become a habit.

As far as I am concerned, the secret to a happy life, especially in your later years, is to help other people until you don't notice your own needs and pains anymore. When the only person you worry about is yourself, all your problems tend to get magnified and out of hand, and you become thoroughly unpleasant to be around. I'm sure I didn't preach all this to her too much, but we had good and frank conversations.

After a few days I was on my feet. I took a walk around the hospital, ending up in a wing used as a rest home. I met Ada and

Mary. They asked me to help them remove the restraints that kept them in their wheelchairs. They asked me if I knew who had brought them there, so they might find out how to go home. It was very sad, and I had certainly gotten in over my head. I told them that we were lucky to be in such a lovely new place and we should just relax and enjoy being waited on. I then bugged out, thankful for my wits and good health.

I have no interest in living in a nursing home. When my husband, Jim, suffered his worsening episodes of Alzheimer's, the easier thing for me to do would have been to put him in a home. It is the right decision for many people, but it was not for us. It was hard enough to get him to go to an adult day care program. The ten years of tending him would have crushed me had I not had that three-times-a-week relief. A bus would arrive at 8 A.M. and return him at 4 P.M.

When I first took him there to show him the program, he dutifully made some little craft project and then leaned over to me. "Why have you brought me here?" he asked. "This is a bunch of crazy people. I am not crazy, Doris." But then he continued in fantasy: "I am a famous author with six books at my publishers right now. So why would you bring me here?" We went home and forgot about the program for another two years. By then he was ready for it and looked forward to the arrival of the little bus. He would be standing there in his business suit, with his briefcase stuffed with newspapers. While others did their crafts, he read his papers all day long, rarely engaging in conversation.

I would use that time for shopping, a long walk, and an hour's swim, remembering Jim as he had been for the fifty healthy years of our marriage. Having the respite program, which I had fought for in our community, was better and much less expensive than having Jim move away from me into a nursing home. He could sleep under his own roof and have breakfast and dinner at his own table, still the happy genius of his household.

I have visited so many nursing homes where the residents stare at flickering television sets or slumber in what I presume to be a drugged half-death.

As for me, I should like to stay at home for as long as possible, and I would pray that good programs are at hand to make caregiving easier for family members. When you no longer know where you are, or who anyone is, then I suppose it doesn't matter. I think the plague of Alzheimer's, however, will soon be cured.

Jim would sometimes come around and be able to think quite clearly. It was heartbreaking for both of us to know what was happening to his mind. He was, after all, a bright and lively thinker and conversationalist. During a long, lucid episode after ten years of this suffering, he decided that his play had run. He told me that he wanted to stop taking food. I said that I understood.

We called hospice people into our home to help him be comfortable for the final eleven days of his life. The process is not to be taken lightly in a moral sense, but it is how this free and fearless man decided to conclude his stay. My son, Jim, and my grandson Raphael sat with him at night, and I held his hand during the days. When he took his last breath, my life stopped, too. It stopped for a long time.

When someone is with you that long, he does not just disappear. I dreamed one night that he came to me in my bedroom and said that he was very cold. He asked if he could get in bed with me. We slept spoon-style, as we always had. In the morning I awoke to find myself at the far edge of the bed, as if he had really been there. I thought he might indeed have, and it was very comforting. I could not have made it through those times without the bits of comfort that came in such ways. I also saw a good therapist during the last year of Jim's life and for a time after his death. It makes all the difference in the world to have a little professional help through such times, and I think it is silly not to do so, if you can find a way to afford it.

These memories flooded back as I wandered the halls of the hospital in Arizona. Everyone was so lovely to me, yet I was desperate to escape. After four days there, I was released. Dear Ralph Langley of California drove me down to Phoenix for a week of recuperation at Dennis's house, where I took time to plan my route ahead. I did manage to steal some time away from my recuperation to appear in the Buckeye Rodeo, near Phoenix. That was a great exertion, but greater fun. What is the point of being in Arizona, I decided, if you cannot be a Rodeo queen? So I grabbed my opportunity.

GrannyD.com

Granny, You are my hero. I am sorry to learn you are sick and will keep you in my prayers. We certainly need more leaders like you. You have inspired me to write to my legislators.
Sandra DeLeon, Valencia, CA—Sunday, February 7, 1999

Hope your walk does some good. I guess I'm just a bit cynical, but we support your efforts. Good luck.
Art and De Friedman, Akron, OH—Tuesday, February 9, 1999

Hi Doris! We all miss you at church, but Nancy updates us every Sunday, and we're all glad to hear you're out of the hospital and back on your feet again. You're such an inspiration to all of us, and we're so very proud of you! Love from everyone.
Laura Woerner, Dublin, NH—Thursday, February 11, 1999

Cheer up, please, Granny!
Jin-Young Kim, Chung-ju, Korea—Tuesday, February 16, 1999

Dusting Myself Off

In Phoenix, my son, Jim, arrived with Ken's generous replacement van and we went shopping for a new pair of sneakers and a water bladder backpack with a sipping straw, so I wouldn't get dehydrated again.

It was time to go back to Salome, where I had taken ill, to resume my walk. We picked up Doug, who stayed with Arizona relatives during my recuperation, and went one hundred miles back into the desert.

We headquartered back at the Manginis in Salome. Frank and my son argued politics, and Doug ate raw greens, shunning Jean's wonderful cooking. Pecan pie for dessert! It looked wonderful, but Doug refused even to pass the pie to Frank when he asked for a second piece. "That would be too much sugar for you," Doug pronounced, looking stern and unwilling to have a hand in a good man's undoing. Frank blinked hard and put up with it instead of punching him in the nose. I had the pie.

Off we started in the morning, often hacking our way through the bushes with our walking sticks to avoid dangerous stretches of road. I couldn't help but give Doug a hard time for a few miles about the pie.

After several days walking, a woman came roaring through the desert on a dust-spewing, three-wheel motorcycle to tell us that the residents of the Morengo Palms RV Park, just ahead, were waiting to greet me. A big man carrying two American flags soon tramped toward us and guided us in for a welcome and petition signing. They understood the issue and were lovely.

Larry, the Salome man who made a walking stick for me from a cactus rib, walked quite a ways with me to make sure it worked. He kept trying to hold my free hand, but I was not feeling that friendly, so I talked with big hand gestures to keep it occupied in the air as we walked. He showed up a second day, further down the highway, when Jim, bless him, was preparing a beautiful Japanese soup for our camp dinner in the desert. Jim is an expert on mushrooms, and this soup had four different kinds of wild ones, plus seaweed and all kinds of floaty things. It was so full of stinky goodness that Doug declared Jim the Saint of the Desert on the spot.

Larry liked it too, and told us quite a few bad jokes and made some advances toward me. Jim said, "I wouldn't mind welcoming you as one of her surrogate sons, but not as a new daddy." With that, Larry settled down. He took a roll of pictures and then disappeared after dinner. A good fellow; a wandering soul.

When we finally arrived in Wickenburg, the town was wild with cowboys and festival booths, as the annual hoedown and parade was about to start. Chris Lytle, our hostess, was a friend of the parade organizer, and I was put in the parade at the last minute. It was wonderful, with stagecoaches, Native Americans, rope twirling, dancing—everything Western.

The town started as a gold mining town in the late 1800s, after Henry Wickenburg discovered the Vulture Gold Mine. The town prospered and eventually turned to ranching. As it is located in the cool mountains above Phoenix, it also became peppered with dude ranches in the 1920s, some continuing to the present day—although the dude ranches today usually seem to have some special health focus, like weight loss. The stores of Wickenburg have covered sidewalks and Western fronts, and there is a sense of fun and youthful wildness to the place. I did very well with my petitions after the parade in the town festival, and was happy to hike past the hospital where I had been on oxygen two weeks earlier.

From Wickenburg, after a day of rest, Doug and I began the walk to Phoenix—a downhill fifty miles to the hot, Sonoran Desert floor. We weren't too far out of Wickenburg when we saw a man standing ahead in the breakdown lane. He was a balding, open-shirted, beer-bellied, gum-chewing roughneck who said he'd seen us in the parade and by golly he guessed he'd get him a picture of Granny D. He did.

Just after that, we found a dead fox on the road, still warm. Doug took him off the road and put him under a tree. He had recently done the same for a fallen, bottle-green hummingbird. The number of dead animals along the road was quite constant, and the carcasses often fascinating. It somewhat bothered some of my fellow walkers that I was interested in these bodies and that I looked closely at them as we passed—the color and texture of their innards and the expressions on their faces are worth looking at if you are not put off by death. Every mile was a biology lesson. Of course, my sense of smell is not what it used to be, which was a blessing at such times. A thousand miles ahead, the coyotes and foxes would fade away in favor of cracked-open armadillos and polecats. Rattlesnakes were always especially interesting, dead or alive.

The fact is, as I chatted to Doug, if you are afraid of death, you are afraid of life, for living your life leads to death. Until you face death and see its beauty, you will be afraid to really live—you will never properly burn the candle for fear of its end. I worry that total fixation on the health of one's own body, for example, is not only a disagreeable narcissism, but may be an indication of an unhealthy fear of death and of living.

Road kill, cell phone calls from media, and people stopping for a snapshot were becoming the stuff of our day. Doug ran off to help a dog that had been slightly injured on the road; Jim Lytle, Chris's husband, drove up with a fax from Ken Hechler, to the effect that the National Association of Secretaries of State had passed a resolution of support for my effort. I read the fax and wondered where Doug had gone with the dog. The cell phone rang, and it was Jim Hightower. I talked with him on the air as I hiked along. That's how the time went.

Splintery, old houses dot the rolling desert above Phoenix. One had a sign that said TIMBUKTU and another, SEWING—FABRICS. I wanted to go up to the doors and visit, wondering what it would be like for a woman to live in such a place without neighbors, but I walked on.

We marched five days to Phoenix, staying a couple of nights with Jackie Gerke and Ed Blum—retirees who live in the desert. Dennis had knocked on their door because they were closest to where I would finish my walk one day, and they were flying an American flag. Yes, they would love to have us. Jackie was her high school valedictorian, a magna cum laude graduate of the University of Wisconsin in physics, chemistry, and math. She taught high school and ran a knitting shop and a residential complex for four hundred mentally retarded people. I tell you all this because you buzz down a highway and glimpse a house in the desert, and you have no idea that such wonderful, accomplished people are living there. I have found that such people are absolutely everywhere. The tapestry of America is very large, and if you look closely, its fibers are golden.

A Senator in Hiding

Two hard days later I walked into Phoenix—this time arriving under my own steam. During the previous weeks, Dennis had still been trying to get an appointment for me with Senator Kyl. He finally called them to say we were coming by, with or without an appointment. He was told that they "were working on it."

Matt Keller, a thirty-something Common Cause fellow from Washington, came out to Phoenix to walk with me for a time. Matt is tall and lean and looks rather like a member of a rock and roll band—perhaps a drummer. He is very sharp and quick to laugh. His job in Washington is to lobby the House of Representatives on reform bills. He and Dennis strategized my route across the city for the next day, including the stop at Senator Kyl's luxury office across from the Ritz-Carleton.

The next morning I walked through Phoenix to the senator's office. I hadn't slept a wink, my mind going 'round and 'round, worrying about what to say at the senator's office. As both of California's senators voted in favor of campaign reform, Senator Kyl was the first "no" vote on my long trek—four hundred miles so far. I wanted to say the right things.

As I walked through Phoenix, more and more people joined me, each carrying flags that said GO, GRANNY, GO! on one side and END THE BRIBE SYSTEM on the other. Dennis gave me a big yellow flag because he said it would make me more visible and safe in the traffic. When I arrived at the senator's luxury office on East Camelback Road, we breezed into the front courtyard with fifty supporters including two high school girls, Lauren and Ashleigh, who skipped class for the occasion. Waiting for us were four television stations, two radio stations, and two daily newspapers. A number of people from different good-government organizations welcomed me to Phoenix, and then I spoke for a few moments.

Toward the end, a staff person from Senator Kyl's office came out and said that the senator would see me inside, but that he would not come out and greet me publicly. That did not go over well with the assembled supporters. Someone spoke up and said, "The lady has walked four hundred miles—can't he take a few steps to greet her in public?" Well, he would not come out. I later told a reporter that I thought previous Arizona senators like Barry Goldwater or Morris Udall would have come out to greet me, even if they disagreed with the old woman who had just walked across the desert. We waited for him to come out for a little bit, but the crowd was getting restless. A chant started up: "Come out, come out!" Dennis went to the microphone and said that we certainly wouldn't get him to come out if we were disrespectful. Then someone started chanting "We'll be nice. We'll be nice," which was rather funny, but it didn't work, either.

We left. One of the walkers, who had driven an hour from Sun City to walk with me, dared to go into Senator Kyl's office and ask if she could use the ladies' room before her long drive home. They refused her. I am quite sure that she would have had a better reception if she had arrived with a campaign contribution instead of criticism.

The press articles gave Mr. Kyl a hard time for not greeting me. The next day, as we were walking through Chandler, southeast of Phoenix, some mechanics came out of a garage to meet me. They had read all about the senator's refusal in the newspaper and wanted to tell me that they thought Mr. Kyl had just done his career some damage, and that they hoped so. Many people came out on the sidewalks after that article. Everyone was full of high spirits for me. "Go, Granny, go" was shouted wherever I went—even from passing cars and trucks—as though we were finally starting something. It seemed clear to me that people feel oppressed by big money politicians and they take glee in any chance for a small rebellion.

I walked out of Phoenix without the company of my dear walking partner, Doug. His strict vegetarianism made it difficult for him to partake of what was offered in the homes where we were guests. He was getting thinner and thinner, and I worried about his health. It was easier when we were camping in the desert, but now that we were nearly always guests in homes, it would get even more difficult. We talked long about it and finally agreed that he was risking his health and the vegetarian issues were dominating our days more than we wished. So we hugged and said good-bye. He took a bus back to Los Angeles, traveling for nearly six hours at seventy miles an hour to cover the distance he had walked with me. Many times in the miles ahead, I would wish he were still with me.

The Reservation

With Herb Weinberg, Matt Keller, and Ken Hechler at my side, I finished the last miles of the Phoenix urban area and began crossing Indian lands on February 26. There is no sign to say you are entering another nation, but all development stops. The land looks as it might have looked two hundred or more years ago, with an occasional small house, surrounded with rough fencing and a few dogs. Here and there are agricultural fields and loosely organized towns, each marked by a water tower.

After a long walk into the reservation, we arrived at Upper Santan, a small village near Sacaton. *Good Morning America* had called a few days earlier to say that a crew was on its way for a live interview from the reservation. We found a little Catholic mission that would provide a picturesque backdrop for the dawn interview, and Dennis and Matt removed a long-dead dog from its dirt driveway. We got the word out through the reservation grapevine, which is faster than e-mail, that kids should come to the mission at dawn if they wanted to be on national television. Dennis bought white posterboards and marking pens in town and passed them around to a few parents who agreed to distribute them to the kids. The signs could say GOOD MORNING AMERICA FROM UPPER SANTAN, or whatever the kids wanted to write. Ms. White, an elder of the tribe, gave me a fine bedroom and lots of good conversation.

In the evening, as I walked down the dusty road, Matt and Herb were atop a low hill, silhouetted against the sunset like two Scarlett O'Haras, shaking their fists at each other and having a wonderfully loud argument about Native American culture. The villagers were watching from their patios and yards. The argument had something to do with all the litter strewn about, centuries of repression, environmentalism, racism, etc. Those two had wonderful arguments from time to time, though I believe they are good friends at some deep and hard-to-locate level. They are both intense reformers. Matt is young. He came close to joining the priesthood, I believe, but instead got a law degree and does the Lord's work on Capitol Hill. Herb has been a reform organizer all his life, in addition to his careers. They are both handsome and wonderful to be around. It is quieter to be with them individually, however.

Herb is an explainer, which would drive Matt crazy. "If you ask him what time it is," Matt told me, "Herb will tell you, but he'll also tell you how the watch is made." Herb is also a tenacious organizer. He will argue with complete strangers about how they are the problem if they are not voting. He gets quite worked up. He is right about it, but one does have to come to the rescue of strangers from time to time. I love his ferocious unwillingness to let people off the hook when they are being the passive problem. He gives no quarter, and he assumes everyone is equal to intellectual battle, which is admirably American. A democracy needs a good sergeant-at-arms like Herb on every block.

After dinner, all was quiet at Ms. White's. Children and some adults were sleeping on the floor and on sofas. Ken decided to sleep in the van. I went right to sleep. I was awakened about 9 P.M. by a large fellow standing at the foot of my bed in the gray light. "Telephone," he said. *Good Morning America* had scrubbed us in favor of a segment on wedding dresses. They would catch up with us further down the road, they said. I knew I should wake up Ken and tell him and everyone else, but I dozed back to sleep. There would be time to tell everyone in the morning, I thought. I

awoke again at 1 A.M. An interesting-smelling smoke drifted
through the house. I got up to find the bathroom and found six
men and women smoking something traditional around the
kitchen table.

Well, Ken rose very early: 4 A.M. He tiptoed into Ms. White's
house, showered, spruced up, and then wrestled his way in the
dark through the fences and cacti up to the highway and then
down the shoulder to the old church. The children were already
waiting in the dark for the *Good Morning America* crew.

When the TV people did not arrive, Ken tried to find his way
home again in the predawn. He found himself behind barbed wire
with dogs barking at him in an alarming manner. Down on all
fours, he slithered under the barbed wire and heard a ripping
sound in so doing. I remind you that Ken is the secretary of state
of West Virginia, a noted historian and author, a former member
of Congress, and an aide and speechwriter to President Truman.
With all that, it would have been inappropriate for his trousers to
be ripped or for the dogs to have bitten him. He was relieved to
find that the barbed wire had scraped but not torn the seat of his
trousers, and thus the secretary returned to wake me and tell me
of the media's treachery.

We went up to the churchyard and found about ten children
of different ages all standing around, looking glum. Grandma
White was nearby in a car full of cardboard signs that the children
had made. Duffy Monahan, a dear friend from home who had
just arrived to walk with me for several days, quickly unpacked
her camera from her bag. We lined up the children with their
posters and took pictures. They wanted to walk with me, so we
did about half a mile down the highway, two abreast. Then we
sent them off to school and kept walking to begin our ten miles
for the day.

By midday, we were very much in the middle of nowhere. Up
ahead, the next small Indian village, Hashan Kehk, had heard of
my approach. Several women of the village dashed off on a gro-
cery run to Casa Grande, an hour's round trip, to prepare a welcome banquet.

Hashan Kehk means "cactus standing." The Pima-Mari-
copas are part of an ancient people who created, by hand labor,

an ingenious network of canals—hundreds of miles in extent—
that turned the deserts of central Arizona into a great agricultural
empire more than two thousand years ago. Newer settlers who
came to Arizona in the 1870s restored the old canals and began
planting crops. The farmers were still the victims of floods and
droughts, so the area did not grow steadily. When Theodore
Roosevelt was president, he repaid a big favor to Arizona—the
territory that had sent him most of his Rough Rider troops for the
Spanish-American War. He arranged for Arizona to receive a federal loan to build a system of dams that would end the cycle of
droughts and floods. The dams indeed kept the canals filled year-
round, which created an agricultural system that assured state-
hood and economic growth. But it was the Native Americans who
invented and dug the original system. The Pima people still farm,
producing the world's finest, long-fiber cotton.

In Hashan Kehk that evening, a large, happy man with a
beautiful, black ponytail prepared the meal that the women then
served on a long feast table. After dinner, I rolled my bedding out
on a sofa in the meeting room. It had been a long day walking in
the heat, but it was a beautiful evening in this village. It was not
quite over, as about six women sat around my sofa in the dark
and watched me as I tried to go to sleep. When I woke much
later, they had gone.

In the morning, a woman from Upper Santan caught up with
me to give me a small, leather medicine bag I should carry for
health. Such things I do take seriously and follow. We were in the
land of very old spirits, and it would only be common courtesy to
honor their traditions and their medicine.

When we departed, Duffy left a small jug of maple syrup as a
gift, with a note saying that the Dequad Indians had taught the
first white New Englanders how to make it.

We had started early, not wanting to wake the village. But we
had not gone far into the desert when a car stopped and two
women from the village caught up with us. They brought us our
breakfast—covered trays with eggs, toast, bacon, tortilla bread,
and a quart of fresh orange juice. They also presented me with a
tiny pair of moccasins and a miniature burden basket with tin-
kling copper ornaments and leather strips hanging down.

After our roadside meal, another man and woman came out to greet us and wish us luck. They were both in their second marriage and had been together for only two years. She had inherited their small cottage, and they had it fenced all around to keep out the wild dogs and coyotes. She was retired from the local hospital, and he still worked every day in Phoenix, a long drive. He said what I was doing was the right thing.

Next, a lone woman walked toward me on the highway. She gave me a hug. "I am a single woman, a simple Indian woman—a nobody—but I want to tell you I honor you. You are walking for me." I was very touched, and my eyes prickled and I gulped a few times. I thanked her, we embraced again, and she left. It began to occur to me that, in the eyes of these people, I had some spiritual power, some medicine. I didn't deserve that honor, but I took it to mean that they hoped that a solitary person, even an old woman living on Social Security, might find a place of respect for the common person, and that place would be for them, too. So I did indeed think that I was walking for them.

I should not want to over-romanticize these people. They are like people everywhere. They have dreams, traditions, and problems. Jim met up with three of their "problems" at a roadside general store one day—drunk and mean. Jim said it was a serious encounter, and he does not scare easily. He saw in their eyes that missing thing that says your own life is not worth much in their company. He managed to get away, but he was worried that they were somewhere on the road, and before he returned to New Hampshire, he told Duffy to keep an eye out for them.

Ken was still walking with me, and at one point he went into the van to rest. Duffy thought I was resting somewhere near the van, too. But I had kept walking, and I thought Duffy had seen me head on down the desert road. When Duffy realized I was not there, I was very long gone, and she and Ken sped along the highway looking for me. I had gone farther than they calculated, so they doubled back to see if they had missed me somewhere. Maybe I had taken a powder in the desert, she thought.

Near panic, she parked in the shade of a roadway overpass and wondered whom she might call. As she stepped around the front of the van, the three big men were standing there. They had materialized from the brushy margin of the road and walked toward her.

It is important, I believe, for us to understand something about Native American men and the problems that haunt some of them. For longer than we can imagine, they were hunter-gatherers and sometimes warriors through these deserts. They had great responsibilities to their families and to their communities. Those responsibilities still weigh heavily upon them, though many of them are not in a position to properly discharge them. Their defeat in the Indian wars still defines their position. Until a just peace is found, and until the great wisdom of Native ways is honored and incorporated into the mainstream culture—providing an ethic of respect and sustainability that can only do us all some good—then many of these men will wander lost in the guilt and self-destruction arising from their inability to care for their families. Alcoholism, I believe, is not in the genes of Native Americans or Irish or anyone else. Unresolved political defeat is the thing. Inability to discharge traditional duties is the thing.

Well, you are probably worried that I left Duffy under the bridge with three tough-looking fellows. I wanted you to understand why it was that when I saw the men walking toward me in the heat of the highway, some fifteen or twenty minutes before they encountered Duffy, I saw three sad warriors returning from an impossible battle with nothing to tell their families.

I could see in them the great facial strength of my Eskimo friends, Teenavick and Narkook, who, when they were alive, always had their dignity because they had their village, their livelihoods, and their ability to take care of each other according to their traditions.

I also saw in these men glimpses of Wahbateeste and Untwinecolten, two chieftain brothers who worked for my Grandmother Tucker when she lived in North Bay, Canada. Hunting guides by trade, they worked a season on the Tucker farm in order to buy a bolt of purple velveteen cloth at the trading post for their wives. At the harvest feast, they did not sit at Grandmother Tucker's great harvest table under the maple tree, but sat some distance away, receiving helpings of food on their red bandannas spread before them on the ground. I am not sure who was excluding whom: They were, after all, chiefs. But there was no proper attempt made to make everyone feel that they could all take their places at the same table. That is still waiting to happen between Native Americans and everyone else. I wonder when Thanksgiving will finally happen and a just peace will truly be devised.

There was something in the facial bones of my grandfather to suggest that his parents were kin to Wahbateeste and Untwinecolten. If I am more the hunter-gatherer than the farmer, which is true enough, then I may owe some of my treasured wanderlust to the distant elders of the men approaching me on the road.

I saw all this as they approached through the wavy heat of the highway, and a great smile came to me. I said hello to them, and they smiled and said hello to me as we passed. They told Duffy, when they got to the bridge, that "the old woman who walks" was way up ahead. Duffy thanked them and drove on to find me.

I will get you out of this long desert soon, but I would like to stop and let you see an Indian graveyard out in these wilds. The earth is piled high over each grave, with a white cross at one end. Each mound is trimmed with vases of plastic flowers and, in some cases, gifts symbolic of the person buried, including favorite soft drinks. The most decorated graves were those of children. In the great, brown desert, a cemetery ahead is a shock of color and gaiety, like an unexpected flower garden. There are many graves of children because diabetes is a plague across the reservations, striking, crippling, and killing as many as half the people in some villages. Dialysis centers are set up in every large reservation town, but not much is being done to really stop the plague. There are many theories about why diabetes strikes these people so hard. One idea is that their genes were adapted over the centuries to subsistence hunting and gathering. Their systems do not know how to handle normal quantities of modern food. I don't know if that is the right theory, but there is no doubt that the people are suffering. Some teachers are trying to get the youngsters to be much more active in running, dancing, and other traditional activities and to limit the kinds of food they eat to more traditional fare. That has a good effect, but it does not eliminate the problem. And it does not seem to affect the number of decorated children's graves you see as you walk.

One more stop: In the town of Coolidge, there is an ancient adobe apartment structure, several stories high. It was one of the hundreds of community buildings constructed by the canal builders of a thousand years ago. To preserve it from the elements, a great roof was built over the whole thing many years ago. It is a national monument, so we walked in and took the tour. After making a very nice presentation, the park ranger asked if there were any questions. A lady raised her hand and then pointed to me. "Is that the woman who is crossing the country on foot?" I believe it was my hat that gave me away. Had I thought that I would have distracted people from the ranger's fine presentation, I certainly would have tucked it away.

The flat, desert setting of the old pueblo was strikingly beautiful. I say "was" because the town council approved the construction of a giant discount store on the adjacent land after I left.

It will no doubt be the final blow to the struggling family businesses in the partially boarded-up business district of Coolidge. The lack of respect for small family businesses was something I saw in town after boarded-up town across America, where the deterioration was so severe that even the graffiti could use some touching up. For a few dollars saved at a discount store, or in an attempt to steal the tax base of competing towns, communities cut their own throats and turn their neighbors from business owners to store greeters. I think the residents of a town should support their locally owned businesses and turn out of office any councilman who gives away the town's economy to the giant retailers from out of state. Those corporations are using their overpowering capital to annihilate small businesses and turn our towns into their colonies, and it is quite the same process that impoverished much of the Third World. It is a kind of self-colonialism: America's corporations are turning upon their own countrymen.

When the economic life of a community is defoliated by pushing all the little family businesses out of existence, there are fewer and fewer kinds of people who can make a living to support their families.

When I was in the hospital in Wickenburg, I was just down the mountain from the town of Prescott, where Dennis's family hails from. He told me about a man named Clayton who used to roam the Prescott streets when Dennis was a child. Clayton was very mentally retarded, and he was easily visible with his very turned-out ears. He often had a lariat with him for rope practice and was known to sit behind the girls in the theater and lasso them during Western movies. The most interesting thing about Clayton was that the downtown businessmen all paid him a few dollars to take their daily deposits to the bank, and those dollars added up to a modest living and a rented room of his own. He provided safer passage than an armored truck for those deposits because the idea of anyone harming this innocent soul was completely out of the question in Prescott. Where would Clayton be today if he were still living? Probably in a group home and probably not enjoying a productive role in a community. It takes small businesses operated by local owners to provide a wide enough spectrum of jobs to accommodate the many, many varieties of people in the world. When people are not accommodated, they are angry and villainous, or they are depressed and self-destructive, or they are homeless and expensive.

I say expensive because we always pay much more on the output side of a problem than on the prevention side. As an example, a terrible, 1993 brush fire in Altadena, in the hills above Pasadena, consumed 150 beautiful homes—some of the barren hills were still visible, though now green, when I walked near them. That fire was accidentally started by the little campfire of a homeless man, a Mr. Huang, on a cold October night. The wind stirred up the fire after he fell asleep. Mr. Huang, I am sure, would rather have been warm in a little apartment somewhere that night. It would have been cheaper to help him than it was to not help him—it always is, if you consider all the real costs associated with excluding people from the economic life of a community.

I came across quite a few homeless people in my walk. In the West, it is perhaps easier to see who these people are, in terms of personality type. Put them on a horse and give them a rope, and I think most of them would be happy, productive, and healthy. Born a century late, they are exactly the kind of people who opened the frontier. Where are our wild frontiers now, where these rolling stones might find appropriate work? That is a question for any good community leader. Simple human dignity and economic efficiency demand creative answers. It takes no creative leadership to build jails and shelters for every personality type that does not fit into the new corporate model.

Good political and community leadership is indeed a matter of making sure that there is a productive role for everyone, so that people can meet the responsibilities they feel in their hearts, find a respected place in their community, attract a mate, and enjoy the respect of their friends and family. When they have that, people are usually no trouble at all, and we can spend our prison money for schools and stages instead. This must be the basis for economic development in healthy communities. Unhealthy communities, I believe, talk the different language of tax base improvements, world-class this and that kind of stadium or facility, and so on, while the people slowly self-destruct with alcohol, drugs, and family abuse.

Sometimes it is a relief to finally walk out of a depressed town and be in the wide spaces again.

Fraternity Boys and Bikers in Tucson

Through the next several days, we walked through the deserts and fields toward Tucson, where velvet green alfalfa and vegetables stretched in rows forever.

A fruit stand just ahead is a joyful thing to see. At such a stand south of Coolidge, a toothless, gaunt-faced woman signed my petition with a flourish. "It ain't gonna do no good 'cause they're a buncha crooks," she said. I asked her adult son, working nearby, how long they'd had the beautiful fruit stand. "My daddy had it first, and I worked on it all my life. This here's my son, and he'll take over it someday." When the three of them had signed, I said I was happy to have the whole family represented. "Oh, no you ain't," the woman said. "We got eleven children in all."

We camped here and there through this patchwork of vegetable fields and ancient desert. I spent two nights in a camper shell stored in front of a house. In Picacho, we camped in the desert, high on a hillside. A breeze came up, and it was very pleasant sitting outdoors for supper. The sloping desert before us, Picacho Pass, was the scene of the western-most Civil War battle.

One day, Nancy Cayford, an old friend from home, and Duffy and I noticed little holes, about big enough for golf balls, all along the side of the road as we walked. Little rodents would dart in and out of them as we walked, like some vast arcade game. Finally, we saw one of the creatures dead on the road: about six inches long with no neck and tiny ears. It had dark brown fur with a ratlike tail and a narrow body. Near this poor fellow were several others, all squashed by the traffic. We imagined that a family must have been moving all together when they met their demise, or they met their fate mourning the first and then subsequent traffic victims, as often happens with other animals on the road, especially mourning doves, who mate for life.

We waved at passing trains. The engineers would sound their long horns. Truckers did the same. Spotting Granny D had become a thing with truckers, as I had been told at a truck stop lunch counter.

Friends came and went. I walked into Tucson on March 5 in the company of two photographers sent by *People* magazine, Eric and Mark, who walked backward nearly all day long, snapping away. We chatted, of course. Eric was thinking of asking his longtime girlfriend to marry him. I quizzed him to see if he was worthy of any young woman.

"We share the work. I help with the cooking and cleaning and shopping—everything." He said in his defense. To change the subject, he asked me how I had managed to stay married for sixty-two years. "Great sex," I said. That took him back a bit. "That's it?" he asked. I said, "No, that's basic. Everything else comes after that." He wanted to know the definition of "great." I said, "When you both enjoy it." Then Mark, who had been down the road, came back and we cut it off. A half-hour later, again alone together, Eric wanted to know more. The road was long, so we talked frankly about marriage. I don't know why my opinion seemed to be worth more when I was walking than when I was sitting in my living room back in New Hampshire, but maybe it is explained by that old saying that an expert is anyone from more than fifty miles away. The longer I walked, the more my opinions were solicited. I was, for the first time in my life, feeling like an honored elder whose views were of some value. It was nice.

A rousing band of Tucson supporters and dear Herb Weinberg joined us near downtown Tucson, and we walked through the city on our way to meet with Congressman Jim Kolbe—another traditional "no" vote on campaign reform. I had been featured on the front page of the *Tucson Star,* so cars were honking and thumbs were up.

We stopped first at a day care center. Dennis was buying some time for more volunteers to arrive at the starting point of the move through Tucson. He said the little kids wanted to talk with me. Sure they did.

I never know what to say to little children. Nice Granny D was in a funk, tired from the miles I had just walked, hot from the sun. I slumped down on the floor with the children around me, wondering if I would ever be able to get up.

So here were the teachers standing in a semicircle in front of me, behind the seated children. Mark and Eric, the photographers, grinned at me as I wondered what to say to these children, many of whom I surmised spoke only Spanish. Dear Herb was in the corner, browbeating the confused day care workers for not having voted.

If you ever miss voting in any election for any reason, even major surgery or an earthquake, you mustn't tell Herb.

I told these dear little children, sitting wide-eyed as they looked up at me, that they should be good, dear little children and always mind what their mommies and daddies and teachers told them to do so they would grow up to be good people and everybody would love them dearly and that they should always stick to a job until it was done like hanging up their little clothes and keeping their little rooms all picked up so they would grow up to be good men and women and everybody would love them dearly. Now how many of you are there? Let's count how many good little boys and girls there are here, one, two . . .

Dennis came forward, seeing I was making heavy weather of this, and asked the children to teach me the numbers in Spanish, which they did. I rolled over, got my knees under me, heaved a mighty heave, and staggered up on my legs like an old cow.

As we walked away down the sidewalk, the children streamed out onto their playground and ascended their monkey bars, from which they chanted, "Gran-ny! Gran-ny!" It may have made some good pictures, but I hadn't yet the slightest idea of how to explain my project to children.

Miles later, as we walked alongside the University of Arizona campus, I heard some young men running down the sidewalk to catch up with us. They were from the Sigma Chi fraternity. At a street corner, they knelt down around me and made me a Sweetheart, singing me their famous song and then adding their names to my petition while Herb berated them for not voting. It was so wonderful, as any woman can imagine. If you ever think life has passed you by and you will never be a Sweetheart of Sigma Chi, take heart. Life is full of miracles.

A few blocks later, we passed a notorious biker bar. They were all outside cheering me and waving their beers at me, inviting me inside for a cool one, which I accepted—though a soft drink, as I was soon to meet with a congressman. I sat on a beautiful Harley-Davidson, owned by a Vietnam vet who said he understood very well what I was walking for and we had better get our country back from the special interests while there was still time. Amen, I said, tilting my drink. The interior of the bar was almost pitch black, cool, and smelling of malt. A road-hardened woman with overflowing, tattooed breasts gave me the most wonderful, crying hug. As I left, they offered to keep an eye out for me on the highways, which they indeed did. They boosted my spirits after the day's hot walk so that I was ready to face Congressman Kolbe. I couldn't have been walking more happily and confidently if I had had a tattoo. I think I would like to have one, actually. I suppose it would say CAMPAIGN FINANCE REFORM, which would probably confuse the tattoo artist. They probably do not have a pattern of that on the display board. Yet.

Unlike Senator Kyl, Congressman Kolbe was kind enough and brave enough to come into his courtyard and talk to me in the company of the forty people who were walking with me—some of whom came along from the biker bar. Perhaps it helped to have *People* magazine with me.

Mr. Kolbe was very courteous. Raised on a ranch in Patagonia, south of Tucson, he had a Western openness and kindly manners that made his flawed politics easy to take. We had a good time arguing in his courtyard and some more in his office. While I didn't much change his mind, he was a gentleman, and I congratulated him on daring to come out and face a hostile crowd. We parted with a friendly handshake. I'm sure he will come around some day and see the light.

I was ready for a weekend rest. A new Tucson friend, Golda Velez, took me to her parents' house. Carol and Harris Bernstein have a large hole in the dirt near the house where Carol, for exercise, has been digging a swimming pool. When it is finished, she will change her exercise routine to swimming. Carol and her husband are molecular biologists at the University of Arizona and the coauthors of a book on the subject. Their daughter, Golda, runs an Internet company with her husband, Al, who is disabled from childhood polio but is not stopped in the least by his disability—though he uses crutches and a wheelchair to get around. All of them have long been involved in justice issues and the politics of reform. Conversation in their home sparkles with current news, wit, and insight. I mention all this just to make the point again that we have no idea what may be behind the curtains of the little houses we pass on any American road.

It was daunting to think of the desert beyond Tucson. Because the interstate did not have a good breakdown lane, I decided to take the back roads through Tombstone and several ghost towns. Matt Keller drove the van, and Ken Hechler and I commenced to walk through the ancient, bloodied dust of what still looks and feels very much like the Old West. Ken had come to Tucson to speak at the University of Arizona with me, so we walked together.

New friends offered homes to us on the road. Heather, a twenty-eight-year-old librarian in a land conservation office, took us into her home filled with books and art, model airplanes, and the furniture of her grandparents. She is a lovely girl, tall and thin, with red hair and porcelain skin. She is a volunteer reader, a scuba diver, and a dancer who once had a commercial pilot's license. She drove us around in a pickup truck, which was fun.

For those who think I must be a Communist to be so against big business involvement in campaign financing, you may suspiciously take note: The next night we stayed with a recent Russian immigrant, Vladimir, and his lovely daughter, a University of Arizona student. Vladimir, a strong-looking man with curly gray hair above his great forehead, had been an electrical engineer in Russia. He was looking for a job as a truck driver when we stayed with him. When I went to bed, he was reading a book on computers. When I woke up, he was still there, reading. He fixed breakfast for me as we talked about his life. They had left Moscow because of the rampant anti-Semitism directed against them. He pointed across the room at all his furniture. "The people in the synagogue here gave us all this to get started," he said, his voice breaking slightly.

We had left a wake of campaign reform TV, radio, and newspaper stories in the towns and cities behind us. Fox Network News said they wanted to do a story about my arrival in Tombstone, so a friend in Tucson, Avery Kolers, made calls to set up the participation of the mayor, the chamber, forty people who were to show up in Old West garb, and so on. Then he had to call them all back when Fox canceled. We were getting used to the hardships of being a soft news story in a hard news world.

Ken had to go back to his duties in West Virginia, but on his last day we had an interesting walk. We compared our lifetime collections of romances and talked about our current needs. I told him that I enjoyed the company of a ninety-one-year-old friend back home, but that I wasn't too keen on the kind of commitment that might put me through the deathbed wringer again. The last ten years of my husband's life were very difficult. I said I didn't think I had it in me to go through that again. Ken was very sympathetic. For himself, he said he enjoyed the company of young women. In politics he meets many, I am sure. "Not that I don't like you, Doris," he said, "but I seem to enjoy the company of young women." Well, I thought, here's an honest fellow; what's he doing in politics?

He told me a story from his old days in the Truman White House. He was with the president, preparing a speech I assume, when an elderly friend of the president's stopped in to show off his young, new honey. Truman took him aside and said, "Now, what makes me think she doesn't know your real age!" "Dang right," replied the seventy-year-old. "I told her I was ninety, so she'd think I'm about to die and leave her everything!" Truman and Hechler, the dogs, har-har-harred over that one, I'm sure.

Far out in the middle of nowhere, near Tombstone, two white-shirted young men on bicycles stopped to walk their bikes with me. They knew who I was, and introduced themselves as missionaries for the Church of Jesus Christ of Latter-day Saints. After they inquired of my religious health, they disappeared over the bushy hills, their black neckties flapping over their shoulders.

Then a woman and her mother drove up and asked if I might like a lift. When I told them that my mission was to walk, the mother leaned close and said, "No one would know!" Instead of taking the ride, I visited with them for a while, learning of their health problems, which were many. It is interesting that they launched into their health woes when I mentioned campaign reform. They made a direct connection, going on about health maintenance organizations and drug companies being in cahoots with crooked politicians. I hope we don't try to stuff all our problems into the political bag, but they were right about the fact that campaign money is building a high wall between patient and doctor.

Tombstone

By the time we got to Tombstone, my only companion was Matt. We walked along the covered wooden sidewalks of the old town, past the real OK Corral, and found the mayor, who gave me a key to the city and showed us around. Later, we tried to buy an ice-cream cone at the Bird Cage Theater, but our money was no good anywhere in town. So we took our free ice cream and sat on a bench on the sidewalk. A beautiful, dark-haired, dark-eyed woman, the owner of the Silver Nugget Saloon, sat down beside us and said that we would be guests in her house, just up the street, and she would show us a good time, which she did.

Pattie "PK" Klesson seemed born to that task. She took us out that night to her Silver Nugget for a drink, then to a nearby steak house for a Western dinner, and finally to Big Nose Kate's for a nightcap. Well, that's why they put hitching posts along the sidewalks in towns like that. They're not just for the horses; they're handrails.

At Big Nose Kate's, PK commanded the guitar-strumming cowboy to serenade me, which he did. A few rounds later, PK had a tug-of-war with a cowboy poet over the microphone, both of them frothing with wonderful verse. And they had to hear from me. Well, everybody in Big Nose Kate's knows everything about campaign finance reform now. You just go check and see if I didn't make them experts—if they remembered anything at all in the morning.

Jim McGiffen, an old friend of my son's, met me in Tombstone. He would take turns with Matt, driving and walking, through the rest of Arizona and New Mexico. He brought with him a laptop computer and a guitar.

The next day, PK got news that a dear friend in Tucson had

suffered a cerebral hemorrhage. Poor PK was in quite an agitated state all day, though she insisted that we stay, as it was my rest day. By night, she was quite ill and had a long night. She was finally dead asleep when we tiptoed out to resume the long walk, leaving a note and our best wishes behind.

Not far down the rocky dirt road, I went rolling on a round pebble and ended up flat. I broke my sunglasses, bruised my hand, and scraped my knees. Otherwise fine. I had packed spare sunglasses, just like Teddy Roosevelt in the Spanish-American War, who had several spare eyeglasses sewn into his Abercrombie & Fitch uniform.

We walked on through the rolling desert hills, coming to a place of tepees and camels called Venture Quest, a ranch for boys with problems. I had a visit with some boys on the porch of the main building, and they were very welcoming and polite. I wished I could have sprung them all out and taken them with me. A grandmother might do them more good than all that wilderness. You cannot raise children well without a family all around.

Pea stone gravel made for hard walking through much of the desert. Pavement is so much easier, but rare where we were headed. The scenery soon changed to a yellow-green grass that shone beautifully in the sun. In the distance were the purple Dragoon Mountains. A hard wind blew at our front, but beautiful sights surrounded us. It may surprise you to learn that the Hollywood musical *Oklahoma!* was filmed in southern Arizona—near Patagonia, a ways west of where we were walking. The landscape is beautiful and always surprising.

We stopped at a rattlesnake farm, so called—they were mostly stuffed. The more interesting features were the huge collections of things found in the desert and on display in great leaning clusters: rusty, broken, old washing machines; washtubs; precious rocks; tools; everything.

Over the next days, we saw odd groups of people here and there, and U.S. Immigration and drug police vans. We were told that we were heading into dangerous areas, as there were people on foot, sometimes well armed, who might like to make use of our van. Our plan was to not think about it.

Along the way we met a young couple, Peter and Sarah, who had been camping in the mountains ahead: the Chiricahuas. At Matt's prodding, I told them we had been memorizing a Robert Frost poem, "Stopping by Woods on a Snowy Evening," as we walked that day, and we recited it to them. They were from Massachusetts and were delighted to hear something from home, they said.

Jim McGiffen, through these long miles, had been advancing the idea that I could help organize all the unorganized reform groups in the country and focus them on campaign finance reform. Environmental and other groups whose efforts were stymied by big money interests in Washington, should come together now, Jim thought, and I should go to some big meeting in Oregon to try to do it. Matt thought there was some merit to the idea, as did my son. Could we really create a groundswell? But any influence I had depended more on walking my course, not taking side trips. I had a long way to go for an eighty-nine-year-old woman, and I knew I should conserve my energy to complete my goal. I would take more and more side trips as my walking confidence grew in the months ahead—and as special circumstances and short-term opportunities to influence reform presented themselves. But for now, I must just walk.

Matt was very patient with me, adjusting his step to mine, and so full of wonderful conversation for the long miles uphill into the Chiricahuas—the mountains of the famed Cochise Stronghold.

Once, in the shimmer of the road ahead, came a strange apparition—a woman on a recumbent bicycle. The odd arrangement of seat, pedals, and chains allowed her to sit as if in an easy chair and see the beauty of the desert, rather than staring at the ground as most bicycle riders must do to avoid stiff necks. She was a forty-eight-year-old teacher from Texas, traveling through. She wore a visored cap with a hard hat atop it, a well-worn windbreaker, and black tights over muscular legs. She was cheerful and outgoing. We watched her depart at quite a fast speed down the mountain we were climbing.

We topped the long grade, with me using a walking stick for extra oomph on the hill and my old hiking boots for traction. We passed into pines and crocodile oaks.

We kept going. Step by step, over the top and down the other side to the tiny town of Portal, where Ken Hechler waited with a box of chocolates. The man was becoming a frequent flier on my account, which was flattering attention from someone who only likes sweet young things.

We all had a great steak dinner that night, and a fine group of honest-to-goodness cowboys joined us at our table to "git a sit-down with this Granny D."

We walked the next day, dined together again, and the following day, Sunday, March 21, we walked out of Arizona and into New Mexico in a place so desolate that not even a sign marked the state line.

Tail Winds in New Mexico

In the last days of March, the wind was fierce in the New Mexico desert near Columbus, but it was fortunately at my back, pushing me down the road in great gusts of sand. Jim McGiffen often walked with me just to steady me. When the wind quieted down, he would talk more about how we should be trying to bring the loose ends of the reform community together. I appreciated what he was saying, but I didn't know what to do beyond what I was doing: walking and talking and replacing dead batteries and flat tires—I had by this time lost count of how many, though they were well accounted for on my credit card statements.

This part of America is culturally closer to Mexico than to Anglo America. In fact, I was now walking in Pancho Villa country. I walked under a great water tower outside Columbus, New Mexico, near where Villa's troops once camped during his twelve-year attempt to liberate Mexico from foreign colonial powers and wealthy landowners. It was all just yesterday, really. I was six years old, in 1916, when Villa attacked the U.S. Army post at Columbus, killing eighteen American soldiers and losing ninety of his own. He was angry because he thought, wrongly, that President Woodrow Wilson had signed an agreement with his rival revolutionary, Venustiano Carranza, giving over Mexican sovereignty to the United States. But he was right about some things. I could imagine General Villa still out there in the sandstorm, as most of his issues are still festering.

The New Mexico wind! It got stronger as we walked. My eyes were soon weeping in spite of my large dark glasses. Large particles of sand sprayed against me and stung like little bullets. I could see only about fifty yards ahead. A wonderful highway patrol officer at one point drove his car right behind me with his lights flashing to protect me from vehicles speeding through the gritty soup. It blew so hard that when I opened the door to the van to get a drink, the wind caught the door and sprung it. It would not close properly after that, letting the wind whistle through. My old New Hampshire friends Charlotte and John Goodhue were brave enough to walk with me through the worst of it.

Between the gusts, the view was interesting. The cholla cacti have yellow blossoms everywhere across the layered horizon of hills. Roadrunners, which are quite large birds, actually run across the road just as in the cartoons, sans the beep.

In Columbus, Mayor Ken Riley introduced me to the three clerks in the adobe office of the mayor and justices. Then I was taken to the school, where second-grade children just learning English recited the Declaration of Independence and the Preamble to the Constitution and the Bill of Rights, as their very proud teacher and I marveled at them. I went on to talk to other grades, and I had a handful of little candies given to me by the second graders. I discovered a way to communicate campaign finance reform to children, finally. I told them that if we change the laws a little bit, it will be possible for them to be elected president or senator someday, if they are good people with good ideas, even if they are not rich. "To make it more fair, then?" a child asked. "Yes, indeed!" I answered.

That evening, there was a potluck dinner in town. I gave a little talk, and a woman who uses hats and handkerchiefs to imitate different characters she has met in her fight against animal cruelty performed for quite some time. Jim McGiffen brought his guitar along and used it well. With guitar and dulcimer music in the background, I had a lovely visit with a fellow who had been forced to retire early from General Electric. His income is a fraction of what it once was, so he says he has learned to live simply. He lives in a trailer with his beautiful, young girlfriend, who said she had been following my progress on the Internet.

Skinny-dipping and Remembering Dundee

The next day, Friday, April 2, and the beginning of the Easter weekend, I accepted an invitation to go soak in some hot springs up in the mountains. The springs are in a tiny community, called Membres, that is not too far from being a commune. Resident artists and people with jobs down in the valley live in little adobe houses scattered about the community. After two years, you can be voted a permanent resident and then you, I suppose, have some voting rights about who else is admitted and how the place will be run.

I arrived as they were getting the big room of the community house ready for a birthday surprise, layering it in pink and purple streamers. Two little girls were perched on ledges above a doorway, holding boxes of inflated balloons and practicing their job of dumping them over the doorway. They scrambled down on ladders and refilled the boxes, then took their positions again. Residents had brought all kinds of foods to the great table. We all were hushed quiet as the happy victim approached.

The birthday fellow, ushered in by three friends, was fully surprised. A very handsome young man, he stood grinning, looking up at the two little girls as they unloaded the boxes on him. His wife came out from the crowd to kiss him and to be picked up and whirled around as the whole room burst into applause. There was such great warmth in the room. I thought, how wonderful it would be to live here in this special village in the hills.

After presents and many kinds of goodies to eat, the crowd moved outdoors for a softball game, followed by a great dinner. On Sunday, the children had an Easter egg hunt before breakfast.

You may find it interesting that while this is no nudist colony, the custom is to remove your clothes before entering the hot springs, which are a communal gathering spot for the adults. You may find it of further interest that on both Saturday, when it was difficult, and Sunday, when it was much easier, I partook of this custom and these waters—slipping in and out at discreet times when the women had possession. Skinny-dipping among these bright and joyful artists was a great balm and a blessing. We talked about watercolors and writing. I told them about Dundee.

And I must tell you about Dundee. I only wish we were soaking in the mineral waters of Membres while we share this story. Perhaps you can do something relaxing on your end.

Jim and I often went on long hikes in the White Mountains of New Hampshire. By long, I mean two weeks. I would carry forty-five pounds of supplies; he would carry sixty. In 1939, Betty was six and Jimmy was four—old enough to come along with their little fishing poles. We were headed for Mount Meader, in the lowest range of the White Mountains, where we knew we would find wild blueberries in profusion.

This was a poor man's holiday, indeed. We were exceedingly poor in those days; we even collected newspapers, wetted them, rolled them up into logs and let them dry behind the stove, using them later to heat the house. And our weekly budgeting was extreme: I would put a few coins in envelopes for each account we owed—the doctor, the grocer—and we would take them around until everyone was paid off. So our camping trips were the only kind of family fun we could afford. And yet they were wonderful. As we were educated and optimistic, we did not feel that we were poor people—we just didn't have any money. So off we went into the jolly woods.

We stayed in the shelters built every eight miles along the

trail. They are three-sided affairs with the open side facing a fire pit. A platform runs the full length of the inside wall and, when layered with balsam boughs, forms a fragrant, family-size bed. Jim says that lying there, with the fire crackling nearby, is his strongest childhood memory of our young family. He and Betty would haul water, collect firewood, and gather boughs to make the big bed. There would be a guest book in each shelter in which to write a greeting. Each signer would comment on how the previous campers had left the site, and everyone made a great effort in that regard. We even left behind crackers, rice, and other foods for those who came after, as did others ahead of us.

The only visitors with no manners were the mosquitoes. The children would snuggle close to me, as the insects preferred me and would leave them alone if I were within biting distance. I would wake up with my eyes nearly swollen shut from so many bites. I was made fun of by Jim and the children as I worked over the breakfast fire with my eyes swollen oddly from the bites.

Early on in the journey, we came to a boiling brook with a little bridge over it. There might be fish in it, someone decided. What happened on this bridge was very significant to the rest of our lives. It is perfect that it was a bridge.

Jim took off his shoes and socks and put a fishing line down into the tumbling brook. No luck. After a bit, he put his backpack on and turned to put his shoes back on. Both kids were running on the bridge. Jim told them to watch out for his boot, but too late. One boot tumbled into the furious water. We looked all over for it, but it was gone. I tossed the other boot in the water, saying, "Let's see if it can find its mate!" But it was instantly gone, too.

"What did you do that for?" Jim said. I reminded him that he wasn't one-legged. He had a pair of moccasins for wearing around camp, so he put them on. Clearly, however, they would not do for the long miles ahead.

We got to the top of Mount Meader, and he sat down on a boulder to relax his pack. In so doing, he upset a hornets' nest and was bitten all over. I made mud packs and covered his bites.

So we were off to a good start.

That night he looked on the map and saw that he could drop down to a place called Mountain Pond, about eight miles away. From there, he could walk five miles to a road, where he could thumb his way to a town and surely buy some new boots. To get there, he could wear my boots without socks, as I have big feet—they go all over the place.

He set out the next day, promising to bring us back chocolates. That, he knew, would persuade me to let him go.

He had hiked about five miles downhill when he chanced onto a lovely meadow. He did so at the precise moment when a woman was standing there. She was very beautiful, with blond hair braided in buns around each ear. She saw him and waved.

Jim, who was always finding beautiful things for me, on that day found Elizabeth, who would become my lifelong best friend.

Elizabeth and her husband, Maxwell Foster, were camping on the land they had recently purchased. It was called Dundee, and like Elizabeth and Maxwell, it would become central to our lives.

The land, an old Scottish sugar farm, included three houses and a number of small cabins—sugar houses—that had been used for boiling down maple syrup. Elizabeth and Maxwell were now having the large house reroofed and renovated as their summer home. They camped in a tent and supervised the work.

Elizabeth called Jim over to her, and she soon knew all about the boots and the hornets and the wife who tosses boots in rivers and the two kids up the mountain. She said they would be driving to town soon, and they could give him a lift both ways.

By the time the three of them got back to the meadow with the new boots, Maxwell decided that he wanted to meet "this woman on the mountain whose feet are so big that her husband can wear her shoes."

With tumblers of grapefruit juice and rum, they hiked up to find us. Max brought his binoculars and let me try them. It was a new world for me to see birds up close; I was very excited about it. He gave me the binoculars to keep, and they were my prize possession for many years, until I gave them to Teenavick and Narkook, my Eskimo friends.

Elizabeth and Max were people of means, though they tried

not to show it too much. Toward the end of World War II, they began to casually develop Dundee into a retreat. They lent out sugar houses to Harvard professors, great artists including Jackson Pollack, and many fine writers. They invited us to join them one weekend, and we had a wonderful time—my Jim was a great conversationalist and voracious reader, and I had ideas to offer, too. The four of us became best friends. Sometime after the war, they insisted that we take a sugar house and consider it our summer home permanently.

Elizabeth and Max dropped into our lives as quickly as those old boots dropped out. They arrived like a heavenly grace, and we had the good sense to say yes. As a result, our lives became a lifelong academic fellowship, where we were exposed to the best thinkers and artists of our day. It was incredible fun, and it lasted for a half-century of spring, summer, and autumn weekends.

After the workweek, we would pack the car with the kids and with great jugs of water, and head up the hill. We fished in the river and climbed nearby peaks with the children. At the end of each beautiful day, we would come down to the main house for dinner, which we adults prepared together and served on a long trestle table—usually for twenty guests or more. The meals were quite fancy, and the conversation was first-rate. We would play charades and other parlor games after dinner, and put on shows in a big shed attached to the house that had been outfitted with a stage, lighting, and a curtain. All the children and adults participated, and my experience with costume making and drama was given full creative license.

In the winter, Jim and I spent many of our winter weekends skiing on our own or with the children.

Jim was always a good skier; I got good in later years. Jim quit when he got older, while I kept at it and switched to cross-country—which I still enjoy and teach. I make a three-mile trail outside my house each winter and try to ski it before breakfast.

Max was a very interesting man. He served during the war with the State Department and was later a partner in a large New York City law firm. He retired at forty-nine and started to write, publishing a number of poems and a scholarly work on Shake-

speare. He was a confidante and critic to many other writers, and
was very well connected politically, which would come into play
when we needed his help with the Alaska project.

Max and Elizabeth had two sons. Robin was educated at Gro-
ton and Harvard, and taught at Berkeley. The other son, Peter, was
educated at Putney and went on to Yale, graduating with honors.
He rode to Alaska with us in the crowded Volkswagen minibus, on
our way to stop Edward Teller from using H-bombs on an Alaskan
village—which I shall tell you about when there is perhaps some
nip in the air to inspire me.

For our long years together as best friends, Elizabeth was
foremost a gardener—one of the first to garden organically in a
conscious and scientific way. There is no activity, I think, more
conducive to peaceful contentment and clear thinking. She was
from French lineage. Her father was the president of the Univer-

*Jim and I with our children, Jim and Betty, on the trail in New Hampshire's
White Mountains, 1939.*

sity of Minnesota and, following that, the head of the Rockefeller Foundation. Elizabeth went to Bryn Mawr, after which she traveled extensively with her father. As a friend, she was full of insight and information and a joyful spirit.

There was a wonderful energy to our little community in the woods that I sensed again in the New Mexico village of Membres. It is a sparkle in people's eyes.

Well, it is time to get out of these relaxing waters and go back to my walk. If I may make a parting suggestion to those planning a visit to the little colony of Membres, it is this: Knock before entering any room, as they enjoy life there and the Easter bunny has nothing on them.

On Sunday afternoon, I returned to the desert floor to resume my walk the next morning, but I felt changed. Whatever part of Dundee had dried out in me in these lonely years had been refreshed somehow. I was more my old self—that is to say, my young self. And that evening, staying in the trailer home of Virginia Hallack, was the icing on the cake.

"Now, Doris. Sit down right here, and I will give you a concert!" she said after dinner.

I sat and sipped my tea as she picked eighteen instruments off the wall one-by-one and played and sang "On the Road to Mandalay" for the rest of the evening. Trumpet, fiddle, flute, banjo, and on and on, with vocals in her high-pitched voice where breath would allow. It may seem comical as I describe it, but it was in fact quite something. Here was a woman in the vast desert of New Mexico letting her every breath make the best music she could muster. Your breath can blow through more instruments than you can imagine, and they were all there at Virginia's.

So she sang, strummed, pounded, and blew her song into the night as I tapped my toes. I imagined that the lizards and the desert hares outside were doing the same, swinging back and forth with a smile and a loving stare at Virginia's little trailer in the desert, all of us amazed at what can be done with the breath of a life.

Under the Crescent Moon

April 17, my last night before crossing out of New Mexico, was spent at Mary Kay Papen's home. The stars there are spectacular. A thin, new moon slid across the sky, boding well for new adventures in Texas.

When the twentieth century was yet a bright, happy youth, unmarked by war, there was an annual performance of a newly minted, three-act operetta in our town's moving picture theater. The sight of a crescent moon always reminds me of it. I stood in Mary Kay's yard, swimming in the stars and in this memory.

The regular offerings at the theater were silent pictures. A large woman played the theater's piano with gusto, accompanying the film action and exciting the children and adults to cheer the heroes and boo the villains. It was affordable, and we all scraped up the nickel to go every Saturday. But the annual musical was even more exciting, for the show played for a whole week and the boys and girls of the town would often get small parts— appearing in line dances or costumed as animals, flowers, or clowns. Unfortunately, tickets were more expensive than for a film, and our family did not have the money to attend. But one year something special occurred.

My dear Aunt Bertha, whom everyone called Birdie because of her name and her beautiful voice, secured the lead in the operetta. In her big scene, she was seated with her beau on a wooden crescent moon that was suspended by wire cables and moved high across the stage as she sang. Beneath her were scores of sleeping children in their pajamas. Birdie told my mother that my two eldest sisters and I might get into the great event if we showed up for rehearsal in our pajamas.

I'm sure that seemed like no bargain to Mama, for she knew we would need expensive new pajamas. Mama normally made all our clothes, often from the same bolt of cloth. We girls came as a matched set when we arrived for holiday services or any big occasion. But mother knew this was a special situation, and she walked three miles into downtown to buy us store-bought pajamas. She had no idea that all the children were wearing two-piece, shirt-and-pants pajamas. She bought one-piece Dr. Dentons, with buttoned, drop-seat bottoms and sewn feet. We were mortified, as we knew what the other children would wear. We would look ridiculous.

"We won't look like anyone else," I cried. "We'll look like babies!" But mother had made her walk and already spent the money.

There was no way for us to not go: Birdie was so excited for us, and it was, after all, an opportunity to be on stage in a real show. So we went to rehearsals, and on the night of the dress rehearsal, Sybil, Vivian, and I appeared in our Dr. Dentons, humiliated but pretending we were doing it just for fun.

The director said, "Well, look at this! Aren't you the cute ones!"

Of course, I wanted to die, ready for his further mocking. But he continued: "Let's see. I want you three in the very front of the sleeping children. You will wake up last and go skipping off, holding hands as you go!" So in this way, as is often the case, the thing that made us once feel different and ashamed was, when we courageously embraced it, the very thing that brought us success.

It was also my first experience participating in the community, and I think it set up a bit of a lifetime fascination.

After the opening show the following night, Aunt Birdie, who herself was a hit, brought us home to Mama, who could not afford to come to the show, and announced that we were the big stars. Mama was exceedingly proud. From that night, we were known in town as "those Rollins girls," which was our family name, and Mama got the lifelong idea that I, particularly, should become an actress.

When I see a crescent moon, I remember sneaking a peek as I pretended to sleep on that stage. Here comes Birdie on her moon, sweet thing but a little too big for it all, with the boys among us tittering to see her bare legs up her dress, and the men in the rigging madly struggling away with the cables to stabilize and move the thing along, and her beau clamping his sweaty hands onto the tip of the moon and onto substantial Birdie for dear life. If things had gone awry, with half the town's children below this moon of Damocles, it would have been the tragedy of the century for Laconia, New Hampshire. There would be a touching memorial yet today crumbling in the old cemetery, with a rusted crescent moon atop, squeaking in the wind.

I enjoyed my balmy last evening in New Mexico, with Birdie singing in the stars above me—a nightingale somewhere. And tomorrow, Texas!

Nick

The dry and wrinkled southwestern deserts are a no-man's-land between life and death. It had been just the right kind of landscape for me to walk out my lonely thoughts about Jim and Elizabeth and the sad slipping away of our lives. The desert was a Zen garden that didn't challenge me to be too joyful or distract me from the thousand replayings of my life as I walked. But it had been enough. As I neared Texas at El Paso, after my rehydration in the springs of Membres and my joyful lesson in breathing in Virginia Hallack's parlor, I was looking forward to the green horizons ahead.

Perhaps what I had done in taking this long walk in the wilderness was a kind of shoving of my old self out on the ice to see if I would please die, or if I would please be reborn into something new, forged in service to my deepest beliefs. In either case, I knew that my old life had run its course. On my last evening in New Mexico, I had an inkling of which way things had gone: The nightingale sang a song I'd never heard before.

And if taking the walk had been me going off to pout about the disintegration of the civic community and my loss of a place at the table, why, I had found so many new friends along the road, and they had entrusted me with so much of their hearts, that I was not feeling the least bit alone anymore.

Things were happening, too. Several thousand people were now corresponding by e-mail. Hundreds had walked. Letters were being written to Congress. Reform organizations that had long worked alone were beginning to talk to each other. Several hundred news stories had raised the issue of campaign reform in a new and emotional way. I felt like a citizen doing an important job.

In these five months walking, the energy and commitment of the young people was the thing that gave me the most hope. Even the often-slandered Generation X members were well accounted for.

A twenty-five-year-old carpenter from Chicago, Nick Palumbo, showed up one day in Las Cruces. Tall, lanky, dark-haired, Nick had jumped on a train to find me. His journey began years earlier when he and a carpenter friend pledged to each other that they would, all their lives, work one day a week for a cause they believed in deeply. I cannot tell you how I felt to hear a young person talk in such a way. It made me teary-eyed.

Nick became involved in the protests against the U.S. Army school at Fort Bragg that was allegedly training South American soldiers in the art of torture. He was among six thousand pro-testers in 1999 at the fort. He also studied nonviolent social change techniques in India. When he got back to Chicago, he was determined to get to the root reason why U.S. policy sometimes favors corporate interests around the world and the theft of re-sources rather than the interests of simple justice. He concluded that campaign finance reform was the keystone issue. He had never used the Internet before, but he sat down at a family com-puter and searched for the term "campaign finance reform." The GrannyD.com site was the first thing that popped up. So he read it, top to bottom, and decided to join my walk for a while. He said he was looking for that magic "power of one" that he saw in the work of Gandhi and King. I laughed when he said that. Once he knew me better, he laughed, too. We also laughed about our first meeting, which was after I had just walked a very long way in a very hot desert. I was dog-tired, almost to the point of passing out, and I just nodded and smiled to his questions.

"You just smiled. I thought I was in the presence of a mystic," he later told me. He wasn't.

He walked for two weeks through the harshest deserts of southern New Mexico. He had a firm grasp of the issues and a wonderful speaking style, so he was a great asset through those towns. He had also become a good promoter, passing out flyers in towns to promote my talks. When he left to go home to Chicago, he did so to work some carpentry jobs and save his money so that he could return to the road, paying his own way.

I would not see him again until Tennessee, but that was when I would most need his help.

Well, Friend, we have already shared three states and a thousand miles. We should perhaps have a little bowl of ice cream and give our eyes a rest.

BOOK II

Coming Alive

On the morning I would cross into Texas, I lay peeking from my covers for a few minutes before rising. Getting all the way to Texas was deeply satisfying, but now I would have to think about crossing a hopelessly large state. The idea was overwhelming, though my patented method of just putting one foot in front of the other was holding up fairly well. I decided that I just wouldn't think about the whole state.

Rising early is natural for me. I take my hearing aids out before bed and therefore can't hear an alarm clock very well. I use my mental clock instead, which works fine if I remember to set it. On the road, I would rise and bathe quickly, bandage up my toes or feet or whatever needed wrapping, then put on my steel corset back support and my clothes. I have special insoles for my walking shoes, so I would make sure they were correctly seated and then lace up the shoes. Last on would be my high-visibility orange vest and my hat. I often wore sunglasses, to protect me not only from the glare, but also from the grit thrown up by passing traffic.

At breakfast, I would have a bowl of cereal and, if I could get it, some hot tea. Then I would go out to where I had left off the previous day and begin. If other walkers were joining me, I would pace around, waiting for everyone to be ready with their water bottles, hats, sunblock, and such. Soon—often impatiently—I would say, "Let's go," and I would set out at a fast pace, holding the big, yellow flag for visibility. That would tend to organize the dawdlers, and they would soon catch up. We started before sunrise, and we therefore had to be extremely careful of traffic in the dark. But the moisture and greens and blues of the dawn were always refreshingly beautiful in any terrain and worth the danger, I thought (others disagreed). I enjoyed my companions, but I also walked many a mile alone, which was joyful in other ways.

My body was never entirely the same from day to day; there would usually be some newly sore toe or something pinching or rubbing or aching somewhere to create an annoying backbeat for the day's trudge—the ache *du jour.* After age forty, it's always something. But after eighty-five, it's always nearly everything.

After the first mile or two, I would somehow disregard the flurry of irate telegrams being sent from the far corners of my body and begin to enjoy the day's company and the landscape. Toward the end of the ten miles, particularly in hot or hilly weather, my concentration would have to go back to each step and to my labored breathing. I became very conscious of the fact that I was soaked in perspiration and looking, I'm afraid, like a drowned rat. I am so vain! Why on earth should I care how I looked under such circumstances—but I did.

My hearing aids were rarely working properly, so unless I made an effort to adjust them to hear a companion's conversation, I walked through silent landscapes, unable to hear even the crunching of gravel under my own feet. I was always conscious of the temperature and moisture of the air as I moved through cooler and warmer pockets in the vicinity of greenery or barren soil. A cloud cover and a gentle breeze were my favorite treasures. Even in regions of hot, dead air, a brisk walk provided a private breeze, and the yellow flag, held forward, gave a flapping shade.

Because I was walking eastward, I had to be conscious of the fact that early morning motorists coming behind me were driving into the rising sun and would hardly be able to see me. So it was usually safer to walk on the left side. I don't know how many times we were nearly hit anyway. I credit our prayers with saving us from mishaps. Countless times, my companions grabbed my arm and pulled me aside when traffic came too close. So, I do not recommend walking along busy roads, especially when side roads or back roads can be taken.

So here we go on a desert morning, bound for the Texas line: The friends are ready. Test the shoulder of the road to see if the gravel will roll under foot or hold firm. Begin the walk, raising the old flag high. Find the curve of each foot that works best to avoid the sharper pains. Keep a straight posture and land easy to keep the dull pains of the spine from spiking too often. Keep an eye to traffic, but scan the ground in front of each step—a fall could be a great disaster, as we ancients are made of china. Wave a hand to the people passing by. Breathe deeply, for old muscles need their oxygen, as old trains need their coal. Remember to frequently take a sip of water from the backpack's plastic tube. Another step and another, chugging along now, with the far horizon sometimes visible from atop a rise or around a bend. Be a good sport and chat it up downhill with today's companions, but save precious breath going uphill. Keep going. One-half mile already down. Above all, grasp that we are here now, in this beautiful place and moment. And so it goes, with always a new plant or animal to discover and the clouds of the sky forever presenting a changing gallery of sublime colors and shapes beyond imagination to distract us from our pains.

Wild Texas

I was welcomed to Texas by several people standing under the Texas sign with cold drinks and snacks and great, pump-handle handshakes. "Welcome to Texas, Doris," they said, simply and beautifully. I took the first step into this new place and then accepted their refreshments and their new friendship.

In the following days, the heat increased, but so did my spirits. I was entering a kingdom of high energy and generous living.

My Friday friend, radio host Jim Hightower, the radio voice of American populist-progressive reformers, was somewhere ahead. I imagined that his buzzing AM radio waves were lassoing me into his great state. I was in the land of oil wells, cowboys, cowgirls, and remarkably large landscapes.

For the first few days of Texas, the road skirted the southern edge of the White Sands Missile Range, most of which is across the line in New Mexico. At the far end of that range, hundreds of miles north, is the Trinity Site, where the first atom bomb was exploded in 1945. The little kid in me looked over the horizon in that direction, hoping to see some interesting cloud. I was in Edward Teller's backyard—the father of the H-bomb and my old adversary.

Somehow I knew I was in for it in Texas. If I needed an omen, it came twisting along the highway one day. My son, Jim,

My son, Jim, advancing the trail with Matt Keller of Common Cause behind the wheel.

had pulled the vehicle over and had climbed onto the roof, the better to receive a distant cell phone call. Just then, a small twister touched down, overturning a nearby motor home and then bearing down upon me. In a great swirl of sand and debris, old Jim tumbled down from the van and ran after his mother.

The thing zipped past me and was gone before Jim even had time to tackle me. I was fine, though a little shaken. Jim ran back to the overturned motor home, where a woman was trapped inside and trying to get out. Her vehicle was hissing propane and was turned onto its door, so the woman was stuck in a dangerous situation. Jim quickly found the propane tank compartment and shut off the valve. Then he kicked in the already cracked windshield and rescued the woman. I mention that it was already cracked because I can just see her insurance company making a copy of this page and sending it to Jim along with a bill for the windshield.

This was not a tornado. Tornadoes come from the dark clouds of colliding weather systems. This came out of the blue sky and is what Westerners call a dust devil. The very hot air near the desert floor tries to rise, but is prevented by a layer of cooler air above. When a weak spot can be found in this cool layer, the hot air rushes up in a violent tube of wind, dust, and debris. Sometimes, a great dust devil will stand for a long while out in the middle of a great valley—a standing wave to adjust the atmospheres of the desert. Or a little one may perch atop a mound of dirt or a raised railroad bed. As many as a half-dozen will at times be visible in a wide, hot expanse of flat desert. They can be small and whimsical enough to just borrow your hat, or they can, as you see, overturn a motor home or visit serious havoc upon the tents of a camp or a desert shack, sending the sheets of a roof high into the blue sky—great, rusted kites that come slicing back to earth some minutes later.

When the dust wasn't blowing or twisting, a dead heat set in. By changing to a southern route, I had let myself in for that. My steel corset felt like a sizzling rotisserie rack—and I was the old bird being roasted. The southern route had also put me in tornado alley, and I would be hiding in a bathtub from the real McCoy before I left Texas.

Grass for Snow

As the gold sun rose high in the morning sky, the flat landscape of earth and stubble shimmered sometimes like snowfields to my old eyes. I yielded to this illusion in order to feel cooler. As my walking companion, Jean Higgs, walked silently beside me, I remembered the time my older sister, Sybil, and I nearly died of exposure on a frozen lake. The memory made the hot miles positively chilly.

The memory was from the first winter after the First World War. I had pestered Sybil to go with me the two and a half miles across our frozen Winnisquam Lake to the town on the other side. There, the Winnisquam Hiking and Skiing Club was holding running races with prizes and free coffee and doughnuts. We could use the new skis Papa gave us for Christmas to get across the lake. They were cheaply made children's skis, but we loved them. I was eight and Sybil was ten.

I knew I could win a prize in any fair running race, but I needed Sybil to go with me, for Papa would not let me go across the lake alone. Sybil didn't want to make the hard, cold trek, but I was relentless. "Free doughnuts, Sybil. Think of it: All you want. And hot coffee to wash them down so you can have more!"

Sybil was overweight, and Mama would always try to stop her from overeating. Her pudginess was not her most important feature: She had taffy-colored pigtails that reached to her waist, big, blueberry eyes, and an angelic face—rather too round, of course. She cried easily and was jumping scared of anything that moved in the dark, but she was very poised and socially fearless. She had tender feelings and was quite literally a ball of kindness—and no match for my cruel manipulations.

I had gotten her little mouth watering, and she agreed that we would ask Papa for permission to go across the lake.

Sitting at the family table that noon, we laid out our case. We would be with crowds of adults. All the kids were going. We had new skis, and you have to use skis or there is no point in having spent money for them. Also, I would surely win a prize.

There were six of us squeezed around the small oak table in our dining room: Papa; Mama; my sister Vivian (eighteen months my junior and my only sibling now alive); my only brother, Rex, (four years my junior); and Sybil (two years my senior). Baby sister Merle would not come along for another few years. Papa, as usual, had come home for the midday dinner from the Lougee and Robinson furniture warehouse, where he handled packing and shipping.

I should mention that I was very proud of this work my father did. The warehouse was an immense world of its own to my eyes, and Papa was its king. He knew where every little chair or thing might be, anywhere within the towering, endless aisles of its six, immense floors. There were no electric elevators yet in Laconia, so my father raised the elevator platform full of furniture—and occasionally me—by pulling on a block-and-tackle arrangement of great ropes with his powerful, glistening arms. The elevator would move through dusty shafts of sunlight streaming from the great windows; electric lights were an afterthought to such old buildings. Papa was not a tall man, but he was strong and sure of himself. He believed in his work and in the company's wonderful furniture. When the hour came for the midday meal, he would leap from the loading dock and whistle home on his bicycle.

Mama usually prepared meat, beautifully whipped potatoes, some poor vegetable cooked to a frazzle, and a baked pie or cake for dessert. Mama and Papa might talk awhile about the ending of the Great War, or about the warehouse, or the neighbors, or our Methodist church, or the new house being built for us.

After Papa and Mama discussed such things, there would be a lull. We children might then respectfully introduce a new subject. We made our pitch.

Papa agreed to it, so long as we promised to stay with the adults and so long as we were home well before dark.

This picture of our little family may make you long for times when there was quite a bit of respect at the family table. It is important to understand why things have changed. There are many politicians who sell "values" like snake oil and will point to the family of old and say, "See, we need more of this," as if all we had to do to solve the problems of an overly commercial age were to become stronger parents and more respectful children. Missing from that argument are the facts. Strong families, in mass numbers, do not come from out of the blue or from our good intentions. Papa never doubted that his hard work would be rewarded sufficiently to take care of us. His kingly power over the world for our benefit was the basis of our family economy and the basis of the system of respect in our family. In today's world, millions of laboring parents no longer have the ability to meet their responsibilities to their families, and everything falls down without that centerpost.

To the men in the front office of the Lougee and Robinson furniture warehouse, my father was a valued and honored employee—a family man with great responsibilities. That was the contract that secured much of society. It was made possible by the idea of an honest profit, meaning a modest profit. It would be going too far to say that the atmosphere of respect in our house came from the company policies of my father's employer, but there is something there. When reliable work brings reliable rewards and respect, you can build a proper society upon that equation.

Now, I don't mean to say that things were so respectful that we told Papa everything. We certainly didn't inform him that we would be the youngest children crossing the frozen lake. In fact, we had a very hard time keeping up. The lake was wind-swept and bitter cold. Sybil trudged behind me, complaining and whimpering—her skis crunching deeply into the sparkling snow. We were the last ones to arrive on the far side, but were still in time for the races. The doughnuts, however, were picked-over, and we were told to take only one each. The coffee was cold. Sybil glared at me, shivering.

They put boys and girls in the same foot race, which I thought was unfair. One of the boys was so tall he should have raced with the adults. I had to be satisfied with second place, which was a big disappointment. I certainly could have bested any girl in town and most of the boys. Sybil poked around the empty snack tables and said it was too bad I didn't win.

It was now dusk, and I worried about us getting home across the lake. Sybil had been so slow coming over that I made sure we left with one of the first groups going back. Less than a mile out, the lacing broke on one of Sybil's overloaded skis, and we had to stop. We tried and tried but couldn't fix it. We were soon alone and in near darkness. The lights of Laconia were twinkling in the distance. She lifted the useless ski over her shoulder and proceeded on one ski and one foot. She was in tears.

"We're never going to make it," she wept. "You go on without me—there's no need for two of us dying."

"You're not going to *die,* Sybil," I told her. "We can make it. Look, the lights are right over there on the shore. It will just take us longer, that's all."

"But I'm so cold."

It was soon clear to me that she was right: We were going to die, and it would be my fault. I should have known this was going to be too much for her.

The cold slowed us more and more as darkness fell around us. I could easily imagine what it would be like to die out there. Curling up in the snow became easier to imagine than ever getting home. I felt badly that the ski club would probably be severely criticized in the weeks and months after our pathetic, double-coffin funeral. It was really our fault for not staying with a group of adults or calling to them when we had a chance. Certainly, the adults had been looking out for us all day, but each group, perhaps distracted by their own laughing and singing, assumed we were with some other group as dusk fell. The ministers would try to comfort everyone and say it was God's will, but there would be recriminations and accusations forever. It would still be going on today in Laconia. I know that for a fact, because I was in Laconia recently and someone a bit older than I am asked if I wasn't one of the Rollins girls from that pajama skit where the girl was singing on the moon.

Suddenly, we heard voices from the darkness behind us. It was a robust Mayberry Quimby, whose father owned the drugstore, coming along with his new girlfriend. They were just barely teenagers, but they were adults to us. They had been late in leaving Winnesquam and nearly literally stumbled across us in the dark. Mayberry produced from his pack a long piece of rawhide and a jack knife to make the repairs. They stayed with us all the way home, encouraging Sybil along and warming us with friction hugs.

And all the way, I worried that it was my selfishness that had put my sister in such danger. It was the first time I really understood that I was a real person, and that I had the power to influence people for good or evil and must be responsible. I had never felt so close to my sister, or anyone, perhaps, until that night. If it was a frightening moment, the resulting closeness was, I think, worth it, as my abiding memory of the night is a happy one.

When I was old enough to go to the town dances, I was chided by the other girls for always saying yes when Mayberry asked for a dance. He was considered quite an Ichabod Crane and was, in fact, a dangerous dance partner: He would hold you too tight, seize your right hand, and pump it for all his life. "Pump-handle Mayberry" was what the girls secretly called him, but never did I. That was another lesson learned: Don't make fun of anyone if you can help it, because you never know what wonderful thing they might do for you under the right circumstances. Of course, sometimes people are too funny, and you can't help it.

Coming out of these recollections, I walked quietly in the heat for a long while, all the hotter, now that the last snows of my imagination had melted. I remembered our arrival home and our quick thaw in front of the red-hot woodstove and our even hotter Papa.

The Big Enchilada

Early in my Texas walking, *New York Times* reporter Frank Bruni appeared. When *The New York Times* comes calling, you rather suddenly feel like a teenager whose parents have just come home early—you check your buttons and hope everything is in its proper place. I was a bit nervous. We sat down at a Mexican restaurant. He was very sophisticated in that casual kind of way. I told him about my concerns for our democracy, but he didn't seem too interested as he ate. I felt a little naive and silly. Then I thought, Well, Doris, just tell him what you feel and don't worry. So I let it all out, telling him my sappy notions of what self-government must be like if we are to be free people. He nodded, raised his eyebrows from time to time, glanced out the window, and otherwise finished his enchilada as I finished mine.

After a bit of a lull, I asked why a big-time reporter had come all this way to talk to me. He smiled and chuckled, and I suddenly felt some warmth. He said he had heard a Texas congressman on the U.S. House floor say that they'd all better get their marbles in order because old Granny D was on her way. He said he figured he should find out what that was about. He went on to say that he thought the Eastern newspapers had passed over the story so far, thinking it was a stunt.

"Well, now, you'll have to tell me if you think it is," I said to him. He said no, he didn't think so.

His news story was excellent, and my fear of being made to look silly was quite misplaced. This moment was important, because *The New York Times* simply owns the stamp of approval for American news stories. With the publication of Frank Bruni's piece, my effort was validated somehow—taken far more seriously by all the other news organizations and by the Washington crowd.

GrannyD.com

I am confined to bed, but my thoughts and prayers go with Granny D. I admire her spunk and agree with her totally. I have written to my representative and senators about campaign reform and hope something is done this year.

M. J. White, Albuquerque, NM—Friday, April 5, 1999

I read about Granny D in *The NY Times* today. She's awesome. I've posted the article in front of my office door to let others know about it. She's a true testament to the idea that one person can make a difference. . . .

Rebecca Long, Sacramento, CA—Friday, April 2, 1999

I'm a college student, and this gives me renewed hope for our country and encouragement for me to take my own chances and make my own adventures and not to be afraid!

Kathryn A. Wolfe, Austin, TX—Friday, April 2, 1999

You are a wonderful inspiration for all of us. I am the Democratic Senator from Michigan and a long time supporter of the McCain-Feingold bill. Your determination will help us in Congress who feel deeply about the need for campaign finance reform keep our eye on the ball. Our good wishes and many thanks are with you as you walk.

Senator Carl Levin, Washington, DC—Saturday, April 3, 1999

Me and my hippie girlfriend think yer great granny!

Geoff Marslett, Austin, TX—Saturday, March 27, 1999

A Land Waiting for Rain

I was walking through the region known as the Trans-Pecos. It is that wing of Texas that tucks under half of New Mexico: Texas west of the Pecos River. In the small towns along the road I could see so many of the same kinds of people I had known as a child in Laconia. Small towns make up for their lack of people by having everyone be more interesting.

One of the first and smallest Texas towns I came to was Cornudas. It is on the map, but just barely. May Carson, the owner of the café there, welcomed me as if she were the mayor and my long-lost daughter. She is tall and slender, one-eighth Cherokee, with a blaze of red hair in a swept-up bouffant. She wears jeans and a cowboy shirt and stands with her thumbs hooked in her trouser pockets. She laughs big when she speaks.

All the truckers, lawmen, and traveling men frequent her café and consider her to be the central attraction of the region—after their own wives, of course. The café tables have legs, which you would expect, but they also have trousers and boots, which you might not. The rafters are lined with thousands of old work caps, each preserved in plastic. Foreign money is stapled all over one wall. Another is covered with embroidered patches and another with old postcards—all covered in clear plastic. The menu is written in pencil on a brown paper bag. The food, both American and Mexican, comes heaped high on oval plates and is wonderful.

In the adjoining gift shop, small, handwoven saddle blankets were on sale for $5 each. That was the best rug bargain I have ever seen, and I am a rug hooker and something of an expert. But you have to wonder what they are paying the weavers, because it is hard work.

May's place is like an old Western movie set, complete with wooden sidewalk and Conestoga wagons. Along the wooden sidewalk are little storefronts, which May built to use as motel rooms or rental apartments. There is not enough water in the area to rent them, according to the government officials who told her to close them down. But one on the far end is kept habitable for passing friends, and we were given that status within a few minutes of meeting her.

I was still with my longtime friend Jean, who had been walking with me for nearly a month—since before Las Cruces. May gave Jean a key to the restaurant and told us to fix our own breakfast, as the place didn't open until eight in the morning—we were starting at six to beat the heat. The next morning, we enjoyed being our own short-order cooks.

As we were walking, three different trucks stopped along the road to see if we needed a lift. "Walkin' or broke down?" one old Native American fellow asked me from the window of his beat-up truck. His pretty, teenaged granddaughter sat beside him. This stretch is slightly hilly, with bare stretches of sand, cacti, and creosote bushes. A red-tailed hawk exploded out from a bush as we passed, circling around until he found a telephone pole a safe distance away where he could keep an eye on us. The next day, May joined us on the road after the breakfast rush. She sponsors a few miles of the highway for litter control, so we picked up as we walked, and she told the story of how she had cleansed her body of cancer. She had first received radiation, which had made her violently ill. She then refused chemotherapy, instead drinking gallons and gallons of water every day. The cancer went away, she said. She drowned it.

We stopped at a small, abandoned house made of stones, and we went inside—its doors and windows were standing open. May showed me the spent matches that indicated immigrating Mexicans had camped there recently. The place belongs to an Arab sheik, she told me, who had never come near it. May once rented it from him, through an El Paso agent, for $50 a month when her daughter and new son-in-law needed a place. They got divorced, and the daughter moved to California. The stone house has not been rented since, and wind and dust and illegal immigrants now blow through its broken windows and doors.

She told me the names of the plants we passed, which I always love to know. Yucca is the tree that the Indians used for soap and other purposes. The root bulb soaps up well. She also showed me grama grass, which is like a wild barley.

I had heard about grama grass when we first arrived at the café from a waitress named Mary, who works there with her daughter. Mary told me about their life. She is a widow running a nearby ranch. Her daughter, two granddaughters, and a grandson all live together and manage the ranch, riding herd, branding, rounding up. Her day begins on her horse, or in a pickup truck hauling fifty-pound bales of grama grass mixed with molasses to her three hundred cattle out on the range. She has one bull for every fifteen cows. Cows, unwilling to bring life into an unwelcome world, will not mate if there has not been rain, and there had been no rain so far that year—a major economic threat to her family. A cow, she told me, can produce for twelve years, one calf per year. Some cows can go as long as fourteen years, after which they are sold for hamburger. Mary's son-in-law did not approve of keeping a cow longer than twelve years, and this difference of opinion was the chief reason he left her daughter, if I understood Mary correctly. She gets back to her house at noon, showers, and heads into May's café to work until 8 P.M. That is how she lives. It seems that all the daughters get abandoned around here.

Mary served us pie that evening. After dinner, her boss, May, took us across the way to show us her mobile home, which she has filled with Western paintings and kachina dolls. She showed me a photo of her cowboy father astride a fine horse. She worries that her siblings are restricting him too much in his old age. His father, May's grandfather, half-Cherokee, came to a sad end after his wife died and his children would not let him entertain other women. When they sold his horse, which he rode every day, he went into the garage and laid out a sheet. He shot himself with the gun he always carried. He was ninety-three and not a thing wrong with him, she said.

I don't know why adult children think they have to interfere like that. It's not only hard on the elder, it makes unnecessary work for the children. The rule should be to assume that people can manage their own affairs unless they ask for help or it becomes clear to everyone—not just the regular meddlers—that some sort of intervention is absolutely necessary. You can make someone helpless by helping too much. When May was telling me the sad story, I was thinking that the old man just shot the wrong person.

May has a walled garden between the back of the storefronts and her mobile home, with over two hundred planted trees and a hand-dug well to keep them all alive. It is her secret garden. Like a cactus, May does very well with the little bits of water she can find.

That evening, we made room on the floor for a girl named Laura who was bicycling through—a microbiologist on a month's vacation. America's roads are dotted with interesting wayfarers, and they pop up unexpectedly and are quickly gone.

The next meal at May's would be our last together for several months, as Jean would be heading home to New Jersey, passing the van to my son, Jim, at the El Paso airport. Her last meal was a burrito. She had a great talk with May's friend Tony, a dark-toned, mustachioed man who waltzed with her between the tables to a good and loud Strauss waltz. It was from a cassette tape she had produced from her purse, the devil. She had it tucked away the way teenaged boys stash condoms for moments of unexpected luck.

Seven men trying to cross the border from Mexico were arrested near the café that day. They were near starvation and in no condition to resist. It is a national disgrace that men, women, and children are dying on these deserts, by the hundreds each year, from hunger and thirst. That is more than ever died trying to get across the Berlin Wall or the Florida Straits to a better life, isn't it? Yet there is little help or sympathy for them as they die of thirst, sometimes holding their babies.

The Trans-Pecos is hardly a wasteland, yet one nevertheless wishes some magic king might pass his sword across the sky and bring rain and green grass and a steadfast Prince Charming or two to these people. The off-centeredness of life in such places comes from a deep off-centeredness in American life, where too few people are masters of their own fates. Who is this land for? That is the magic question that, even in the asking, could begin to bring forth balance and bounty.

Cloudsplitters

Walking on alone, I had a strong wind at my back, and there were big mountains ahead that I would have to climb—a seven-mile steep incline through one of the southernmost passes of the Rocky Mountains. Dominating the horizon through that pass was Guadalupe Peak, the highest mountain in Texas—over 8,700 feet high.

There are a number of people who make a big project of traveling around and climbing the highest peak in each state. I think that would be great fun, and I could certainly do some of them, even at my age. Florida's high point, Britton Hill, is only 345 feet high. We could all do that one, even in wheelchairs. There are four other states with high points under 1,000 feet. We shall skip Alaska's Mount McKinley, which is over 20,000 feet.

I am familiar with the high points in my part of the world. Mount Katahdin is Maine's. Each clear morning its summit, Baxter Peak, is one of the first spots in America to be warmed by the new day's light. I climbed it nearly sixty years ago with my husband and children, when they were six and eight. We also took our Irish setter, Ginger. There are difficult passages, such as the one called Knife Edge, where one must do some fairly serious rock climbing. We pulled our way up with the help of bits of iron that previous climbers had left sticking from the cracks. My husband climbed carrying not only his pack but also Ginger. This got to be quite a chore for Jim, and when we found a little cave we thought we might leave Ginger there in a nest of sweaters long enough for us to make the last dash to the summit. But as we departed, poor Ginger set up a howl of such unearthly terror that we went back and satisfied ourselves that we were within a spit of the top. If I ever return to finish the job, I shall not take a dog.

The highest point in New Hampshire, next door, is dear Mount Washington in the White Mountains, which I have climbed often. From atop Washington, you can see 150 or so miles to Mount Marcy in the Adirondacks, which is New York's highest peak.

Marcy is a special mountain, where several deep lines of American reform history intersect. Its summit is an altar of granite blocks, covered with green lichen and great cracks. When you stand on the summit, you are standing in very interesting footprints. Just to your north, down the valley near Lake Placid, is the old farmhouse of John Brown. This is his mountain, and he must have many times stood on this rock like Abraham and thought about his sons, his God, and his nation. Surely, it was upon such a rock where he resolved to start the bloodshed that would end slavery. He is not a sympathetic character, and I do not wish to romanticize violence as a method of social change, but here he stood.

The Iroquois name for Mount Marcy is Tahawus, meaning "cleaves the clouds." The Iroquois were clearly impressed with the way the mountain cut the clouds and made the rain pour. The name also refers to someone who tells the truth and shakes the heavens. There is a Russell Banks novel about John Brown, called *Cloudsplitter.* The title is taken from this mountain, the slopes of which, by the way, give birth to the Hudson River, which deposits the soil of this mountain far into the Atlantic Ocean.

This summit is also the very same place where Vice President Teddy Roosevelt stood on the day he learned, from a messenger who ran up the mountain, that President William McKinley had died and he had become president.

As Brown split open the gathering clouds of abolition, so Roosevelt would split open the clouds of populist reform that had been gathering since the end of the Civil War. The rise of powerful railroads, oil companies, and monopolies had pushed Americans—particularly farmers—into a corner, and they responded by creating the populist and progressive movements at the end of the nineteenth century. Theodore Roosevelt would be the man to make their reforms happen.

That two heaven shakers, John Brown and Teddy Roosevelt, should have shared the same American Mount Sinai is beyond curious. Of course, if we could see the world as it truly is, I think we would see that every twig of it represents infinitely deep mean- ing—we are just blind to the language of it.

Roosevelt the populist reformer, in whose cool shade I was walking, was a Republican—a Lincoln Republican. We may have forgotten what that meant. Let me give you an idea of it.

My father was a Lincoln Republican. Abe Lincoln was only a generation gone when my father was born. That means Papa grew up at a dinner table where Lincoln was remembered and honored. You can't imagine how Americans idolized and mourned Lincoln—Northern Republicans, anyway. If you are old enough to remember how America felt after John Kennedy's death, or how England felt after Diana's death, you will have a small sense of it. You must remember that there was no television or radio to change the subject back then. The much longer atten- tion span meant that there was time for everyone to read all about Lincoln's life, hear countless speeches about him at the civic meetings, countless poems and odes at afternoon teas, and time to form opinions about his best writings and his best decisions. Many writers simply made a career of writing about Lincoln. In an era when industrialization was challenging the family-based and faith-based values of America, the memory of Lincoln was something to hold on to for dear life.

The words Lincoln left hanging in the air for people to pon- der were words of democracy and tolerance—"a government of the people, by the people, and for the people" and, of course, from his second inaugural address:

> With malice toward none; with charity for all; with firmness in
> the right, as God gives us to see the right, let us strive on to fin-
> ish the work we are in; to bind up the nation's wounds; to care
> for him who shall have borne the battle, and for his widow and
> his orphan . . . to do all which may achieve and cherish a just
> and lasting peace among ourselves and with all nations . . .

Now, who can do better than that? These words were a spir- itual meditation for America to think upon for many long years. They certainly helped move America forward toward democratic and social reforms.

In 1912, when I was two years old, former president Teddy Roosevelt, a true Lincoln Republican, was deciding to get back into the game. He had served out McKinley's term as president and been elected to a term of his own, during which he pushed through antitrust, pure food and drug, forest conservation, and fair labor regulations and many other reforms. When his second term was over, he went on a long safari and wished William Taft, his successor, well.

When he returned, however, he found that Taft and his own Republican Party had backpedaled on many important reforms at the behest of big industry. The soul of the party was in a tug-of-war: It was the Main Street family businesses and farms versus the big railroads, oil, steel, and the rest. In short, it was the struggle for human scale. Big money won.

Roosevelt was a human being with his eyes and heart wide open to life. I think we all have that energy for living that TR demonstrated, but we do not all have our eyes and hearts open wide enough to let all that energy out constructively into the world. When it cannot get out, it coils inside us and energizes our darker corners. Not so with Teddy! When he encountered a whole system of political and industrial corruption, he was naturally disposed to attack it with all his considerable force.

He ran against Taft in 1912. He rounded up enough delegates to take the nomination away from Taft, but backroom backstabbing at the convention gave it back to Taft. Roosevelt ran as a third-party candidate on the Progressive Party ticket, which assured victory to the Democrat, Woodrow Wilson. That probably didn't bother Roosevelt very much, as Wilson was also a great reformer. World War I, however, soon changed everything, deflecting America's reform energy until it reemerged three generations later—as it always does. It came after World War II in the form of the civil rights, free speech, ban the bomb, antiwar, and the women's and gay rights movements.

That fight between the human scale and giant scale, left unresolved in the Progressive Era, is now returning for some kind of epic confrontation. Campaign finance reform is a part of it.

Don't let me get lost. I am walking uphill in sight of

Guadalupe Peak, the highest point in Texas, walking alone in very dry desert. The muddy Rio Grande is now off to the south. It comes from headwaters far to the north in the San Juan Mountains of Colorado. My son, Jim, has come back from New Hampshire to skip the van ahead of me. It is getting quite hot, even in the morning, and the road is steep.

If we stop at the summit, we can look back and see May's little café, a shiny spot in the gray expanse. Such valleys are where we live. We invest our lives there. We raise our children. We pray our prayers. And the difference between a good valley and a bad, and between a good life and a poor one, is very much a function of good, unselfish leadership and vision. Why is it that some nations around the world go so terribly wrong, devolving into mass brutality? Well, it is a matter of leadership. Even good constitutions are not enough if the leaders are not unselfish and high-minded, unwounded by corruption. Without such people, the land becomes a wasteland. With them, we do all right. The land is, after all, a paradise, if we will let it be so.

May Carson is a good and unselfish leader to her little community. I saw well-wrought communities wherever I walked. But above them, at the state and national level, there is only wind and dust, I am afraid. So we cling to the words of people like Roosevelt, just as our fathers clung to Lincoln's, and we hope for better times, better leaders—doing what we can for each other as we wait for the clouds to gather and the rains to come.

The clouds were certainly not gathering in the Trans-Pecos as I walked through it. Everything was dry and crispy, hot and thirsty. I cut south to Van Horn. Far ahead was the oil country of Midland and Odessa.

GrannyD.com

Hello Granny D! I met you today with a friend of mine. We were in the little cafe where you where eating today. I think you are a very strong woman doing what you are doing to make this country better for you and me. I know you meet a lot of people on your way across the country, so I don't know if you will remember or not but that's ok. I just wanted to let you know that I am praying for you and may God bless you all the way.

Beverly Brisco, Hobbs, NM—Wednesday, May 5, 1999

Dear Doris, I wish we could prevent catastrophes like the gift to the banking and credit card companies Phil Gramm and Dick Armey are attempting currently. There has to come a point where the people of this country matter as much as the money of the big contributors.

Carole Gandy Haynes, Dallas, TX—Wednesday, May 12, 1999

More power to you, GrannyD. You are really an inspiration to all of us young'ns—I'm 72—to clean up the worst Congress and White House that money can buy.

Mary Meany, Somerville, NJ—Wednesday, May 12, 1999

The Long X Ranch

About 160 miles west of El Paso, the Long X Ranch spreads over mountains and valleys for as far as you can see. When my son, Jim, advanced the trail and knocked on the doors of several little houses in the area, the people were friendly, but they said he really should go to the main ranch house and talk to Mary Jo. They pointed up the long, sloping valley to a green clump of big trees at the base of chalky hills.

The white adobe ranch headquarters dates to the 1880s and is nestled in those trees next to a spring. In back of the main house is a line of stone bunkhouses, all with made-up beds and bathrooms, just in case someone might stop by. Actually, up to forty people could stop by.

Mary Jo Reynolds told Jim that they would love to have me stay, along with Jim, and Ken Hechler and anyone else in our bedraggled, sweaty little party. Ken had recently arrived to put in some Texas miles.

When my feet finally got me there a few days later, Mary Jo met me at the door. She was very trim in new blue jeans and a blue shirt—her dark hair pulled businesslike into her cowboy hat. Ken and I sat back in the great central room of the ranch house as she continued her day's business. She stood in a corner, her fists on her hips, listening to the top hands of the ranch offer opinions about what needed doing yet that day. Usually deferring to the advice of Rick, the top hand, she quietly suggested what should be done first and how it might be done best. After four generations of Reynolds men and women running this ranch, there was no question in anyone's mind that she had said just the right thing. She was then off on horseback to some far range, leaving Frank Escobedo, the ranch handyman, and Laura Furlong, the cook, to mind me and Ken.

Dear old Ken watched the condensation streak down his tea glass and then said he had some news.

"Doris, you have inspired me. I am about to do something crazy."

I didn't know what he was going to say next. My mind was racing. I had been looking at the exquisite Indian rugs on the floor.

"I think that if you, at your age, can walk across America, I can do something, too, as I am only eighty-four. I have decided to run for Congress again." His cheeks were still red from the day's hard walk, but their glow seemed pure cheerfulness now.

"Well, Ken, if that's what you think you should do, I certainly think you must try. You are in good enough shape for it, and you know the issues." I went on and on, encouraging him.

Frank, the ranch handyman since 1951, took the two of us out for a Jeep drive through the upper part of the ranch. We rode for hours, as the ranch spreads through ninety-seven thousand acres. The Long X was once many times larger, as it goes back to a time when it included immense tracts in several parts of Texas. Each generation has carved it up for the next batch of heirs. Mary Jo is the great granddaughter of the man who founded it. He was a good friend of Charles Goodnight of *Lonesome Dove* fame, and a photo of the two old friends hangs near the mantel.

When we got back from our ride, Dennis Burke had arrived from Arizona. He had met up with Jim at the El Paso airport and taken over the van. Jim headed back to New Hampshire. That's how we were always patching things together.

The men and women who work the ranch are better-looking than any cowboys or cowgirls ever dreamed up by Hollywood. Their eyes are bluer and squintier, their wide-brimmed, white hats are wider and more stained with character. Their spurs jingle and their leather chaps and holsters squeak as these men and women pass you in the room and say, honestly, "Howdy, ma'am." They defer to Mary Jo with tips of their hats and assent to her orders, yet they all eat at the same long table for breakfast, supper, and dinner. Laura Furlong's husband, Rick, whose mustache takes a square turn south to his chin, is the foreman. Their teenaged son, Clay, and a nephew, Jesse, are the main hands. Other hands come and go with the seasons. Two huge, blue-eyed dogs bark inside and outside the house when you first arrive. They are not so much guard dogs; they are just happy to meet you.

The boys were not much for politics, except to shake their heads at the mention of those people in Washington: "Not the kind of characters you would want to ride all day with," Rick said, describing how the economics of ranching are controlled by Congress to a great extent—especially in regard to the import and export of beef. Rick interrogated me over supper, as the others let him. There was general agreement over the table that the politicians are in the pockets of the wrong people.

But talking politics doesn't last long over a ranch meal. There are other problems to deal with, right after supper, that must be discussed. The immediacy of things is refreshing: Ranch life is a world apart from modern, industrialized American culture where things are scheduled on pocket computers and there never seems to be a satisfying ending to anything. On the ranch, the colt gets born; the herd gets moved; the fence gets mended; it rains or it doesn't. A person's connection with the earth is constant and intimate, and one's position on the food chain is quite visible and a matter for vigilance.

Life is exuberantly laid bare: The cowboys and cowgirls of the valley were not much for urban discretion, and I so enjoyed, for the three days I headquartered there, a swirl of news about romances and jealousies. Stories were told in the kitchen, which was big enough for a good bunch of folks. There is a beautiful, old stove, great cooking vessels, and a fine view up the hill. Stories were also told in the dining room, around the long, trestle tables across from the fireplace.

One of the stories was about a fresh mess at another ranch down the valley, where the woman owner married a rotten city fellow who tried to poison her by taking breakfast to her in bed each morning and putting something in it along the way. The ranch hands grew worried that she seemed lazier and lazier each day, finally not coming out of her bedroom much at all. She was saved only by the fact that the cad met a richer woman and sped off, taking half the treasures from the ranch house when all the hands were off on a roundup. I repeat the story so that you will see that the same human problems that plow up the peace of the cities plow the rest of the nation, too. We are not a boring people, which is to our credit. And in Texas, especially, I think there is a tincture of some aphrodisiac in the branch water. Perhaps energy seeps into the subterranean rivers from those vast stores of liquid energy being pumped into the pipelines by those countless, copulating metal sculptures that dot the landscape east of the Long X. Or perhaps it is ranch life generally, where one sees so much nature all day long and does not want to feel left out of the fun.

One evening, I watched from the edge of a small, round corral made from posts stuck in the ground at an outward angle like tightly fit flower petals. Inside, Clay Furlong was breaking a colt with great patience and caution, and with very few, but important, words of advice from his father, perched nearby. The young colt would be calm and easy; then he would bolt. Then he would be easy again, as the young man walked him around and around and gradually introduced him to a bridle and then to a small saddle. We watched this as the sky grew dark and a million stars and a brilliant red Mars came out.

It is indeed star country: The University of Texas McDonald Observatory is just forty miles down the road, next door by Texas standards. Bats flicked around over the corral, barely visible against the western sky, where only a faint wedgewood glow remained. Soon, and by bright starlight, the boy was riding the colt. The creature, its head and tail high, seemed to be fine with it. The evening air was filled with dust and the sound of hooves and low conversations: Clay and his father over here in the corral, and Mary Jo and some of the boys over there, evaluating this new addition to the workforce. By 8:30, when the last color was gone from the sky, we had all turned in. I was so comfortable to be in a place where the sun again measured my day, telling me when to get up and go to work, and when to go to bed. You can get a great deal done in such a day.

In the blue dawn of the day I left; Mary Jo and the men came around to the front of the ranch house on their horses for a quick good-bye. I was leaving to bite off another ten miles of highway, and they were off to bring some of the herd from the parched upper range down to a valley where there was still some grass. I silently prayed they would have some rain soon. They tipped their hats as they do, and turned to gallop off in the early light, with Mary Jo in the lead.

The Grasshopper Queens

When road builders cut a notch in a hill, they produce a fine geology exhibit, revealing the wavy remains of ancient oceans and forests, now deformed into hills and mountains by the unimaginably slow press of continental drift. The layer cake cross-sections do make you think about all the history under the surface of your life. The hills and valleys of our own personalities are, of course, the product of a lot of piling up and wearing down of the already bumpy terrain with which we were born.

In the West, these road cuts are not much overgrown with greenery but are exposed. In the land between the Long X and Toyah, I saw the chalky white layers of ancient seabeds, with crustacean fossils eroding out, to be easily picked up beside the road. A mere eighty million years ago, this was the edge of a great ocean that has shrunk to become the present Gulf of Mexico. Had you been standing here about sixty-five million years ago, hiding out from dinosaurs perhaps, you would have seen a great flash in the southern sky, millions of times greater than the Trinity atom bomb explosion. It was a giant meteor crashing into what is now the northern shore of Mexico's Yucatán Peninsula— straight across the Gulf of Mexico from Texas. It sent a great wave of debris that now forms a stony ridge along southern Texas. It sent so much dust into the air that the weather changed, causing dinosaurs to die out everywhere in the world. It may interest you to know that the sixth major extinction of species is presently under way on earth. This extinction is the first man-made one, and it certainly will not stop until our own long-term interests are again the business of our governments.

My passage through these hills was indeed a fossil outing, as I was still walking with my old friend, Ken. He entertained me away from my walking pains with his lively, hand-waving stories about politics and Harry Truman and beautiful, talented Margaret.

"She was terrific on the piano, you know," he told me again. I wished he was about to begin describing some intimate activity atop a grand piano to make these miles more interesting, but he was not. So I nodded and listened—his heart is still so dedicated to her.

While he regretted not winning her hand, I think he has always needed his solitude as much as I have needed belonging. He is a thinker who does not seem to mind being on the outside looking in. That is torture to me, and that is why I spent so much of my life trying to get on the inside. Finally getting there, however, is never what one expects.

When the shoulder of the road narrowed through a construction area just west of Toyah, Ken and I walked single file and it became impossible for me to hear him. I should have told him so, instead of letting him waste his wonderful prose and sonorous voice on the long piles of dirt and the lizards scampering atop them. I just walked and hummed my old Girl Scout hiking songs to myself, and waved to the workers clustered in projects every few miles. When we could walk two-abreast again, I asked Ken to summarize what I had missed, and then I told him what I had been thinking about during the last several miles: my great, single-file Girl Scout hike with Sybil when I was ten and she was twelve—in the first Girl Scout troop in Laconia.

"Do you want to hear about it, Ken?"

"Why, yes, Doris. Tell me the whole damn thing; I love the Girl Scouts."

"I bet you do," I muttered very much to myself. He was angry that I had missed so much of his wonderful storytelling. But it was my turn. He perked up to the story when I described the dark-haired Tucker sisters, who were both tall, good-looking, and single. He suspended from his thinking the unfortunate fact that they were long gone from this earth.

These wonderful but hapless ladies sent an announcement around to our school that we should go over to the Congregational church if we wanted to join Laconia's very first Girl Scout troop. Sybil and I discussed the idea as we skipped home for noon dinner. When it was proper to speak, we asked if we could become Girl Scouts.

Papa sat thinking until he knew what he thought. "They're nice girls," he said of the Tuckers. "Too bad they didn't catch them a couple of men at college. I suppose it's time they have to think about doing good deeds instead." That is how I remember the conversation.

Mama wanted to know how much it would cost. She was the treasurer of the family, making the payments on our small cottage and feeding and clothing a houseful of children on Papa's small pay. Saturday was payday, so on Friday night she would rush around looking for our pencil, with which she would put down each sum we owed on a scrap of butcher paper and scowl at the bad result. When we said scouting was free, Mama smiled wanly, her intuition knowing better.

Every girl in town wanted to join, so they had to draw lots to see who would be the lucky ones. Sybil and I made the grade. We danced home happy to be Girl Scouts—finally among the luckiest girls in Laconia, which seemed to wipe out the fact that we were among the poorest and were often reminded of that fact. But now we were in!

The Tucker sisters generally had no idea what we should do at our meetings. At the first gathering, they broke us into four patrols, eight to a patrol. Each patrol was to form two lines. Miss Barbara Tucker stood in front of the assembled troops and said, "Now we will learn the Girl Scout oath. Put your hand on your heart and repeat after me."

After we repeated the oath three times, she dismissed us. That was our first meeting. All that fall, winter, and spring, we met in the basement of the church, mostly forming straight lines and reciting the oath. On our walks home, Sybil and I practiced the oath to each other, and increasingly, others walked with us— we were making friends. I was elected the leader of our little patrol.

We indeed became a group. Each Friday, our voices rang out over the eight rows of four-abreast, no-breasted girls. And we all learned the Girl Scout laws. The big moment was when Miss Barbara said we would learn to march, because, come summer, we were going into the mountains on a big hike. We cheered.

The rest of the meetings were devoted to reciting laws and learning our little paramilitary marches. We did squad-lefting, squad-righting, halting, marching backward, marching forward.

At a meeting in the spring, the Tucker sisters appeared before us resplendent in green uniforms, looking like grasshopper queens. Ahhs and oohs spilled from our little hearts. We were told that we could have our own uniforms for three dollars each.

Sybil and I earned our money at twenty-five cents per hour, sitting for the next door neighbor's little girl. The job went well, though I was usually the one stuck telling stories to little Cissy until she fell asleep. Then I would find Sybil in the kitchen sneaking a spoonful of marshmallow fluff and trying to wipe it off her nose when she heard me coming. We would read the neighbors' movie magazines and would talk about our dreams of romance and glory.

It was the only time I could read such material, as our own home was filled with mysteries and historical novels—plus Western adventures for Papa. Every Monday, Mama would walk to the pink granite public library and come home with a bag full of books for the week. She and Papa went through so many books that she would put a little pencil mark on page 56 of each book read, so she wouldn't check it out again by mistake. Occasionally, the librarians would spring clean and go through the books with an eraser, which made Mama furious.

Our lives became dedicated to the coming hike. When the great morning finally arrived, the Tucker sisters had arranged for a gentleman friend to carry us all to the foot of the mountain in his big, open truck, along with our supplies. We were each to bring a blanket, a whistle on a lanyard we had made, a dollar toward the cost of supplies, and a sack lunch for Saturday noon. To save hauling, we would just sleep in our uniforms—Spartan living, indeed.

We climbed into Mr. Philbrick's great truck. "Gee," Sybil whispered, "I hope you don't get sick." Motion sickness was my weakness. I concentrated. I breathed. I took life one breath at a time, as is sometimes necessary. I made it.

The truck left us at the base of the mountain. In eight rows, four abreast, we combed across the first meadow like brave invaders, with Miss Barbara in front and breathless Miss Elizabeth in the rear. On the trail at the top of the meadow, we proceeded in rank, though the girls on the outside had to step through the high brush and ivy. Well, this is madness, I thought. Miss Barbara's whistle blew a halt—three blasts. The stop was for a conference between the sisters, who had never climbed a mountain and had not provided in their plan for the narrow trail. The value of our long months of training was in question.

Her voice quavering with disappointment, Miss Barbara announced that we would henceforth continue up the mountain single-file. This was a great relief to me, as the outboard girls of our patrol were up to their thighs in what looked to me like suspicious ivy.

We continued, our paper-bag lunches in our right hands, our

left arms swinging as we sang. Poor red-faced, short-legged Sybil, so full of marshmallow fluff, was soon sweating and puffing miserably. "I sure would like a cup of water," she said uselessly, as the Tucker sisters had forgotten about water, and none of us had thought to even ask about it—even a patrol leader, who might at least be concerned enough for her troops and her sister to do some planning. Sybil's condition worsened until she plopped down on the trail and let the girls pass her. I stayed with her until she recovered enough to continue. We were last to the campsite with its little stone cabin. The other girls were scattered under the trees eating their sandwiches.

After lunch, we located a trickle of a spring and had a sip, and then Miss Elizabeth led us to the chilly summit of the mountain.

The evening's fare consisted of half-cooked hot dogs and beans—a great many beans for such little girls.

After dinner we stood in a circle around the fire, sang our songs, and recited our Girl Scout oath and the Girl Scout laws with our hands over our hearts. Finally, a good-night prayer and we were off to our sleeping spaces in the cabin. Poor Miss Elizabeth and Miss Barbara were all in. They were barely able to walk by the end of the evening, casting long, stumbling shadows in the light of the campfire.

In the cabin, curled like rows of shrimp on the hard, plank floor, we whispered for an hour before falling off to sleep, one by one, in the thick and stinky atmosphere of friendship.

Blanket-muffled trumpetings marked the passage of time as we drifted off to sleep. Had there been a static spark anywhere in that methane-rich mess of wool, the great tragedy of Laconia—the town spared Aunt Birdie's dangling crescent moon—would have been the loss of half the town's young girls in a hillside explosion of unknown origin.

As it was, we packed ourselves in the open truck the next morning, blew our whistles and sang until we saw the roofs of town, and skipped home from the church to tell Mama how wonderful it had been. She would spend a good part of the next Monday cleaning and pressing our uniforms, which were a terrible mess and, Mama reminded us, had cost a fortune.

Purple Glass

In the old railroad town of Toyah, Texas, where the ruined buildings of a once-beautiful main street stand vacant, Berta Begay offered shelter to me. She owns an extra house across the road that
she keeps for visitors, usually affiliated with her church. Though
she had never met me or heard of me, she was glad to welcome
me and let me stay in the house.

It is a little yellow bungalow near the railroad tracks. The
kitchen has linoleum floors creatively held down in strips with up-
holstery tacks to the old wooden floor. It is cooled only by the
open doors and the overhead fans. The yard is dirt with a little
grass, and everything about the house is well ordered and clean.
She said I would be welcome to stay there for as long as I needed
to, if she could first have a chance to clean it and make sure the
linens were fresh. That would be my evening home for the next
several days as I walked the final miles to the Pecos River—com-
pleting the Far West.

Berta, a beautiful Native American and Hispanic woman,
each evening visited us with a basket of bread and other wonderful dishes. When Berta stands and talks, her very dignified posture and great smile are powerfully charismatic. She said her
daughter, whose name is Misty Moon to describe the night she
was born, was soon to graduate from college as an agricultural
scientist, after which she will have large college loans to pay off.
Her son, whose name is Dearheart, is a medical technician at a
community hospital, living with a beautiful girl who is in the military and who was "soldier of the year" at her base. Berta's husband, Steve, is an expert machinist at an auto parts dealer in
Pecos. He named their son, knowing that the boy would have to
defend his name with his fists, which he has done. Berta is the
postmistress of a nearby town. She is rightfully very proud of her
family, as they have come a long way in one generation, thanks to
their hard work in a land of opportunity.

There is a collection of lavender antique bottles in the little house. Berta collects them in the desert as her mother did before her. The pharmacy in Pecos, thirty miles away, once had a large collection of them also, when Berta's mother traded bottles for her children's medicine—that's how far and how fast they have come.

Clear glass found in the desert is often a shade of lavender; the color is caused by long exposure to the sun. Glass used to be made with the additives of manganese and lead, as you may know (I did not until recently). The lead gave glass a sparkling clarity. But lead became expensive and scarce during the Civil War, as it was in demand for bullets. Without lead in the glass, the manganese would cause the glass to turn purple after long exposure to the sun. Around 1915, the manganese was replaced with selenium by most glassmakers. Selenium does not turn purple. So a purple bottle found in the desert was probably chucked there sometime between 1864 and 1915. Lavender bottles overfilled Berta's breakfast room table. They would catch the morning light like a beautiful, Impressionist painting. The lead that is not in the glass is, instead, in many a soldier's grave. This beautiful color, like purple hearts, commemorates sacrifice. I examined a few of these old vessels—about my own age, colored by many a long day.

Berta helped introduce me at Toyah's tiny city hall. The two women clerks invited me to speak the next evening. As I walked into town the next day at the end of my ten miles, there were posters up at the gas station and general store out on the highway, promoting my talk. Government moves fast in Toyah.

Many townspeople brought food to the evening event. Berta brought delicious cold snacks made from prickly pear cactus paddles. I saved some for breakfast the next morning. If I ever doubt that I am a tough old nut, I can remember that I had cactus for breakfast in Texas. It is very tart and tasty, by the way.

The dear event was so like something from my own small town childhood, where a visiting public speaker was always a great opportunity for a gathering and some food. The highlight of the year, in my youth, was a great summer crowd of speakers and entertainers called the Chautauqua meeting. A big tent was erected on the Pearl Street Playgrounds, the largest open space in Laconia. Speeches, entertainment, and potluck dinners were planned for the whole week.

As a child, I went for two reasons: The fun reason was that there were dramas performed—like one about the villain foreclosing on a mortgage and putting the farmer's pure daughter in harm's way. I loved drama, and got myself a part in any play put on by the Women's Club, the Elks, or The Grange. So I was in the front row when the Chautauqua dramas were presented. I did not care for the way they portrayed rural people as rubes, however, and I once told the actors so afterward. "Farmers don't talk that way in our town," I told them. My uncle Charlie was a farmer so I knew.

Adults went to hear the political speakers in order to learn something. The great progressive-populist movement had caught fire at such meetings in the early 1890s, and great speeches at those meetings kept people informed, interested, and fired-up.

Mama believed that our family was too poor for any of us children to ever attend college. She decided that the Chautauqua would be a place where we could hear great lectures and get some education. She saved to buy us all tickets, and we indeed sat there and got educated alongside Mama. I remember how she would later describe the salient points of these speeches to her two friends, Lizzie and Delia.

The Chautauqua was an important place where you could meet candidates and ideas. The idea of spending a great amount of money on a political campaign was unheard of. Of course, the Internet now has great potential for getting information to people without cost, but there is no substitute for meeting someone in the flesh, shaking a hand, looking in an eye, hearing the timbre of a voice, and seeing how a person does with other people and with hard questions.

The fellow who really started Chautauqua, Bishop Vincent, is memorialized with a wonderful statue at the Chautauqua Institute in Chautauqua, New York. The institute still has wonderful speakers and educational events there, but it is not the road show that I knew, and it is not as politically oriented. Bishop Vincent's granddaughter, by the way, was Elizabeth Foster, my best friend for so many years.

I told all this to Martha Fleischer, a new friend from Connecticut, as we visited after the Toyah meeting. Martha is a strong-looking beauty who came to America from Hungary as an eight-year-old. Her family was fleeing the Nazis, and just in time. After seeing me somewhere in the news, she drove all the way out to Texas to walk with me, staying with me in Berta's charming house. Ken had gone home. We fixed a simple pasta dinner and set up a table under a tree in the yard. Martha had been delayed by severe tornadoes that had ripped through Texas and Oklahoma. She stopped to help the Red Cross in a small town, and had stories to tell. When the twister approached, the teachers had ushered eight hundred children into a central hallway—all the town's school-age children. After the storm, the hallway was the only part of the building remaining: The town's children were saved. In the school parking lot, a parent was nearly sucked out the window of her Jeep, but she was saved by the fact that her diet had not gone well and she had become wedged in the seat belts and window. So if you ever need a reason to take a little chocolate break from your diet, remember that, under the right circumstances, it might be a lifesaver.

Following my talk in Toyah's community room, there were heartfelt comments from the townspeople about how they could no longer politically defend themselves and how corruption was literally dismantling the town, selling off the beautiful historic buildings for their bricks and changing the rail service that had once been the lifeblood of the town. As I left, Berta folded a letter into my hand. It was a long and beautifully written letter about her town and about her religious beliefs. The letter concluded:

"God has a mission for all of us, though we often don't know the details, so therefore we trust. When you pray, please remember this little town." Well, I do indeed remember in my prayers this community of kindness and reverence.

Berta loves her country and has worked hard to take advantage of the opportunities it provides. But she cries for the poor people of her town. Under her backyard tree where we dined, she took my hands and said that she understands my mission: "Everything depends on cleaning up the system," she said.

What Berta feels, and what so many people along the road feel, is political abandonment.

With all the progress we have gained during the modern era, let us not think that we are necessarily better off than the tribal village whose elders gather at the council fire in an evening to discuss the needs of the village and its people, and to manage the common resources of the village to best serve those needs. Where is our council fire? The antigovernment people will tell you that it is at your church and in your home, and that is correct. There should be council fires there. But Berta and a thousand people along any road you wander down will tell you correctly that the community needs a council fire, too. They do not have one. They do not have the power to manage their common resources, and those who have the power are misdirecting it for their own benefit. That is the feeling.

An old woman, obviously in very impoverished circumstances, pressed a can of government-issued food into my hands one day along a desert road. She did not think I looked hungry, but she wanted to give me something to help me on my way to Washington, so that it would be her trek, too. Many others did the same, telling me that when I said the system no longer represented the people's real needs, I would be speaking for them when I got to Washington. There is no one for them to complain to who will listen, except a crazy old woman walking by.

Center of the World

The town of Pecos sprawls west along the Pecos River, with the rail station and restored hotel on the north end of town, and the Buck Jackson Rodeo Arena on the south. The old post office and city hall are beautifully kept up, as is the town generally. Tom

Rivera at the chamber of commerce met me in his office and took me out the side door to a luminous, tree-shaded patio, where there just happened to be a big, annual luncheon to support the museum. The townswomen were there in colorful pantsuits and summer hats, and they had dragged along their men, who were very good sports and seemed to be much enjoying the piles of barbecued beef, potato salad, baked beans, and frosted white cake. After lunch, Tom told me where the biggest crowd in town would be the next night. There would be a "big do" at the Buck Jackson Rodeo Arena. Everybody would be there. It was an all-night walk-a-thon around the track for the Cancer Society. "Sure, Doris. You can say a few words," he said after calling Nancy, the organizer, at the health association.

Word travels fast, especially when everyone listens to the same radio station. The next morning, I was walking along the highway when a truck with two highway workers pulled over to say that they had just heard all about me and they sure were coming to the arena to listen to me.

That night, I stood atop a flat trailer in the arena and gave my first speech to a large crowd. The track was lined with little luminarias—Mexican candles—that were more beautiful in the dark, so they turned the arena lights off. I gave my speech by flashlight as people walked around the track and others gathered in the dark to listen. It was a beautiful evening. I didn't talk much about campaign reform, of course, because they weren't there for that. I talked about how we dedicate ourselves to important causes as a way of turning pain and fear into beauty.

The next morning I walked from the town to the famous Pecos River. It was a modest stream, really, as the region was in drought. But it was wide enough to do what it has done through our history: It is the boundary of the Far West. Since I had walked across all of the Far West, this was too special a moment to just go across the concrete bridge. So I took off my shoes and socks and waded across, in no hurry to get out of the refreshingly cool water.

Very near the river, Mary Jo Reynolds, on her way back to the Long X after a trip to sell some cattle, pulled alongside the highway in her big, white Cadillac and visited with me as I rested. She was wearing jeans with a jeweled belt and a tucked-in, white, pure linen shirt. She looked very elegant for a cowgirl. She talks quietly, which was just right for this nearly silent setting, where the dry grasses whisper in the warm Texas breeze.

FROM THE SPEECH AT THE BUCK JACKSON RODEO ARENA, MAY 14, 1999

Never be discouraged from being an activist because people tell you that you'll not succeed. You have already succeeded if you're out there representing truth or justice or compassion or fairness or love. You already have your victory because you have changed the world; you have changed the status quo by you; you have changed the chemistry of things. And changes will spread from you, will be easier to happen again in others because of you, because, believe it or not, you are the center of the world.

GrannyD.com

Dear Granny D, As I read your words to my eleven-year-old daughter, Josie, I was filled with such emotion that I had to pause to regain my voice. As this became increasingly difficult for me, Josie came and stood beside me and began reading the beautiful messages to me. In 1982 I began activist work, and soon found that it was no longer a job, but a calling. I have spent too many evenings in the last 7 years, most of Josie's life, working and organizing neighborhoods around important issues. I believe that is part of my job as a mom to make this world a better place for them. Sometimes, in a small, underfunded office like mine, the Fort Worth Texas Clean Water Action office, it's easy to get discouraged. My drive and determination to carry on has been renewed. I would like to call you our family's political granny.

The Hendersons, Cleburne, TX

A Texas Do-Si-Do

My hometown friend Nancy Cayford and a young Common Cause man, Hunter Schofield, were with me when we headed east from the Pecos River on May 16. Gallant Hunter hadn't walked a mile before he flew in front of me to stop me from stepping on a coiled rattlesnake beside the road. We backed off as it flashed its fangs and rattled its tail. We watched in fascination until the beautiful thing slithered away.

Being back in Nancy's company was very comforting. She is young enough to be my granddaughter, but considers herself a girlfriend. We go to the movies together back home whenever Phil, her stamp-collecting husband, goes off on a trip. Nancy has rare sensitivity to others. She has spent six or seven years helping the residents of an Indian village in South Dakota, which she visits several times a year. Currently, she is helping them put their beadwork on the Internet. She does this sort of thing quietly, and works on church and town committees. If I had to defend the reputation of America by pointing to one person, she would be a fine pick.

So would Val Wilson, whose ranch we happened upon east of Pecos. She had been trying desperately to find us when we knocked on her door.

Val was in the middle of the political fight of her life, trying to stop a plan to dispose of nuclear wastes in the area. Her representatives were no good to her, as they had all been fattened up by contributions from the waste company. She was on her own, and for some reason she thought I could help. It was, indeed, an issue I had some experience with, from many years earlier. But I didn't think I could do much just walking through. The Wilson Ranch became our headquarters for the next several days of walking, and she took me with her to some gatherings where the opponents of the dump were demonstrating. I was glad to at least be another body in the crowd. Before we left, Hunter, who is a good political organizer, spent quite a bit of time helping them plan their future course. It is very hard work being a good citizen when your representatives have been bought off. Val walked many miles with me as we talked about what she might do. For fun, she taught me to pump my arm in the air to make the passing truckers honk. She has driven trucks and done many other great things in her life.

Val passed me to other friends, also reformers, up ahead. From here on, through the rest of Texas, I was passed from partner to partner in a do-si-do reform dance that got faster and wilder as I went.

In the town of Monahans, I thought they were going to change the town name for me. It was all the work of a local radio man, Allen Martin. His deep voice, filtered by a soft mustache, pours out like honey to the trucks on the highway and the little ranch houses dotting the far hills. His station carries Jim Hightower's program, so he knew all about me and told everything he knew to every person with a radio for one hundred miles. Trucks stopped all day long with fellows jogging their stomachs across the road to give me a hug and tell me they heard all about me from Martin and Hightower. He had also put down the microphone long enough to call up the town judge and put together a welcome reception. Everyone in town turned out for Granny D Day—by court order.

So the towns were incredibly kind to me. In the terrain between them, I began to notice a gorgeous variety of thistle, with a purple fringe of leaves and a center of cream-colored petals. Mesquite bushes still covered the land, and a gray grass grew between them. Oil wells, each looking like a praying mantis with its head nodding up and down to a ten-second beat, dominated the view in every direction as I approached Midland.

Midland is all about oil and rodeos. Soon after arriving, I found myself at the Dos Amigos bull riding ring. All around the dusty ring are good shade trees and long tables with chairs. In the ring, men challenge the bulls and the men lose. But how well they lose is the game, as in life.

Everyone was having a good time socializing and watching the riders nearly get killed every time. There was only mild drinking, I noticed. Not being able to hold your liquor in such a place is evidently unacceptable. Personal responsibility is considered an essential part of manhood, and manhood is celebrated in a town like Midland.

Many of the bull riders were very young men, strutting about in tight blue jeans, with colorful cowboy shirts tucked in over their trim bellies and brass and turquoise buckles. Very pretty girls—lots of them—were available to admire the young men. Boys the next size down, looking more like walking cowboy hats, were decked out like their fathers and big brothers, and were twirling ropes, strutting about, and taking turns riding wild and dangerous lambs in the boys' ring. Very young girls admired them. Big brothers, little brothers, sisters, mothers, fathers, grandpappys, and grandmoms were all there. The gender difference in such a place is just as clear as it can be. I am not sure what kind of mythology is at work at such an event, though I suppose when you ride a beast you become one with its power, which makes you quite a satyr or at least a very bright peacock.

Everyone in and around the ring stopped twirling and strutting long enough to be respectful—and I include the bulls, who stopped snorting—when the owner stepped into the arena. He welcomed them in his wonderful drawl, and then he invited me to say a few words about my mission. They yahooed for how far I'd walked. "You are something else, Granny!" a cowboy yelled. More yahoos, and then back to their dusty business.

The folks from the local ballpark found me and asked me to throw out the first ball at the game the next day. That sounded fine, but I hadn't thrown a baseball for a good eighty years or so—and never in a real game. I worried that I might do a poor job of it. I like baseball and thought, out of respect for the game, I should put in some effort. I am a pretty decent athlete, I told myself; I just needed to get some pointers and give it some practice.

Even when empty, Rockhound Stadium is very impressive, with a semicircle of seats reaching heavenward. Nancy Cayford and I worked our way through passageways to the field, where a man exercising there directed me to a canvas bag full of balls. He showed me how to step forward with my left foot, then raise my right arm and throw. I don't know how good a ballplayer he really is, for I followed exactly what he said and yet I fell exactly on my bottom. Nancy and the fellow, Moe, hoisted me to my feet. I practiced late into the evening, hoping to not make a fool of myself.

The next day, the seats were filled with screaming schoolchildren, all there on the free, first day of the season. A large group of children sang "The Star-Spangled Banner" while others played along as best they could on their violins. I was escorted to the mound like Marie Antoinette to the blade. Now here is a crowd that knows how to laugh and point, I thought—and I was not so old that I would not feel like a shamed little child if they did so. So I took my position and nodded slightly to the catcher. He nodded slightly back, as if we had done this for years. The crowd grew silent, with occasional, far-off whoops that faded as I went into that silent zone of concentration. I sent my left foot forward and my right arm into rotation. The ball sailed over home plate and, thanks to the absence of a batter, right into the catcher's mitt with a good slap of leather. The children went wild. I then immediately retired from baseball, going out at the top of my game.

A lovely thing about Midland was the first smell of rain. The clouds had been gathering all through these days, making the walk enjoyably cooler. The clouds opened up near Big Spring on May 27. Nancy and I dashed into a general store and purchased some plastic drop cloths to walk under. They were bulky and crackly, but did the trick. It poured so hard we could hardly see, and we were up to our ankles in cold, fast-running water. I was happy for Texas to finally get a good drink.

The bright, new look of everything after the rain made me feel like a child on a garden walk. At least six different varieties of yellow aster lined the road, plus more of those purple and cream thistles. Deadly nightshade; coneflower in four different shades; many nameless purple flowers, white flowers, and flowering yucca, were all quite different from the June bloomery in New Hampshire. No clover here, no Indian paintbrush or white daisies; no Queen Anne's lace, lilies, buttercups, trillium, or lady's slippers.

Beyond the roadside flowers—a project of Lady Bird Johnson's, by the way—were alternating fields of prickly pear cactus and brushy areas of creosote and cacti. The mantis heads of oil wells poked up everywhere. Their constant beat marks the passage of time in this part of the world, and never was there a more perfect clock to remind us that time is money.

Roadside Biology

We stopped to see two centipedes, about four inches long, rowing away from each other like Viking ships from what we hoped had been a happy tryst. They were quite beautiful. Several new kinds of anthills spread out near the road in great, flat circles. The half-inch red ants had pulled dark red sand from far below the earth, making their circles look like the scenes of explosions. I longed to open up the center of one to see the city below. I am fascinated by the precision of such societies, and it always makes me feel somewhat of a slacker. How does each ant know what to do? I suppose it is like the cells of our bodies knowing what kinds of cells to become. If you, as a cell, see cells on either side of you that are becoming nose cells, then you look at your DNA map of the whole body that each cell carries and you say, "Aha! If these are my neighbors, I must be this one here," and you become a nose cell, too. Maybe that is how ant colonies operate, in some sense. I think it is also how human groups function, which would show the importance of picking your peer group very carefully, for they fix your position on the map of self-development.

I also suspect that our parents imprint us very early with an idea of who we are. When I was seven, I overheard my mother telling her friend Lizzie Hughes that I was the most difficult of her children. "She's not like the others. She's different. Sometimes I wonder if she's mine at all, like I found her in a basket on my front doorstep," she said.

As I consider it now, it may have been her way of saying that I was very special, of almost bragging on me. But I heard it another way—that I did not belong, that she did not feel close to me. Her words plunged deeply into my heart and, I think, changed my life. Such words are indigestible. It is up to each of us to take the indigestible grit and decide if it will cause a wound or a pearl. I think I used that insecurity well—which you can do if you are conscious of it—but it has indeed been central to my life. Parents must be careful to imprint upon their children the idea that each child is loved and special and worth attention. Somewhere deep in the subconscious, which is a very stupid place as you know if you have watched a hypnotist, we unquestioningly believe our parents and accept their opinion of us. That opinion, good or bad, becomes the blueprint for our lives.

The imprinting of a positive self, I believe, constitutes the first half of good parenting and grandparenting—certainly the first five years of it. The other half consists in helping children build self-reliance, character, and empathy by gradually and thoughtfully expanding their participation in responsible duties. By character, I mean the ability to follow through with a resolution long after the mood of the moment has past.

A child can survive even when this is all done poorly by the parents, but it takes a great deal of self-repair work!

Just past the great ant colonies, a young reporter named Allison came walking toward us.

Now, you are going to think I favor women too much when I describe Allison. While I am straight laced—and straight unlaced!—I have never shied away from the simple fact that women are about the prettiest thing on the planet. They need to be, of course, if our species is to prosper.

It was near Big Spring, which is a nice, watery-sounding place from which a Venus might be expected, where young Allison appeared on the road to interview me for the local paper. She was only eighteen, bright-eyed, beautiful, and very thin. She wore a white, underwearlike top and skin-tight jeans. There was not an ounce of fat on her body, and she was full of joyful questions. "I hate her!" Nancy whispered when she had the opportunity. When old women look at young women, especially beautiful young women, we are struck with such a mix of feelings. If we were fortunate in our girlish years, we can remember what it was like to be young and attractive, which is the essence of being female in this culture. When you see that very essence walking beside you in tight jeans, and you know that such a person is still inside you, still wanting to look beautiful and turn heads, well, it is difficult. All I can say is that, over the years, you get accustomed to the loss. But it is always difficult, made bearable only when it is exchanged for some respect. Young women like Allison give older women such a gift when they show them respect and friendship. Not that we wouldn't trade positions with them in a second, but the loss of youth and beauty is made bearable.

Walking along with Nancy and Allison, thinking of my time as a young bride, it struck me that it was past time to put fresh flowers on Jim's grave. I hadn't even thought about it recently. I called my son in a panic, but he had already taken care of it. So, you see, other things come up in life and you aren't always worried about the mirror and gentlemen's eyes—there is love and duty, art and intellect, daily routine, and, of course, adventure.

Dear Nancy said good-bye, and my old friend Martha Raymond arrived to walk in her place. Martha runs a travel office in New Hampshire. My son taught her to swim in Dublin Lake when she was a little girl and he was a lifeguard, like his father. We walked and talked toward Fort Worth with the horizon falling away on all sides of us as if the sky were a blue bowl over us and we were upon a great, fertile dish. In such a place you can see the truth of the matter that you are the center of the world. We were walking among plowed fields. Just up ahead were real trees—nearly two thousand miles of desert coming to an end.

Well, I had come to love the desert, I realized. I would miss it. When you live most of your life in green New England, you might think of the desert in the way that a young person thinks of old age. But you find that it has its own beauty. It is an acquired taste, to be sure.

Through the Looking Glass

Somewhere between Midland and Fort Worth, I stepped through the looking glass. I don't know precisely where it happened.

The first sign that I was in a strange new world came when an elderly man from Fort Worth joined me on the road. He told me that his second wife had died of cancer after he had kept her alive with herbs for many years. She dropped dead the minute she stopped taking them—against his advice, of course. "They opened her up and found she had a mosslike substance all inside her skin, but all of her organs were in perfect condition," he insisted. He went on to tell me that his third wife, now ninety-one, takes her herbs religiously under his direction. Well, I would think so—the stories she must hear! I met her the next day—deaf as a post. She came with three other elderly women, all confused about my mission despite a number of go-rounds. I went to the vehicle and produced a copy of a *People* magazine article that had just come out and some petitions, which pleased them, but they kept trying to understand what this was all about and getting it wrong.

I know storytelling well enough to know a comic first scene when I see one. The stage was being set for a zany burlesque, complete with tornado, and it soon opened while we were staying in the incredible rooms of Mulberry Mansion, a bed and breakfast. It is a place of mirrors, chandeliers, huge glass bowls, porcelain washing pitchers and basins, mammoth vases of artificial flowers, artificial green vines draped about, a full-sized artificial stuffed duck, deep carpets and dark colors, statues and statuettes galore. Victorian pictures are framed heavily everywhere, and even a charming young boy appeared, dressed as a dining room server in velvet pants. Queen Victoria was declared dead nine years before I was born, but here she was, evidently alive in Texas, decorating the bejeebers out of this wonderful old home. All I could do was stare in admiration of it all. Martha Raymond stared, too.

We were there joined by Shené Hoffpauir-Casey, the young, fit, dark-haired webmaster of the Reform Party of Texas, who was opening all the populist doors of Texas for me. She was in the process of learning website design so that she could be a free woman. She had just driven all the way from Oklahoma, where she was temporarily living with her mother. She said Mulberry Mansion was one of the prettiest places she had ever seen. So we three stared.

Martha took turns driving the vehicle with Shené as we walked through the region. Shené was selling me on the Reform Party. They weren't crazy, she said; they were dedicated to tax reform and other reforms—campaign finance reform, too. And Ross Perot, she said, would do whatever the party decided was best. He would step down if they thought that would be best. Or stay, if they asked. She said she had pulled things from my website and shared them with party members, and they were all getting excited to meet me, especially Jeanne Doogs, the state chairman.

As she talked, I was getting a picture of the populist side of the reform community. It was a little different from the reform community I knew back home, which I suppose are the old progressives. I could see we had a great deal in common, and I could see how the gathering clouds of these two movements might come together if a serious effort was made.

As we walked and talked, clouds were gathering. On June 7, they broke loose in pulsing sheets of rain and hail. Luckily, we were just about back to Mulberry Mansion when the worst of it hit. The Sweetwater tornado warning siren began to cry as we splashed up the walk and ducked inside. Shené was in town somewhere, finding cover. Martha hurried me along the halls of the mansion to the bathroom, where a great, iron bathtub, seven feet long, offered shelter. She piled in every bit of towel and sheet she could find from the linen closet, and we crouched in the tub, underneath it all, as the wind outside grew to a wild howl and the building began to shudder. Well, with such a fine craft, I almost wished we could go up for a ride in the clouds and look down from our tub. But the siren stopped, and the wind and rain died down, and we climbed out—the ride canceled. Mulberry Mansion survived with only a scattering of broken branches to say that a disaster had come to call but changed its mind just before knocking.

Martha headed home to Boston shortly after that, leaving me in tears to see her go. I almost always hated it when people left for home. It made me homesick to think how nice it would be to sit in my old chair with a cup of tea and a good book.

I was soon walking beside fields of twelve-foot corn. I was with seventy-five-year-old Ted and Dot Beland, complete strangers who had flown out from California to walk with me because nobody else could, and because they saw a comment to that effect on the web page. What courage! They were appalled by the condition of the vehicle—bad tires, leaky hoses, rusted wheels. They took a deep breath and took over the operation. We became instant friends. Dot had been a nurse practitioner and Ted an engineer, so they were the perfect pair to keep an old lady and an old van going. They are nature lovers who had always camped and hiked with their children, as had I. Walking ten miles a day was a great effort for them, but they did it.

Shené picked me up and fetched me to the Reform Party state meeting in Austin, where I was scheduled to make a small speech. We drove first to a hotel restaurant where I was to meet the great one herself, Jeanne Doogs, chair of the Texas Reform Party.

Jeanne nearly cha-cha'd through the dining room to meet me. A woman in her early fifties, she has sparkling, silver-gray hair cut in a slant from her chin upward toward the back. She has big, blue eyes, a young girl's laugh, and thousand-watt charisma—by which I mean she enjoys life and shows it. She was wearing a white dress-thing that ended in shorts instead of a skirt, which was just the right outfit to celebrate her Betty Grable gams, slim waist, and absolutely Ann Sheridan bosoms. I hope you—and she—will excuse all the Hollywood references, but they are easy shortcuts. Can you now see her greeting me, with her arms outstretched, striking a pinup pose? Well, that's Jeanne Doogs you're looking at, and there was no question in my mind why she had been chosen as state chairman: She was Texas herself—the very image of free, voluptuous, yee-hah living.

She is political to the bone and packed with information. At her home, later down the road, she would stack up a dozen books on campaign corruption for me to read right then. "Oh, Doris, this one's good too. You have to read this one. You'll love this one. We can talk about it later."

Clint Smith, a black man who had organized the Reform Party's welcome dinner for me at the restaurant, invited me to his grandmother's home the next afternoon. He was holding a church fund-raiser there—a sausage plate dinner where I met his 102-year-old granny. She let me cut pieces of sausage and feed her as we talked. When she understood about my walk, she insisted that I eat all the sausage on my plate to make me strong. It was the first time in a long time that someone older than myself was telling me what to do, and it felt nice to obey like a good girl.

I then removed to a rusty chair under a tree and visited with the neighbors, who were competing with flies for their sausages. I learned that Granny would be moving in with one of her children, and this old house would be turned over to the neighborhood to serve the homeless. A minister named Sister O introduced herself. She ran a nearby church, for which this event was a benefit.

Later that afternoon, I spoke at the Reform Party State Convention. Ahead of me on the program was a young woman, perhaps seventeen, speaking about the plight of the Zapatista Indians, rebelling in the Chiapas region of southern Mexico. They are considered by many to be the first rank of fighters in the war against globalization and corporate domination, so they are something of cult heroes to many reformers, including the young speaker. The Zapatista leader is the highly secretive but obviously well educated and sometimes humorous Subcommander Marcos.

The Reform Party, to put it mildly, liked my speech. A fellow who sat near the front of the crowd and seemed unresponsive during the speech came up to me afterward and said I was a regular Winston Churchill and it was the best damned speech he had heard in a very long time. I relate this not to brag, but so you will understand how it came to pass that the Texas party insisted that I give the opening address at the Reform Party national convention later that month in Michigan. If I am any good at giving a speech, it is because I took my studies seriously at Emerson in Boston, where I went to college and where they took great pains to teach me proper elocution before they expelled me in 1931.

Sister O had invited me to church the next morning, and I thought it would be a good idea. At breakfast, just before church, in walked Ken Hechler with a big smile. So we went to church together, along with Clint, Jeanne, and Shené and her friend Barbara. The service was a rousing one, filled with singing and dancing, and we all were asked to take our turns speaking before it was over. My hearing aid was on the fritz so I missed quite a lot of it, but Ken said it was all very interesting.

I was still in a daze from it when we left to go to the statehouse steps, where Bill Stouffer of Texas Common Cause had put together a barn burner of an event with a pantheon of Texas populist speakers and a crowd of just under a hundred. Jeanne Doogs spoke, and ripped corporations up and down for bribing democracy to death. She wore a red-striped skirt, a bright blue blouse, and a silver stove-pipe hat. Then Jim Hightower himself, who could talk us all into taking off our clothes and doing a rumba if he wanted, showed me what public speaking is supposed to be like. There are only a few people in the United States who can do it, and he is one of them. He is not terribly tall by Texas standards, but his talk is so straight that you don't notice. He was wearing jeans and a white cowboy hat, which contrasted nicely with his jet-black hair and mustache. He ended by giving me a rousing tribute, and the crowd was chanting "Granny D for president" by the time he was finished. That was just for fun, of course, and it gave us something to laugh about as we began the long ride back to Abilene.

If you want to know how good a speaker Hightower is, I will tell you that a thunderstorm formed up as he spoke and it rained and thundered our whole way back, which made the trip cool and interesting. Also, Ken Hechler rode with us, as he wanted to walk a spell with me. He kept looking at Shené's beautiful black ponytail bouncing on the seat in front of him as she spoke about how well the events had gone. He was flirting with her terribly—a great weakness for dark-haired girls, I have noticed. Young ones.

GrannyD.com

As a former candidate who got outspent by insurance and medical lobbies, I applaud your efforts and am once again energized by your work.
Brenda Rotramble, Decatur, TX—Thursday, June 24, 1999

Dear Mrs. Haddock, As an American living overseas, I often feel like I lose contact with the ideals of our great nation. Reading about your efforts has reconnected me and inspired me. I wish you a safe and happy trip, and pledge that I too will work to achieve your worthy goal.
David Millette, Tokyo, Japan—Monday, June 28, 1999

Go, Granny, go. A senior myself, I bought in-line roller skates. There is nothing finer or easier on your feet and knees than gliding. When I get really good, I will skate from door to door with your petition! You make my heart sing, Granny D.
Jan Chastain, Reno, NV—Monday, June 28, 1999

Our Traveling Circus

The walking trail from Abilene to Fort Worth got a little crowded. There were Shené and Ken, a woman reporter from Tokyo, Australian cameramen filming for the Discovery Travel Channel, German television, *The Boston Globe, The Christian*

Science Monitor, and many others. Just up ahead, *Good Morning America,* Diane Rehm, *ABC World News Tonight, NBC Nightly News, George* magazine, and several other big interviews were set—many the result of John Anthony's work. Some of the late-night shows were making wisecracks about me. One of them said I wanted to get to Washington to speak to the president—Herbert Hoover. I thought that was pretty good.

Also walking was self-nominated presidential candidate Jeffrey Peters of the We the People Party. Jeffrey, who is a fine gentleman and who helped me a great deal, cleverly uses the device of a presidential candidacy to talk about campaign finance reform and other sensible reforms all over the nation.

In the middle of all this growing activity, John McCain asked me to fly to New Hampshire to stand with him as he announced for president. I wanted to go, but I thought if I did all these fun things I would never get to Washington, so I sent my regrets and kept walking.

I must say that there was a nightmarish quality to much of this. I had a clear idea that Doris Haddock must not get too wrapped up in this Granny D person. I was just me, taking steps across America instead of taking steps around my garden. It was not a great thing I was doing—I was hardly a brave American hero. Yes, I was looking for attention for my cause, but if I let all the attention go to my head, I would be doing the unforgivable thing of fooling myself. I had this conversation many times in my head. Having my son, Jim, nearby also helped, as he would never shrink from staring at me through his eyebrows if I seemed a bit pontifical or petulant.

There were often crowds now along the road, and more hands to touch and hugs to receive. Sometimes the reaction was a great mystery to me—like that of a young black man, perhaps in his early twenties, who had come out of his sickbed at his mother's suggestion to stand at the end of his driveway to see me pass. When I approached, he broke down and wept for no purpose that I could understand. I held him and made light of it, but he continued to weep and became unable to stand. I don't know what this is, I said to myself. It may or may not be good.

Jeanne Doogs walked and walked, always wearing a great outfit and overflowing with energy. While she is naturally animated to an extent that I would have considered beyond improvement, I was proved wrong one morning when she got ants in her pants.

Just beyond Baird, Texas, in the deep purple of early dawn, a scrawny little terrier dog started to follow us. She was covered with fleas and burrs, ticks and dirt, and walked with her head and tail dragging. Jeanne whisked her away. I hoped she hadn't taken her to a pound somewhere, as Jeanne is not shy about doing what needs to be done. But Jeanne and the little mutt reappeared at the end of the day, both looking like a million dollars. The doggie had been given a shampoo and a cut, shots, a fancy collar and leash, and a full day of self-improvement discussions with Jeanne— head and tail were very high. Jeanne later had a little orange safety vest made for her, so she would look like me. This doggie was to walk with me for many miles. When Jeanne headed home, at the end of my Texas adventure, I asked her to take care of the doggie, as I did not know in whose home I would be a guest, and I was determined to travel as lightly as I could. But DJ the dog and I were joys to each other through Texas, and we marveled together at some of the more unforgettable sights: like a fence strung with very large catfish heads in fearsome degrees of decomposition.

I made Fort Worth on July 1. John Anthony met me there. I had talked to him countless times, but never met him before. There he was, a young man in his late twenties, dark hair and athletic build. He knows many of the members of Congress and all of their voting records on campaign reform, so having him join me as an organizer was quite a plus. He had quit his job at Common Cause to go on the road for me and manage the growing crush of reporters.

Both Fort Worth and Dallas were brimming with kindness. I was supposed to meet with the full editorial board of *The Dallas Morning News* for fifteen or twenty minutes, but the meeting went on for over an hour and was great fun. They wrote a beautiful editorial supporting campaign reform. It was one of the political highlights of my walk.

It was interesting and wonderful to see so many women highly placed in news organizations, especially so in Texas. Women reporters, like Nellie Bly, have been around since before my time. But now they are running newspapers.

GrannyD.com

I am so proud of Ms. Haddock's conviction and determination. Feeling patriotic, as I always do on the 4th of July, I cannot express my gratitude emphatically enough that we live in a country where one person can make a difference, even if she dares to challenge the mighty. Thank you for your example. My three daughters and I applaud you.
Rebecca Morris-Chatta, Little Rock, AR—Sunday, July 4, 1999

Granny D., First read of your monumental effort today on the front page of *The Boston Globe*. I intend to write my Congressmen and demand campaign finance reform. Keep up the good work.
Scott Malcolmson, Watertown, MA—Monday, June 28, 1999

The Jeffersonian Hi

On the far side of Dallas, I finally had time to just walk again and relax. Much of it was alongside a beautiful man, Golam Mohammed, who had come to America from India ten years earlier. He was walking with me to celebrate the dream of America in his heart. Frankly, I think anyone from nearly any other country in the world who could have seen the America that Golam and I saw—all the kindness, openness, and the relative lack of class distinctions—would have applied for a visa the next day.

You cannot imagine what it means for most people of the world to be able to walk down a country road, shout a "Hi!" to someone working in a field, and to get a wave and a "Hi!" in re-turn. We take that sort of open friendliness and absence of class barriers for granted in America and other free and democratic countries. What the writer Richard Rodriguez calls that "Jeffer-sonian Hi!" is rooted so deeply in our dream of equality that we do not even see it. But people from many other parts of the world do. On many continents, the passerby would never think to call a greeting across to a stranger. And, if such a word were indeed sent across a field, the worker might just stare, wondering what this person meant and whether it was appropriate to speak in re-turn.

"Howdy!" Golam, with his dear subcontinental accent, would shout to a fellow working on an old truck. "Hi!" the reply would come, usually with a wave.

Walking with Golam made me see America through his eyes. Those days with him also made me reflect on the violence and cruelties in so many parts of the world, as the nuclear tension be-tween India and Pakistan was much in the news. How can people with such common history be willing to kill each other? Then I remembered a moment in my own childhood kitchen, and I un-derstood. During the First World War, there was a moment in-deed, the memory of which enables me to understand much of the horror that goes on between the villages of the world. My mother became that thing that we see in the saddest news stories.

Mama lost her only brother, handsome Rex, in the opening days of the war. She did not first hear the news by telegram: I was one afternoon playing dolls on the floor with Sybil when I looked up and saw the clear image of Uncle Rex, beautiful in his Cana-dian uniform, clearly projected onto the red portiere that hung on the doorway between the living room and the kitchen. There he was, jug-handle ears and all. "Why, there's Uncle Rex!" I said. I was delighted to see his image, however unexpected it was. My mother turned white and slumped into a chair. "Oh, my God! You see him? He's been killed! My darling brother! My only brother! Those butchers—those Germans!" Uncle Rex was the only son of my grandmother's seven children, all of whom adored him—especially mother. She commenced a nervous breakdown.

When my father came home from work he found no supper,

only a weeping wife and two little girls crying because their Mama was crying. "Now, Ethel," he said, "Dotty, is only a tiny girl, and you don't know that she really saw Rex. She only thinks she did."

For days, mother was not to be cheered. Then the letter came from Grandma Tucker, saying Rex had been killed by the Germans. There was also a letter from Rex's captain, which Grandma Tucker had copied out and which was reread so many times over the years that I still know it by heart: "Your son, Rex, suffered no pain. I held him in my arms as he breathed his last. He murmured, 'Oh, Mother,' and then he closed his eyes and was gone." Well, this was probably the standard propaganda letter sent to all the unlucky families, but we bought it.

The fact that I had seen Rex did not disturb me. I was only four, and I did not know it was unusual. Mama said I was born with a thin membrane over my head. It is called a cowl, and an old superstition says it is the mark of a prophet or seer. Years later, she showed me the remains of the thing, which the midwife had stretched over a little paper bag. It seemed to have a spider web pattern. I asked her to burn it, as it horrified me. That, unfortunately, is how children react as they grow older: They turn away from any special ability that would make them different. Of course, I think it is normal for children to have good access to what I suppose is the collective unconscious. It is a shame that we suppress it. My mother, like most women of her day, was very much fascinated by the spirit world, and read tea leaves with her friends. Always believing that I had powers, she would ask me to tell her where things were that she had lost, and I could usually tell her where they were. I thought nothing of it, which may have been the correct response: Children, after all, are very observant and often know where everything is.

The confirmation of Rex's death sent Mama into an even more frenzied state. Insanely, she decided to take action. There was but one German to her knowledge in Laconia. I will omit the name as the family still lives there. My mother decided that this man must die. She spent the day sharpening the one butcher knife we owned. She was actually planning to go stab the poor fellow to death. When my father got home he took the knife away from her and said, "Ethel, dear, if you murder him, you would be arrested and put to death and his little children would be father-less. And I would be left alone with our little girls and what good would that do?" So she gave up the idea of killing him, but she still plotted to get even somehow. When I look at the troubles that southern Europe and Africa and northern India have, remember-ing mother's reaction helps me to understand how violence and hatred can come in wartime. It is a mental illness of grief.

There is a little bit more to this story: My father got a job in the Quincy shipyards and worked there through the war. Mama sold our furniture and the house Papa built, and we moved to Quincy. Papa found us a nice little house, and he filled it with beautiful mission oak furniture, which was then the rage. I thought it uncomfortable compared to our old, overstuffed Vic-torian furniture. He took the job because Uncle Allie came to La-conia in an automobile to tell him it was his patriotic duty to join him at the shipyard. That was quite a day in town, because there were only two other automobiles, both owned by doctors, and this was the first one ever seen that was not a doctor's auto-mobile. Children and men gathered around the front of our house to look at it.

After the war, we returned to Laconia. Papa returned to his old job, and he and Mama had a new home built for us. It is in-teresting that, in 1918, a man who worked in a furniture ware-house and a wife who did not work for pay at all were able to build and own a home for their family. Of course, it helped that we had no expenses for cars or car insurance, as the town was built compactly so that a bicycle and a pair of shoes would do.

The people who bought our old house had suffered a fire, so Mama bought the land back and had a brother-in-law build us a new place. In the meantime, we stayed in a tenement apartment and went to the Harvard Street School where I got moony-eyed for a tall, cute fellow with yellow curls and big blue eyes. He was the son of a certain German.

"You better not tell Mama," Sybil said unnecessarily. The poor, young fellow! If it hadn't been hard enough growing up

German in America during the Great War, he also had the bad luck to be a poor reader. He had a devil of a time in class when he had to stand and read a passage aloud—everyone snickered, including me. He got into a fight one day with another boy, and he used his little pocketknife, wounding the fellow enough to send him to the hospital. After that, his mother had to meet him at the schoolyard gate before and after school, so that the incident would not be repeated. My mother said she wasn't the least bit surprised by the boy's actions, "given his blood line."

Well, the stars had certainly moved into place for a perfect Romeo and Juliet story, with a stabbed Tybalt and all. But our new house was soon ready, and Sybil and I were transferred to the closer school. Thus I was deprived of a fine and tragic story to tell you now, eighty-two years later. The fact is, I was relieved to not have to deal with my affection for him. I was happier to have him as a family enemy, perhaps because I was so often on the outside of things, and it was a relief to have someone further out than myself. Having enemies helps us feel we belong to a group—it is one of the dark sides of belonging.

I ran into the blond boy again years later high on a mountain ski run. We came to a stop several feet apart, and I was staring straight into his blue eyes. I was a wife and mother of two. He looked dashingly marvelous. I was delighted that Mama hadn't hacked up his family. I wished then and now that I had done something to rescue him from what must have been cruel times, when I was more interested in having a useful enemy than in following my own heart.

Walking with Golam, I wondered if I had matured enough over the years to do it differently now. Could I stand up for those I cared for, even if the whole world were against them? Yes, I think I have learned to do that. The price of doing the right thing and of following your heart is always, in the end, the best bargain.

Thunder and Rain

The end of the Texas road was finally just ahead. The Self family of Rockwall gave me a headquarters for much of the walk toward Arkansas, and Scott Self took me night sailing on a lake. I sat back and looked at the sky and a beautiful shooting star. It shot across the sky to the north, reminding me that I had to make a trip northward, myself. It was time to go to Michigan to speak before the Reform Party convention. I had been going over my speech for days.

I flew to Michigan with John Anthony and Paul and Donna Truax. When we arrived, we made a reform walk through parts of Detroit with Senator Carl Levin and several dozen others. I made remarks along the way, as did the senator, who is a great supporter of campaign reform. The dark clouds gathered as we walked. We picked up some interesting people along the way, particularly a young black man, perhaps in his early twenties, who danced as we went along, always chatting it up or jiggling around, singing bee-bop to himself. He had four front teeth missing, but that didn't stop him from laughing and smiling. He was quite ingratiating. When we reached a fruit stand, an older man who had also joined us— he was bearing a big flag with a picture of the round earth—offered to buy fruit for one and all. The dancer was first to take him up on his offer, and at that point I realized how poor and hungry he was.

Along the walk, the cracks in the sidewalk, which I try not to step on for the usual childhood reason, were wide enough to support clumps of chicory with their bright, blue blossoms. These plants were often joined with white Queen Anne's lace, and the two of them blanketed empty lots, covering the litter and grime in a lovely way. I made a mental note to remember the little flowers in my journal that evening. I knew there was a great deal of memorable business ahead that day, and it would take an effort to remember these little ones.

As I crossed the country, a number of people expressed surprise that I would spend a full two hours with my journal each evening before going to bed. "Aren't you too tired for that?" was a common reaction. I have kept a journal on and off through my life, and I do recommend it to everyone. A journal book and a good pen are, I think, especially perfect gifts for any young person, boy or girl. Don't let them do it on a computer, as those files will get lost someday. And give them a way to secure it, like in a locking cash box, or they will not report honestly.

If they can get into the habit of reviewing their day and even their dreams in writing, they will have a healthy, bird's-eye perspective of their own life. They can watch what they are doing and make sense of it. That daily investment in their own life is also a statement to themselves that they matter, and are worth reporting on. It nudges them to make each day count and to get things done. In years to come, having those journals helps a person relearn lessons that might have become misplaced, or to suddenly understand something, milking a new lesson from an old experience. When you remember enough lessons learned, that is the beginning of wisdom and real happiness. I don't mean happiness in the sense of giddy fun, but in the sense of a joyful acceptance of life as it is—the glad "Aha!" of life understood.

Most important, journal writing can be an exercise in seeing. It is so easy to go through the day and through life without really seeing—and I mean the kind of seeing that a blind person can do as well as a sighted person: the taking in and processing of everything around you. To the extent that you can perceive all, I think magical things happen for you. It is perhaps a way of approaching the divine, and activating it in service to your goals.

I do suspect that, at some deep level, we are privy to all kinds of information that might be useful to us. Some people believe that there are no accidents—that we have enough access to the timeless truth of things to be able to avoid or collide with trouble, if we really want to do so. I think there is something to that. So, when Teddy Roosevelt was up there on his horse on the ridges of San Juan Hill, the only man on horse in a swarm of bullets so thick that they said the sky darkened, something divine within him knew the paths of each bullet, telling him when to turn here and when to duck there. In this way, those wholly dedicated to a serious mission often are able to survive the impossible hazards against them. Somewhere in all this must be an argument for the efficacy of prayer.

So many people along my trek commented on what became known as "Granny luck." We always arrived just when the parade was there anyway, or when just the person we needed happened to be right in our path. I am not so sure that such things don't come naturally from paying close attention to everything around you, even the flowers in the sidewalk. If you think about how we use the sense of touch to petition the divine, as with rosary beads or prayer shawls, or if you consider how we try to find luck by massaging a worry stone or a rabbit's foot, or blowing our breath over dice, or touching a successful team member, it does seem that tactile connection with our surroundings—which is the first of many stages of awareness—is connection to the divine. Or it is pleasant to think so.

Of course, when you fully dedicate yourself to a good mission, the floodgates of heaven open up for you, beads or no beads, sending you whatever luck and resources you need. If you can make a creative crack in the crust of the world's deadly abstractions, the divine will rush up, bringing great bounty with it. God does seem to favor gate-crashing heroism.

During our walk through Detroit, the clouds had been gathering. By the time I was taken to the Reform Convention hall, the weather had become a serious problem. Minnesota governor Jesse Ventura, who was to make a great speech that same evening, could not get through the weather, as the Detroit airport had closed down. The ferocious thunderstorm raged outside as I opened the meeting with my remarks. I had sufficient material for a twenty-minute speech, but their reaction caused the thing to stretch out for forty minutes. C-SPAN covered it live and ran it again later, which got campaign reform another few drops of attention in Washington.

I think the Reform Party's policy plank in favor of campaign finance reform would have been high on their platform with or without my remarks, but we certainly helped nail it tightly in place.

The following evening, after I had listened to some good speeches at the Reform Convention, a tall, walkie-talkied woman in a gorgeous green suit approached me and, unaware of an old joke, asked me to "walk this way." Well, I couldn't have walked that way if I had been fifty years younger. But I followed in my own style through the crowd, through a number of locked doors that opened at her knock and call, and down a very long hallway to one more room. When I stepped inside, I was standing in front of Ross Perot, who was ringed by his businesslike assistants. Ralph Langley, my old helper from California who was a big Reform Party booster, was present and making introductions. Mr. Perot asked if there was anything he could do to help me along the walk. "Anything at all. You just have your people make a list of what you need and get it to me," he said in his trademark voice.

Well, I think everyone should have the pleasure of hearing a billionaire prince say that to them someday. After the meeting, which went on for some time and was very cordial, Ralph took me back to the lobby and he lit up a victory cigar. For some reason I felt suddenly queasy, and I had Jeanne Doogs take me to a ladies' room, where I was ill. I don't know if I am allergic to cigars or money. Cigars, I hope.

I never sent Mr. Perot a list, as the point of my walk was to protest the role of big money in politics, but it was a fantasy moment that has become a great memory. I shall send him a copy of this book and ask him if there is anyone described along the road to whom he might like to offer some help.

The fact that the speech was broadcast on C-SPAN was very important in moving the message forward. We were making campaign finance reform fashionable and were demonstrating that it connects emotionally when it is stated truly. The strategists from several presidential campaigns were looking over our shoulders.

On July 25, I flew back to my place on the road, the town of Mount Pleasant, from which there was only one more week of Texas walking. Mount Pleasant is not nearly so high as the mountains on the western edge of the state, where I had entered Texas three months earlier, but I found the rolling hills of the Texas Piney Woods region quite enough of a challenge and very beautiful. Through hilly areas, I always tried to end the day at the top of a hill, to make the first mile of the next day something to pleasantly anticipate. Stopping at the crest of a hill is satisfying anyway, as one can often look back at the distance covered and feel some satisfaction and also a little melancholy.

I did look back at Texas from these hills and imagined I could see all my new acquaintances in that great grail of life that stretches eight hundred miles from the Guadalupe Range to the Piney Woods. I wished I had the eyes to see them all, from May and her friends at the café in Cornudas, to Mary Jo and the boys at the Long X, to Berta and the kind people of Toyah, to Jeanne and the unsinkable Reform crowd, to Golam and all the interesting people of Texas who so effortlessly transcend any stereotype you might naively concoct for them. They are all doing fine, as I thought about them—perfect as they are, moving through their lives, heart first. If they are not completely and forever happy, well, there is no room for that in this theater of the soul. All that we can do is to strive to be conscious of it all and to make our lives the meaty products of our deepest values. Every twig of life is meaningful, I believe, and is given to us for our own divine purposes that one day we shall remember.

When I arrived in Texarkana at the Red River edge of Texas, the mayors of those twin cities were there, as was old Ken, coaxing me across the continent with another bit of chocolate. Bob Waters, a longtime Arkansas reformer, also met me at the border to be my guide and helper for the miles ahead.

Well, here I am remembering my Texarkana chocolate and I am thinking that this writer and her reader friend, now two thousand miles into this story, merit a little treat and a rest in a sunny room.

From the Reform Party Speech
July 23, 1999

On the road so far, I have seen a great nation. I have felt it hugging my shoulders, shaking my hand, cheering from across the way. I am so in love with it. I know you are, too.

See the appendix for more of this speech.

GrannyD.com

I heard your Reform Party speech over Minnesota Public Radio today. It was one of the greatest speeches I have ever heard. You spoke truth. More than that, you held the nation in your heart. We must all learn to do the same. Thank you for reminding us of what we can be as a country and who we can be as individuals. I am deeply grateful and inspired, and wish you the best in your efforts for all of our sakes.

Robert Geis, St. Paul, MN—Wednesday, July 28, 1999

The only way we have a hope of reducing the horrific gap between rich and poor in this country is to lessen the grip that the rich have on decision making in this country. Right on, Granny D!

Linda Goertz, Portland, OR—Saturday, July 31, 1999

Hello Granny D. Your courage and commitment moved me a great deal. I'm a Japanese newspaperman working in Osaka. Money has affected our moral fiber and our free elections here in Japan, too. May God continue to give you energy and strength to continue this great mission safely and successfully.

Yoshikazu Nakaii, Kobe, Japan—Thursday, July 29, 1999

BOOK III

Beyond Hope

I crossed the Red River out of Texas, leaving the American West and entering the South. As I am an old Yankee, the South has always seemed a little foreign to me. That would no longer be the case when I would leave the South at the Ohio River, many miles ahead. It took me nearly ninety years to feel like a whole American.

A woman who lives on the Arkansas side of the river, and who read about my coming, stood at mid-bridge to welcome me to her state. Mayors and governors are nice, but this was always my favorite, most comfortable kind of welcome.

Well, if you are in the market for some August humidity and some dead polecats and armadillos, I cannot recommend this stretch of road enough. It is beautifully green and the people are kind, but I was drained by the drenching steam heat. I was constantly stepping around a great collection of unfortunate armadillos, presenting themselves nearly every tenth mile. It was as if some armadillo Spartacus, fleeing Arkansas, had been captured and executed with all his followers along this road.

I kept up a smile for Ken and for my new friend, Bob Waters, who would dedicate his every day to my walk through his state.

Just inside western Arkansas is the little town of Hope, which as you know is famous for its watermelons. I spit seeds in the watermelon festival seed-spitting contest, and I came in last in a speed-walking race. I stopped by Bill Clinton's boyhood home: a bright and cheery house fronting on Hervey Street. The street passes below the high window of its attic bedroom and dips down below a railroad overpass, which is flanked by grassy banks. Right behind the Clinton home, like its subconscious, is a dark home on an overgrown property that was the boyhood home of his ill-fated associate, Vince Foster. The upper windows of the two homes are within whispering distance.

Between Hope and Arkadelphia, an old man yelled from his house across the road and waddled down his driveway, waving one hand and holding his stomach in check with his other. He was in dirty bib overalls with a work-stained shirt. He shook my hand and gave me a great, nearly toothless grin. "I been workin' in the barn all mornin' and peekin' out to see if you'd might come by," he said. A newspaper, *The Hope Star,* had run my story on the front page, he said. He told me he raises goats and chickens. He pointed to his wife, waving at me from the porch. "I'm just an old red-necked farmer is all," he said. "Raised four kids right here and they's all doin' well. Since retiring, me and my wife been travlin' all over."

Well, you see, that's when his redneck act started to fall apart. Under questioning, he told me that he had traveled much of the world, and I could tell he was a well-read and thoughtful gentleman. But with most strangers, I'm sure he can get away with his backwater persona. I said, "You're no redneck, Joe. Admit it!" He exploded in laughter and turned to Ken: "She's a feisty one, ain't she!" Indeed—another one right out of the phrase book. So much of what we take as regionalism is now only half real and half a kind of nostalgic playacting. I should know: I'm from New England.

There are deep regional differences among the very poor, however, who are not homogenized by higher education, corporate life, frequent travel, and television. Actually, television doesn't do much to blend us together as one culture—at least not as much as one might expect. I think part of the reason is that we tend to watch things that are already comfortable territory to us, so we don't stretch ourselves. And part of it is the pure passivity of the thing: You don't learn unless you are actively engaged. I can watch *Beverly Hillbillies* reruns all day, every day, and I am still not going to refer to swimming pools as "cee-ment ponds." Someone who already does, however, can watch *Frasier* reruns forever and still not crave tickets to the opera.

On a moral level, however, I do think programming matters. The human values celebrated in old shows like *Andy Griffith* and *M*A*S*H* were a healthy weekly tonic for our youngsters and ourselves. Today, of course, we are given poison to swallow by our local television and cable companies, and we should make more of a stink about it with those local executives as a personal matter. They will say that they are only following orders in poisoning our children. We should not accept that answer.

I say this because people have always told stories to their children around the flickering campfire, and those stories formed the culture of that community. Our flickering campfire now is the television and computer screen, and wise adults need to be in charge if our culture is not to devolve into a *Lord of the Flies* horror. I am not arguing for censorship, but for wise adult writers, producers, and broadcasters, whose value systems are brave, mature, and complex enough to resist the reptilian, single-minded pursuit of profit. We must, I think, resist the mass acquisition of production companies and broadcasters by corporations who care only for bottom lines and stock values.

So many people along the way told me that they felt overwhelmed by the pressure of commercial culture on their children—a culture of evil selfishness and brutal exploitation. The culture of a good nation must not be at odds with the work of parents. Maybe you are one of the people who bristle at the idea that it takes a village to raise a child, but you must agree that the village, at the very least, must not work against the family's attempt to teach values, respect, responsibility, and love.

Despite the hard pressures, there are strong and happy families yet in America, and I met many of them.

Bonnie and Tommy Blusberg, who put me up between Hope and Arkadelphia in a home with their five children, spread out a map of Arkansas and showed me where rice is grown (mostly in the southeast of the state) and where soybeans are grown (mostly in the middle of the state). There are also pine forests here and there, and chicken farms everywhere. The Tyson company delivers baby chicks to the little farms and picks up fat chickens eight weeks later. That's about it, Bonnie said, folding the map and adding that Arkansas was the second poorest state after Mississippi.

Pine lumber is indeed a big business in the hilly parts of Arkansas. On the road, huge trucks raced by us with logs dangling out at dangerous angles, sweeping the shoulder and sending us scurrying. They must not stick out as far as they seem to, or there would not be a mailbox left in Arkansas. At the sawmills, logs were heaped in piles of sufficient extent to cover a small town. Sprayers kicked great jets of water over the logs; a mill worker told me that they must keep them wet so the logs don't crack. If the logs crack, little bugs get in and, when they die, leave a green streak that makes the wood less valuable. At least, this is what I heard though my old hearing aids.

At the end of a particularly hot and muggy day, we came upon a flatbed truck full of watermelons parked unattended in a grove beside the road. An old coffee can containing a few dollar bills was perched on the corner of the truck's bed. It was a wonderful treat. John and Mary Rauh, friends from back home, were with me and sprang for the dollar.

The next day we walked into Arkadelphia through sweltering 105-degree misery. But here was heaven: a real town with a fine main street and lovely shops and homes. We had a lemonade at Percy Malone's drugstore, which was filled with lively teenagers at the lunch counter. The sight of them sent me back to Laconia and the highlight of my adolescent life: the 25-cent banana split at the drugstore every time I could save up such a fortune—the cost of five movie tickets.

The central part of Arkadelphia's downtown was flattened by a tornado in 1997, only two years before my walk. It was restored to beautiful standards and in record time. The center of the damage was Percy Malone's drugstore, which has been rebuilt from scratch. It fits nicely with the historic buildings nearby. Percy introduced himself to us and told us the whole, harrowing story of the tornado.

I don't know how Arkadelphia got such quick and first-class disaster relief from the federal government, but they did.

In other news, Percy Malone is one of President Clinton's oldest and best golfing friends. Percy's computer at the old drugstore was where the huge and important "Friends of Bill" mailing list was managed for the president. Moments after the tornado, Percy got a call from the man in the White House to ask how everybody was doing—and the computer, Percy? How's the computer? Well, the backup disks were fine.

Now, the fact that the leaders of Arkadelphia knew the president may or may not have helped them get faster and better assistance from the government. I think the government *should* have helped them quickly, and I'm glad they did. But this may be a case study to demonstrate that access is important in politics. We need to look at how people get that access. Friendships and loyalties and long histories will always create access, and that is fine. But being a citizen in a district should automatically come with pretty good access to the elected representatives.

Giving money to a candidate cannot help but translate to access. It is a natural thing, even though it is wrong. The public official who provides special access for his or her campaign donors is stealing that access away from the citizens of the district to whom it rightfully belongs. But as long as there are big political donations, there will be that sale of stolen goods.

Interesting that this case study in access should come just as I was walking with political activists John and Mary Rauh from back home. John said we do not have to have big political contributions in our politics at all.

After lunch at Percy's, John sat down with me and with the others walking with us and made the argument that getting "soft money" out of politics is important, but it wouldn't do the whole job. Soft money is money given to *political parties* by corporations, unions, and the wealthy, so that the laws limiting what can be given directly to *candidates* are circumvented. The parties, in turn, give that money to the candidates. John said the real solution is the public financing of campaigns. Well, I knew something of that because Dennis helped get such a program passed in Arizona, but I was about to learn more from John and Mary.

Here's how public financing works: First, it's voluntary, so there are no constitutional questions about limiting anyone's rights. The candidate who wants to participate has to personally collect a certain number of qualifying signatures and small contributions—usually in the five-dollar range—from people who live in the district. This demonstrates community support. Someone who has long been active in a parent-teacher group or scouting or some such thing will have an easy time of it. People who have not helped their community will find it hard sledding. When the candidate meets these requirements, the campaign receives advertising money from the state election fund. The candidate must agree to neither raise nor spend any other money. That neatly gets special-interest contributors right out of the picture. The cost of such a system is about one-tenth the cost of paying off special-interest contributors with tax breaks and other favors.

John at that time was working on the Bill Bradley campaign in New Hampshire and had pushed Bradley into coming out strongly for public campaign financing. John said I should start talking it up, too. I am from New England and John is from New England, so I told him I would think it over. It would have been rude to just give in and not show the proper amount of obstinacy. But I knew that what he was saying made sense.

His presentation, which was given in a little meeting room we borrowed downtown, was very eloquent, as usual. As he began to speak, a light rain started to streak the windows. It soon became a downpour that filled the streets of Arkadelphia, rattled the windows with thunder as he made his big points, and baptized us near to drowning as we dashed through the curb-high streets after the meeting. Well, I can take a hint.

That evening, my new friend Percy Malone invited the mayor and a few dozen people from Arkadelphia to come into his drugstore for a special summer picnic dinner and discussion. He moderated a wonderful brainstorming session on campaign finance reform. Believe me, the people who are closest to the system know it needs fixing. I thought this would be a good group on which to test the acceptability of public financing—there was a great mix of people there. I expected to see some serious resistance from somewhere. Not a bit: Nearly everyone agreed that public financing of campaigns is what needs to happen. Seeing how well the idea was embraced in Arkadelphia made me suddenly realize why it passed in conservative Arizona as well as liberal Massachusetts—people are of the opinion that the old system of raising contributions for campaigns is just beyond hope. People are ready for something new and something cleaner. Public financing has also passed in Vermont and in Maine, where it in fact began. As we were wrapping up the evening at Percy's, I gave John Rauh a wink to let him know that he had made the sale with me.

I don't think public financing is really very radical. When I was a young girl, it was expected that the town would put up a speaking platform in the park before an election and the townspeople would come out and hear all the candidates. The community has an interest in making sure that the voters know all the candidates and what they stand for. That is the theory behind public financing. Our towns—many of them—are now big cities, and the only way we can all talk to each other is through broadcast media.

The following day, a fellow driving a garbage truck stopped to say hello. I pulled out my petition and wondered if I could work public financing into the conversation. But he didn't let me get that far; he said campaign finance reform is an okay idea, but the big problems in America are the capital gains tax and the inheritance tax. He said that he gets his political information from a Christian radio program, and they've been talking about those issues for quite some time. I looked again at his conveyance, and I sincerely asked if these two taxes were big problems for him personally. He stared silently at me for a moment and blinked. He said he had to get back to work, but was glad to have met me. I think it is fascinating how the poorest of people have had their own political interests hijacked by the wealthiest of the wealthy, who have sometimes been able to use religious fundamentalists to push their agenda. I don't know how they do it, but it is ingenious. Maybe it's just the fact that the fundamentalist preachers make so much money from these poor souls that their typically self-serving sermons turn naturally to their own tax problems.

GrannyD.com

I came through Texarkana yesterday and was grumbling about whoever was slowing the traffic. I read about her in the paper this morning. Had I known, I would have stopped and given her a hug myself. I am in full support of her idea! Hope to see her in Little Rock in a few days.

George Freeman, Little Rock, AR—Sunday, August 1, 1999

Hi! I am only 15, but I read about Granny D in the paper and I think it is a terrific thing she is doing. People today need to follow her example and fight for what they believe in! YOU GO GRANNY!

Cassie, Hot Springs, AR—Monday, August 2, 1999

Granny, Hi. I go to Rosemead High. My Government teacher spoke to the class about you, and it impressed me very much. Recently I did a research paper on Cesar Chavez and how he boycotted and held strikes. It inspired me to try and do something to show that we as citizens also have the right to express ourselves freely. You, like Chavez, are contributing to that change. If I could, I would be out there with you. Hey, I could even keep you company and maybe more people would be inspired the way you have inspired me. Good luck.

Michelle Medina, Rosemead, CA—Tuesday, August 3, 1999

Heard you on radio. Will write my letters.

Larry Cox, Lanesville, IN—Thursday, August 5, 1999

Dividing Lines

Through the long, green, humid miles, stopping here and there at roadside markets and cafés, and often walking in the company of Judy Smith, a black woman who was running for Congress, it was hard for me to imagine that race relations had ever been such a defining problem in Arkansas. Perhaps I did not see the injustices and cruelties that local people see, but what I did notice was a good amount of friendship between the races. If that is so, we have indeed come a long way quickly. That cannot happen without strong leadership—not only from political leaders, but also from artists and writers, Rotary Club presidents, mayors, school leaders, Little League coaches, brave neighbors, and so many others who, when it was difficult to do so, did the right thing by including everyone and presuming brotherhood and equality. Their collective courage has made us a much better country in the space of my lifetime. It is certainly still a work in progress, as there is yet a mountain of difference between being born white in America and being born nonwhite.

When I was a young girl in Laconia, I was barely aware of the fact that other races existed. I didn't even have much of a conversation with a black person until, after high school graduation, I took a summer job at a small hotel in Nantucket. I took the job to earn tuition money for my first year at Emerson. It was the summer I learned something about prejudice.

I was the first of the summer workers to arrive at a small hotel called the Old Parliament House—an important, historic building that is still on the island.

For a few days I was doing nearly all the jobs, which at least let me learn how the place operated. I would soon be sharing the work with Ida Thomas, my first black acquaintance. She arrived with her ten-year-old son, Jimmy, and her twelve-year-old daughter, Dilsey. Ida was a very big, beautiful woman with a youthful spray of freckles across her face. Her hair was separated in carefully parted bunches, each bunch held by a different color elastic band. She was warm and energetic and a good mother to her children. Her son, Jimmy, was to wallop the pots—which meant to wash them. Dilsey was to help me wait on the guests in the dining room. That meant standing behind guests and fetching the courses and anything they asked for and then cleaning up.

Ida's husband had died eight years earlier. They had worked hard so that he could go to Howard University. He had graduated

My high school portrait, 1927.

after four years of driving a taxicab at night and studying between customers. He and Ida also took care of an apartment building so they could get free rent. When he graduated, he expected to be able to find a good job, and so they started having children. The good job never came, and he died of a heart attack in his cab. She told me it was a broken heart, really. His death sent Ida and the children into deep poverty and into many horrors.

I had never heard of such misery and unfairness outside of a Dickens novel.

In my journal that night, I made note of how a few tears had rolled down Ida's cheeks when she told me her story, but that her face was otherwise expressionless, almost cheerful. Her voice was as steady as if we were talking about the weather. I wondered how much misery it takes before you can report sorrow in such a matter-of-fact manner.

The next morning I taught Jimmy how to get out the lawn furniture and arrange it just so, as the lady owners had shown me. I had been putting them out each morning and taking them in each evening, even though no customers had yet arrived. The ladies were establishing our routine, I explained. Jimmy thought it was a waste of time, which it was.

His attention was captured by the roar of a Stutz Bearcat sports car that pulled up to the house next door. This was the house of the island's Episcopal rector. I had been watching the comings and goings at the house, and knew that the young blond fellow in the car was the rector's son, Peter. He always came by this time of morning to pick up his sister, Temple, for tennis. I also knew that she had just graduated from The Cathedral in Washington, and Peter had just finished his freshman year at Harvard. Miss Crosby and Miss Farrington, my employers who owned the little hotel, had told me all about them.

"Some car," Jimmy said.

The screen door of the rector's house banged open, as it did every morning, and Temple ran out, swinging a tennis racket. She was wearing a sleeveless tennis dress that showed her summer tan. Peter sat revving the engine. His tan skin and blond hair matched hers, as you might expect of twins who played tennis, went to the beach, and sailed together each summer day according to a clockwork schedule. Each evening they went off to a party somewhere on the island—she always in a pastel summer dress from her considerable collection.

This was 1928. I had read the book *The Great Gatsby* the previous year, when it was new in the Laconia library. I had no idea that such beautiful people actually existed until I saw them with my own eyes.

After the Stutz roared away, Jimmy and I were silent. Temple is just my age, I was thinking, and she has such a beautiful life. I don't know what Jimmy was thinking.

Miss Farrington, like Miss Crosby, was a dear. She had a palsy of some kind—her hands and head would shake if she stayed still for too long. She therefore kept busy. Beautiful at seventy, she wore her white hair piled in short curls. Her blue eyes were unfaded by age, and her crisp, gingham dresses were always the perfect definition of trim and prim.

In my first days, the two women wasted no time in getting me accustomed to hard work.

Miss Crosby taught me how to spring clean, which was back-breaking. She was a large woman who would attack a room with a mannish stride, flipping mattresses, rolling up rugs for merciless outdoor beatings, and pulling furniture away from walls for sweeping and wall washing. She had a hint of a gray mustache and a few chin whiskers and straight gray hair. Later she showed me how to fix the breakfast tray that she and Miss Farrington would share. She gave me exacting instructions about the breakfast and the tray. I was to run out the last minute and pick a flower and put it in a bud vase before I delivered the tray.

The next morning I prepared breakfast, snatched a rose, and carried the huge tray from the kitchen through the three dining rooms, through the front entry hall, through the parlor and finally into the master suite, where I stopped in momentary shock. Miss Farrington and Miss Crosby, wearing matching, prim, white nightgowns, were reading together in the huge bed. A large bank of pillows was stacked behind them. The household's two collie dogs, Sandy and Rusty, were lying on the bed waiting for their tidbits. It was a lovely domestic scene, just a little new to my experience.

Miss Farrington was from a famous Boston family with ancestors buried at the old Granary. She later told me how she had rescued Miss Crosby many years earlier from the unfair accusation of taking sacramental wine from their Nantucket church. The real thief was the alcoholic woman making the accusation, Miss Farrington said. "I was the only one on the whole island who would stand up for her." She invited Miss Crosby to take refuge in her great house, and they had been very close ever since.

Ida, Jimmy, Dilsey, and I shared the attic, which was divided into three living spaces by old curtains hung on ropes tied to the rafters. There was also a space filled with old packing cases and a jumbled pile of broken furniture. That's where Jimmy slept on a cot. Ida's space was at the far end, looking out over the rectory garden next door.

I often found myself at that window after dinner, waiting for the moment when Temple and Peter would head off to a party in the Stutz. My routine thus became linked with theirs.

I was once nearly introduced to Temple. Miss Crosby and I took the collie dogs for a long run on the moors every afternoon—I happily did the running with them. After the run, we would do errands in town, including a trip to the post office to check the box. One day Temple and her mother, Mrs. Blodgett, were there.

Miss Crosby greeted them and said how beautiful Temple was these days. Mrs. Blodgett said she was a very satisfactory daughter. The whole post office, about thirty people, listened in on the ramblings of the island's upper crust.

Temple and I smiled at each other, and I thought we were about to be introduced. Instead, Miss Crosby handed me the mailbox key and motioned me on. I could hear them chat about me as I checked the box.

"Oh, yes," Miss Crosby said, "Doris is a very nice girl. She works like a horse. I was telling Julia last night that she works like a horse. She does put me in mind of a thoroughbred pony—got some class to her. We picked us a winner this summer, all right." I was dying of shame.

I grabbed the mail and made a beeline for the car. I didn't speak to Miss Crosby all the way home, answering her running commentary with curt grunts. Miss Crosby looked mystified, and I heard her tell Miss Farrington that she thought I didn't feel too well. A horse, indeed! What must Temple have thought? I wondered how *she* would like being compared to a horse. I'm sure I was being too sensitive, and I could have laughed at the horse talk and introduced myself to Temple, but the class difference between my life and hers was like thick plate glass. So I ran.

I told the whole thing to Ida as we worked in the kitchen. She understood and said there would be other chances to become friends with Temple and Peter. "They just next door," she assured me.

I taught Dilsey the fine art of waiting on people in the dining room when the hotel started filling. I had learned the skill the previous summer, working in a New Hampshire hotel with a high school friend.

After Dilsey and I served the guests breakfast and cleared the tables, I would help Miss Crosby clean the guest bedrooms while Dilsey and Jimmy washed the dishes and set tables for lunch. After lunch, we had two free hours and could go the beach. I went with Jimmy and Dilsey, which caused a stir. The whole little beach was for servants like us. But there was a rope down the middle of the sand, running right into the water and out to a buoy. White servants were to swim on one side of the rope, black servants on the other. I didn't know what the rope was for, and wasn't paying attention to the fact that all the people here were white, and all the people over there were black. I just plunked down in the sand with Dilsey, and Jimmy jumped in the first water he saw. He was having a marvelous time running and swimming about and splashing the other swimmers. He was in the white section and the swimmers were getting upset. The black people were watching with concern.

"Get this little n—rboy out of our water!" one of the bathers screamed to the lifeguard. Others joined in. The lifeguard came down to talk to Jimmy, but Jimmy went running away, yelling and splashing.

"Ain't this a public beach?" he yelled at the lifeguard, who was dodging around after him now.

Jimmy headed up to dry ground, spraying sunbathers with sand as he went, until the whole beach was in an uproar.

I sat stupefied. Things finally settled down, and Jimmy was far out at sea for a long while, where you couldn't tell which side of the rope he was on. Walking home, I said it was stupid that they had two sections. I said the good thing about it was that he made the lifeguard get some exercise.

I had rather liked the looks of the lifeguard, even if he had chased Jimmy around. Remarkably, he was from my old high school, two years ahead of me. I had a dossier on him in my head: He had been senior class president, captain of the debating team, and president of the student council, and he played football and baseball—I thought he was quite something. And here we were, stranded together on this romantic island. Walking home from the beach, I was blissfully dazed by the possibility that fate's heavy hand might be in motion.

Back at the little hotel, Dilsey told Ida all about Jimmy's antics. I defended him, but Ida sat me down for a lecture after she sent Jimmy away with a strong swat.

"Jimmy's got to go by the rules, and there ain't no help for it." Tears welled in her eyes as she talked.

"Dilsey says you and her sat down on the beach together. She can't do that, or her people will think she is a white-lover and that won't do. You just don't understand these things. We can be a family in this little kitchen, but it's a world of our own. Let's just love each other in this kitchen and forget the rest of the world," she said.

I relented. It was a profound challenge to my sense of fairness, and I relented. Such things often must knock several times.

Dilsey and I made the best of it, sitting together right next to the rope but never letting it actually come between us, or sometimes pushing some sand over it. Jimmy would go in the water where he was supposed to, but he would often swim under the rope and pop up on the other side just to show them—just to put his body in the way of an injustice, as we must do.

In the hotel, we worked hard and sang together. Dilsey, especially, had a beautiful voice. Dilsey and I learned gospel songs from Ida, and she learned the popular songs from us.

I told Dilsey that she could earn her way in the world with her voice. She said maybe if she were white—otherwise I was crazy to say it. If I had known about people like Josephine Baker, who was then singing her second season in Paris, or young Billie Holiday, who was just about Dilsey's age and already singing, I could have encouraged her properly. She had no thought that a black woman could make a good living doing anything.

Not long into the season, Temple and Peter had a party in their backyard. Japanese lanterns were hung around, and a punch table and small dance floor were laid out on the lawn. In the evening, a three-piece band arrived, followed by dozens of young people in beautiful summer clothes. Ida, Dilsey, and Jimmy watched from the attic window.

I just sat on my bed, writing in my diary. But Ida peeked around my curtain and said, "You know you want to see this. No harm in watchin' people have a good time." So I crowded up to the window.

It was a beautiful scene, with gorgeous people and piles of food. The band included a piano player, a drummer, and a saxophonist. They were quite good, and so was the dancing.

Temple wore a white gown with layer upon layer of dotted tulle, joined at the narrow waist by sparkling white cloth. Peter was with a pretty redheaded girl I hadn't seen before. She was in an orange, tight-fitting gown. Actually, I had never seen him with any other girl but Temple, and I felt a little jealous—even if I had picked out that lifeguard for myself. I suppose I was living in two worlds: I would settle for the lifeguard, as no Apollo like Peter was likely to drive into my life in a Stutz.

As his date watched, Peter stood, bowed extravagantly, and headed for the punch bowl.

"That Peter sure is hittin' that punch," Jimmy whispered. We had fully opened the window to better hear the music and conversations.

"Yes sir, he's gettin' looped," he added.

I didn't see it. He seemed fine to me. Besides, liquor was against the law, and I said I didn't think they would risk having it in the punch at the rectory. I was defending him.

"He's got a flask, then," Jimmy said.

The music suddenly got louder as they launched into "Yes Sir That's My Baby." Then, without warning, Dilsey, from right beside me, started singing with the orchestra as loud and pretty as if she were on a Broadway stage.

All eyes below looked up to our window, as I backed away into the darkness. "Stop it, Dilsey! Stop it!" I said. "They'll see us for heaven's sake!"

But Dilsey was in full swing, and she didn't hear me or care. She was swaying with the music and belting it out as if she were on a Broadway stage.

When the song ended, I heard wild clapping and yelling from below, and I peeked out to see Dilsey's audience all gathered along the white picket fence. Dilsey leaned out the window, bowing and waving to them.

"It's Dilsey," I heard Temple say below. "It's Dilsey. I hear her singing all the time. She's wonderful, isn't she? Dilsey! Sing us another song, won't you?"

The orchestra struck up "My Blue Heaven" and Dilsey was off again.

"Ida, don't you think you must stop her?" I pleaded with her mother.

"She's having a good time, Dotty. Let her go on some."

"I hate it. It's like the white folks from the plantation house coming down to hear the darkies sing in their cabins. I can't stand it," I said.

"You just a little jealous. They don't mean no harm. Dilsey is having a special time, and that don't come too often."

When the song was over, everyone applauded and cheered again, and then went back to the dance floor for the Charleston. Dilsey sat back, breathing as if she had just run a mile.

"You were good, Dilsey," I said. "Really, really good. Some day you'll be singing for a big orchestra. You wait and see." She just looked at me like she was condemned by a fatal disease. As far as I know, that performance at the window may have been the highest moment of her life.

We watched the party for a while longer. Dilsey leaned back against me, stretched her arms back, and hugged my neck. I wondered how Temple knew her name. I wondered how much she knew about us. She knew I was a horse, of course.

I went back to bed, listening to the music and feeling a little guilty. Watching the dancers longingly from afar made me think of how I had mistreated my sister Sybil. My friends and I were party-going, cigarette-smoking flappers, and poor Sybil just wanted to be one of us. Mama made me take her along to dances for a while. Sybil was always miserable in the corner, and she finally refused to go. She was overweight and plain, and I was embarrassed to have her around. I did nothing to help her into our little crowd. When she stopped coming along, I was relieved. But when I got home, she would always ask me how the evening went, pumping me for every detail.

There was a big dance ballroom in nearly every town. Laconia was a little too small for one, but the nearby town of The Weirs had a fine hall on the shore of Lake Winnepesaukee. My friends and I went there on the summer evenings of our high school years to dance everything from the Charleston to waltzes.

Great bands came to play. There were no tables and chairs; you stood between dances with your two girlfriends, with whom you had probably come on the trolley car and with whom you would ride home on the last trolley. If you were a good dancer, light on your feet, and if you didn't try to lead or get too romantic, you would be sought out as a popular dance partner. When asked to dance, you were likely to be booked up, so you would say, "You can have the fifth," and he would come back five numbers later. We had dance cards and little pencils, as no one's memory was good enough to remember everything. My two girlfriends and I would dance every dance—fast numbers, slow numbers—and we were quite good. Sybil wanted to hear every detail when I got home, picking over the bones of my evening.

She watched from afar, just as I had been watching Temple and Peter. I hadn't before grasped the cruelty of not letting her into my circle. In the Nantucket attic, I felt miserable about it, as I feel miserable now—so many years later.

Dear Sybil passed away at the age of forty. She wanted to be thin all her life. She was finally given a thin body at the very end, but it was from cancer. She showed me how her old robe could wrap fully twice around her slim body. "Look at me, Dotty! And all I had to do was die!" She had come home from the hospital after unsuccessful treatment, and her skin was jaundiced. She was a respected nurse in our town, and would, in a week, die and leave her son the four apartment buildings she bought and fixed up, room by room, with her own hands. She had done the most to care for Mama after Papa died. She was always a wonderful, caring person; I was a flapper.

But in the Nantucket attic, when it was still not too late to decide to be a good sister, I promised and promised in my prayers to be kinder, and I drifted off to sleep.

I awoke to the sound of screaming at about 1 A.M., an hour after Temple and Peter's party ended. I put on my robe and dashed across to the window. Ida and Dilsey were already there.

"What's happening?"

Temple was on her front porch, her father holding her in his arms. Her mouth was wide open and she was screaming, screaming. Her father, his body lurching with great sobs, picked her up and carried her into the house. Two policemen were standing around near the front steps.

"What is happening," I asked again.

"Peter got himself killed," Ida whispered. "The policeman told Reverend Blodgett that Peter crashed his car into a telephone pole on the way back from taking that redheaded girl home. Temple must have overheard them talking, just like Dilsey did, 'cause she came out screaming. I don't know if Mrs. Blodgett even knows yet. Sad, sad, God Almighty sad."

"I told you he was drinkin'," Jimmy said as he arrived at the window, his hair at every angle. "He musta had him a flask, just like I said. That was some car, too." Soon there was a great cry from inside the house as Mrs. Blodgett was told. Ida and Dilsey and I were crying and holding each other. Jimmy was watching out the window and repeating his earlier observations about a flask and the car in endless variations, now become a Beat poem atop our sobbing.

Three weeks later I saw Temple at the post office. I had not seen her outside her house since the accident. She was with her mother, looking white and thin. Miss Crosby went right up to Mrs. Blodgett and said, in a stage whisper that could be heard all over the post office, "How are you both doing?"

Mrs. Blodgett said they were bearing up as best they could. Temple was leaving for England the next day for the rest of the summer, she said.

"I'm sure that's the right thing," Miss Crosby said. Temple gave her a wan smile.

For the first time since I had laid eyes on her, I did not want her life. I did not want to be her. I did not want to bear the loss that she would now bear for the rest of her life. I only wished we were friends so that I could comfort her. And while I did not want to be her, I was aware of the social division between us and it still made my stomach ache to think about it. I shook it off for the moment. I was being selfish to think about it at such a time.

"Temple, and Mrs. Blodgett, I am very sorry for your loss," I said. "Thank you, Doris," Temple said, taking my hand, which I let her take—overcoming an instinct to pull it away. It was the only time we ever spoke together. She had remembered my name. Rhymes with "horse."

As the weeks rolled by, I found myself at the beach whenever I had a moment free. I was a good swimmer and made a long, daily swim. I invented a stroke so awkward that it forced my special lifeguard to offer some tips when we finally met at an island party. Before the end of the summer, we were a steady item, sharing all our growing-up-in–New Hampshire stories. I told him about my long night on the frozen lake with Sybil. He told me how he and his friends in Lakeport had set up tiny ski jump ramps for skiing, and how he had exaggerated it, listing ski jumping on his college application to Amherst. That caught up with him when—because he was the only freshman who had listed the sport—they insisted he go to Dartmouth to try out for the Olympic ski-jumping team. He found himself standing atop a sky-high jump, saying a prayer and pushing off for a defining moment of his life. Being first to jump, he did not know that there was a chain across the landing ramp. It is something they take down when they open the hill, but someone had failed to do it. He had to sail over the chain to live, and he did. He survived, and had a story to tell for the rest of his life. I wish I had a tally of the times I heard it. But the first time was the best.

We shared more stories and more time together. Our relationship would go on for sixty-two years.

Ida cheered me along as I told her every little thing about this Jim fellow. "He sounds fine. You caught youself a good one," she said as we worked and sang in the kitchen that amber summer.

When we all parted at the end of the season, the four of us hugged and kissed in the front room, as Miss Farrington and Miss Crosby hovered about and wished me every success at Emerson and invited all of us back next season. Jim arrived to carry my bag down to the boat. We walked by the Blodgett home, which looked a little bedraggled, with a few weeds and some bushes dying from lack of water. The pastor was still there—I had seen him glumly come and go. But there was no life in the place.

Jim had heard all about Peter and Temple, some from me and some from around the island. When we were past the property, I mentioned that I would never forget those twins. "He sure made a mess out of that Stutz," Jim said. "That was a nice car."

Men are so sensitive.

As I walked toward Little Rock, I wondered what had become of Ida and Jimmy and Dilsey. I had lost track of them less than a year after that summer. Are Ida's grandchildren and great grand-children doing well, like mine? Has it been a happy family story in the long run? As I walked, I prayed that to be the case. Certainly God, unconstrained by time, can hear our prayers today and act upon them ages ago.

GrannyD.com

Granny, I am a 70 year old crippled with arthritis, but in my mind I am marching along with you. God's speed and my prayer for your successful finish of your journey. I sent a note to my senators and congressman with the comment that you speak for all of us. Good luck!
  Evelyn Alexander, Vass, NC—Saturday, August 14, 1999

I wholeheartedly agree with your ideas. I am a Republican who is disgusted by all the money that flows around campaigns. The forefathers of this great country intended for even the poorest man to be eligible for the presidency, not just the richest!
  Amy McGowan, Fly Creek, NY—Saturday, August 14, 1999

Granny: Please don't forget us Apache and Zuni American Indians. We want you for president.
  Geronimo Rafter, Shenandoah, PA—Friday, August 20, 1999

Granny D, I'm sitting here late at night about eight blocks from the Capitol Building. Capitol Hill is quiet tonight, even more so knowing that you are out there, making your way to my neighborhood and into the hearts of the people you meet. I feel you in my heart, too, Granny. There are many, many of us here in support of you.
  Joseph Dress, Washington, DC—Monday, August 23, 1999

Dear Granny D. I just read about your effort on the Internet, and I became so touched by what you are doing. I am Swedish and we don't have the system of election campaigns that you have in America, but I believe, and many others along with me, that big moneymakers are having too much influence on world politics today. I hope you are in for a great success Granny D!

Anna-Lena Stalnacke, Stockholm—Monday,
August 23, 1999

Little Rock

If Jimmy and Dilsey had children, which I feel sure they did, they were in that next generation that simply refused to go along with an unjust system. They would have been just a half-generation older than the eight, brave teenagers who walked through jeering, threatening mobs that first day of school at Little Rock's Central High School in 1957.

The Little Rock Eight were not just any teenagers, by the way. They were chosen from among many volunteers because they had shown that they could stand up to the taunting and not strike back. They could be counted on to keep their cool, and they were also good students. They were trained and trained before that morning by Little Rock's fearless reformer, Daisy Bates.

Ms. Bates was still alive when I walked into Little Rock in 1999, and she had given me some advice on whom I should meet and where I should speak. She died a few months later, and the president of the United States attended her funeral. What raw courage they all had had! I cannot imagine being that brave.

So my first stop, walking into Little Rock, was Central High School to pay my respects to that history. I imagined my old Nantucket friends were walking with me, so that we could share our amazement at how far our society has come with the help of love and courage. I gave a short talk to the Central High students, who were very sweet to me. From the school toward the center of town, there were about fifty walkers with me, including Congressman Vic Snyder, who, as we walked, promised he would continue to push for campaign reform.

I rested at the home of Marlene and Roy Verdery, who had walked quite a ways with me. Marlene is a reform activist, and Roy is a gerontologist—the perfect couple, as far as my needs were concerned. Roy had noticed my worsening limp, and he sent me to a doctor friend. The doctor said I had a ruptured sheath of the second toe, and further said I should have surgery to fix it and then take a week or so to recover. That did not suit my plans, so I wrapped it tighter in the morning and tried not to limp in sight of Roy.

Before I left Little Rock, I spoke at the First Missionary Baptist Church from a podium where Martin Luther King, Jr., once preached in the 1960s. I wanted to start making the point that campaign finance reform opens the door for civil rights progress. This was the place to make that argument, I thought.

The church, I am sure, has not changed much since he was there: A great pipe organ stands behind the altar; a balcony wraps around the sides, creating an intimate space filled with women and girls in beautiful pastel dresses and young and old gentlemen in fine suits.

The preacher's voice was like a great foghorn, cutting through life's murky troubles. "Give your troubles to God," he repeated in a hundred ways as the congregation punctuated his phrases with "That's right" and "Amen." It was just wonderful. No promises, no reprimands, just give your troubles to God, said so many times and so many ways that it finally soaked deep into your old bones. The congregation sang hymns with muscular vigor. The children's choir and men's choir were superb. Then, dear God, it was this old white woman's turn to speak. I felt like a white-bread sandwich at a Paris banquet.

Just the same, how wonderful it was to approach that podium and put my hands upon it. I had been making an effort to learn more about King and other great lights of nonviolence ever since

I began my walk. I was very aware of Dr. King when he was alive, but lately I had been learning the details of his techniques, which came from Gandhi and which were a revelation to me. I was very much in school again. And to be in this space where he had stood was amazing to me.

From the Speech at the First Missionary Baptist Church
September 22, 1999

The teaching of nonviolent political action is a five-fold technique that we must always remember. It must be taught in our schools. It must be remembered wherever people gather with the intention of improving their community or their world. Here are the five steps. . . .

See the appendix for more of this speech.

Well, I made some friends, indeed. People gathered around. A reporter from *Slate* magazine was there and wrote that the congregation eyed me suspiciously at first, but ended up on their feet cheering. This was important to me because I so wanted to find the emotional linkages between civil rights and campaign reform. The next big city along my walk was Memphis, and that seemed like an opportunity to further strengthen the connection.

I Mistreat Ken

In the evening, I delivered a talk at the national convention of Young Democrats serendipitously being held in Little Rock. I disappointed Ken by not using some of the ideas he thought would be good for my speech. That had also happened earlier on the road, at another big speaking engagement. Ken had strong ideas about how I should present my issue at large gatherings. He thought I should always speak extemporaneously, while I felt better with notes or a text. And he made other suggestions, which I worried were not enough about campaign reform and maybe a little too much about Ken and myself. But I understood that he was now in a political campaign of his own, and I did try to mention him whenever I could and have him stand beside me when national cameras were rolling. After all, Ken in Congress would be a great weapon for reform, I reminded myself. He had his eye on that ball.

But the Little Rock event created hard feelings. The next morning, over breakfast, John Anthony, who was now traveling with me, confronted Ken about how he was using my walk for his own campaign purposes. Ken turned red with anger and could barely control himself, but he did, sometimes holding his head in his hands to get hold of his cooler thoughts. He turned to me and asked if I agreed with John. It was one of those moments where truth, loyalty, love, and vanity are competing for your voice, and there is room for only one. I made the wrong decision, and said that we must focus on the reform message more. In retrospect, I don't know if I was really defending the message, or my own glory at center stage. His face crumpled. He took my comment as a profound, personal rebuke.

He did not walk with me for a time after that. I felt awful that I had hurt one of the most noble men in America. But I also thought of him as family now, which made me believe that we would be friends again somewhere down the road—perhaps when I walked through his own West Virginia. I resolved to write him a long letter to get back in the swing with him, and to get the sore spot out of my gut.

Before he left for home, I caught him on the front steps of Marlene and Roy's home, reading from my copy of Marianne Williamson's book *The Healing of America,* which I had been reading and loving. He looked up and said it was just the right medicine for him. We smiled, and I told him to take the book with him on the airplane. He pulled a miniature chocolate box out of his pocket and gave it to me. One of the three truffles had been raided, but the remaining two were delicious, filled, as they were, with the milk of human kindness.

When a prince is unkissed, he changes before your eyes. Poor Ken was wearing a too-big shirt and too-short shorts that he had worn too long on the road. He was not looking like the man who had so charmingly presented himself in Pasadena, and this deflation was my own fault, really. We have to keep our princes up, because there is such a shortage of them in the world today, as single women and quite a few married women know so well.

After Ken left for the airport, Roy and Marlene took me to an open-air market where we stopped for lunch at a pasta booth, called Grass Roots Pasta. The four young men who own the little place happened to know all about my walk and were very kind.

One of them, Jason Rhodes, twenty-two, looked at me with amazement.

Jason had been stewing about the poison of big money in politics ever since his days at Hendrix College, when a guest political lecturer, Dale Bumpers, the retired and much admired U.S. senator from Arkansas, told the class that no amount of yelling and screaming by government reformers was going to do any good until we put a stop to the corrupt way campaigns are financed. Jason studied international relations and learned how multinational corporations are essentially buying up governments through the use of their almost unlimited cash in elections. He actually got quite dejected over the dire condition of our politics, which he thought the average citizen did not understand. It is awful to be alone with such information. When he heard me interviewed on NPR's *The Diane Rehm Show,* he took heart that perhaps other people were catching on and might try to do something. On the Web, he started following my progress across Texas and then into Arkansas. He was making plans to find me in Little Rock when I walked into his restaurant, starving.

He was on the road the next morning as we began walking. He walked the whole ten miles, full of joy and good questions and comments. He worried that the speeding traffic next to me was a great hazard, and he became my guardian angel, keeping me to his safe side like a gentleman. He then returned to his restaurant to tell his partners that he needed to rearrange his life for a while. He walked with me for a week near Nashville, and later shared the final six weeks with me, from West Virginia into Washington.

Money in Politics Is Not a Bloodless Issue

As I walked away from Little Rock, I did not know that Ken was, at that same time, walking in West Virginia on another matter. Ken is, of course, Mr. West Virginia, and he felt an obligation to be among those marching from Marmet to Blair Mountain to commemorate an uprising of oppressed coal miners that had taken place in 1921. The miners marched in 1921 for their right to organize. Their uprising began in the small town of Matewan, West Virginia, when the mayor and police chief sided with striking miners who were being evicted from company housing. The sheriff and the mayor were shot dead by the coal company's hired thugs, and a full insurrection followed. Three counties were soon in open rebellion. Federal troops and air strikes by the Army Air Corps were called in against the miners. The uprising was subdued, but the miners won the right to organize the state's southern coal fields.

So, in August of 1999, right after he left me in Little Rock, Ken joined thirteen other marchers to commemorate this pivotal historical event. Because he and the other marchers are also active in trying to stop "mountain top removal," in West Virginia—the bulldozing of whole mountains and the filling in of entire valleys in the pursuit of coal—Ken was a marked man.

Ken and the other marchers were met by forty thugs, pelting them with eggs, tomatoes, and spit. Believe it or not, these people brought their children along to watch. The thugs said that Ken and the marchers should go home or someone was going to die that day, but they kept walking. Ken told them to remember Martin Luther King, and to not respond to the violence with violence. The thugs pulled Ken away from the other marchers and surrounded him, kicking and pushing him until he fell. Others were beaten and thrown down, too. A twelve-year-old girl looked out her window and called 911. Sheriff deputies finally came before anyone was killed. The officers arrested one of Ken's fellow marchers, but let the bad people go. Later, despite photos that identified twenty of the thugs, and despite the fact that Ken was the West Virginia secretary of state, the prosecutor could not be persuaded to take them to court. Why? Well, because coal money going into political campaigns has made West Virginia a hard place to get justice. The prosecutor who refused to press the case against the thugs went to work for the area's major coal company the very next day, and hardly anyone thought a thing of it. Finally, an honest judge intervened and the case is now moving toward justice.

It was not the first time Ken had faced the violence of King Coal.

In 1968, a mine cave-in in Farmington killed seventy-eight miners. Ken remembers many of their names, even today.

He was a congressman from West Virginia at the time, so he went to visit with the widows—expecting only to extend his sympathies. But the women asked him to do something so that it would not happen again. Mine disasters were at that time considered an inevitable hazard of the business. But, the more he looked into it, the more he saw that proper mine safety procedures could prevent cave-ins and prevent black lung disease.

He wrote the Federal Coal Mine Health and Safety Act of 1969, and he had to fight the coal mines, half of Washington, and even a corrupt mine union to get it moving through Congress.

He brought the widows to Washington to meet with every member of Congress, and with people in the Nixon White House. The corrupt mine union back home, led by Tony Boyle, tried to undercut his efforts.

The union membership knew better than to listen to their own leader. Some forty thousand miners went on strike in the spring of 1969 to support Ken's bill, despite Boyle's commands to stay on the job and shut up. Ken led a rally of six thousand miners, and he held up a twelve-pound stick of bologna as his reply to several West Virginia county medical societies, which had reported that black lung was not such a bad thing.

Every conceivable pressure came to bear on Ken. The Rockefeller family was against the bill, so pressure was applied throughout Congress.

Ken says that Congress was different then: Money didn't decide every issue.

His bill passed, and Nixon threatened a veto. Ken brought the widows back, and he told the world that Nixon would be "putting razor blades in the Christmas stockings of America's miners" if he vetoed it. Nixon reluctantly signed it in private, leaving the widows, who had at one point been invited to watch him sign, waiting in a room in the White House. Ken was waiting in a snow-covered car outside, having not even been invited indoors.

Nixon's helicopter whisked the president toward Air Force One and Christmas in San Clemente. Ken would take the widows to the station and then return to his small apartment.

He did it. There used to be hundreds and sometimes thousands of coal mine deaths each year. Now, there are a dozen or two. The scourge of black lung disease used to be commonplace among miners. Now, it is fought with strict health provisions for air filtration in mines. Ken has saved many thousands of miners' lives and improved their health, and yet some of them, in favor of raping their own landscape for cheap mining methods, were there kicking him with the other King Coal thugs.

I suppose, if you live long enough, people forget what you have done for them. I serve up this reminder here with a scolding that would be quite hot if it were in person.

Soon after Nixon signed the bill, the fellow who organized the forty thousand miners to strike in support of the bill, and who was the logical man to take over the union after Boyle was discredited so completely among the miners, was murdered, along with his wife and his daughter. It happened on New Year's Eve. His name was Jock Yablonski, and he was a good friend of Ken's.

The five men who murdered the Yablonski family also planned to kill Ken, but were immediately caught. They had been hired by the head of the corrupt union, Tony Boyle, who got three life sentences for the murders. The case was a federal action, by the way.

You cannot imagine the courage it takes to go up against such people. Ken was even threatened and roughed up in the corridor of his Washington office by coal toughs. He never flinched. He never asked, as many members of Congress now do, if they were for or against giving a campaign contribution before he asked if they were for or against the interests of the people he represented at home. If we had a Congress full of Ken Hechlers, can you imagine how different our everyday lives would be? We swim in such corporate exploitation today that many people think it is all normal—they cannot see it.

By the way, when he was in Congress, Ken used to regularly bring groups of teenagers from West Virginia to Washington for a full workweek—children from every high school in his district. The kids would pick issues, talk to members of Congress, and write position papers, which they would share with Ken. Many of those children are still his friends and are involved in West Virginia public life.

How many current members of Congress are so dedicated to truth and justice that they could afford to have bright and idealistic children watching over their shoulders all day long? That program should be adopted by every member of Congress, in some form or another.

The Greasy Limpopo

I walked through the heart of Arkansas with many people who were both friends and sworn enemies of President Clinton. Those telling me stories about him would lower their voices, even out in the open country at dawn, as if the commander-in-chief's people might be hiding in the blooming soybeans or the tall, dewy grasses beside the road. We passed great lagoons that looked as if they should be teeming with snakes and other dangers, the perfect backdrop for these whispered stories of intrigue.

The green scum of the lagoons had a wild, dead smell that mixed with the sharp, now-familiar aroma of armadillos who had been too slow in their waddling jaywalks. The little swamps, which had something to do with the fact that I was covered with mosquito bites, made me think of Rudyard Kipling's "The Elephant's Child": "Good-bye. I am going to the great grey-green, greasy Limpopo River, all set about with fever-trees, to find out what the Crocodile has for dinner."

Wide-loaded trucks zoomed around the curves of the narrow road, almost sending us diving into the swamps innumerable times. I thought we might make better time in a canoe. That would also have been easier on my left foot, which was smarting a good deal. I wished dear Doug Vance, the young vegetarian I had started my walk with, was there to bandage it up as only he could.

Late one morning, a car pulled up alongside me as I walked. The window rolled down. I am not one to imagine dangers, but the car coasted along silently and I had a sense of dread about it. The driver, a woman, shouted to me. "Granny D?" I said yes. "Granny D, have you been saved? Do you believe? Are you born again?" Well, of course my deepest spiritual beliefs are not necessarily something I share on a drive-by basis, so I smiled and waved at her. She continued to roll along, giving me a dreadful feeling. I finally said to her, "When I was ten years old, I was saved, dear," which was true.

She flashed a great smile and said, "Oh, that's just what I wanted to hear!" and she revved the engine and roared off.

Verba Belmore was my best friend for a long while when I was ten. Verba was Baptist, and my father allowed me to desert our Methodist-Episcopal church for a few weeks to go to Verba's services. I wanted to do this because the Baptists were holding a revival, and Verba told me how wonderfully handsome and thrilling the traveling minister was. And so he was. At the end of a service, he urged all those who loved Jesus to come and be saved. Verba and I went up and were saved. I didn't play cards for many moons afterward, because cards were the tools of the devil and not to be touched. I was insufferable and would not even play Old Maid with my sisters. I'm sure that if Jesus were baby-sitting, he would have encouraged me to be a better sport—I was being a spiritual snob. That is not the most direct path to enlightenment, which I believe takes a lifetime of difficult and open-minded exploration.

Despite my occasional fears, which were usually unfounded, everyone along the road had only kindness to share with me. My accommodations were usually provided by the people I met along the road. Ralph and Nancy Washburn put me up because their son and his wife and two children had met me along the road east of Little Rock. Often, one host would call friends in a town further ahead, passing me along. Always in the background, making sure that things worked out and that hosts knew what to expect in the way of my early schedule and the occasional buzz of other walkers and the press, was dear Bob Waters, who worried himself into a heart attack for me. It struck him shortly after I finished Arkansas. He survived it, thank God.

A young fellow in a tradesman's pickup truck, Matt Howard, stopped to give me a walking stick made from Arkansas Ozark cedar. He had made two of them and burnished them until they became very comfortable to the hand. One was for himself, and the other for his father. His father died before he could give it to him. He said he would take his father's walking stick and give me the other. The stick is just right for mountain climbing, and I shall use it to climb my Mount Washington one day.

Other people stopped too, as I was becoming something of a traveling picture pony. When workers came off the graveyard shift at a small plant along the road near Lonoke, some of them came back a few minutes later with their sleepy children in tow for a photo. Poor, groggy dears: What do you suppose they thought it was all about?

This was the Mississippi Delta, where rice and soybeans grow in muddy fields. The rice is a lovely light green in late August, and later turns a wheat color. There are fish farms where catfish and minnows are raised, and here and there you will find someone raising chrysanthemums and, I was told, marijuana for a little extra cash. The first cotton fields came into our view, which would soon take over the panorama. Their green bolls had not yet popped open.

A young black woman, taking lunch out to her husband in the fields, walked with me for a while. She had heard me interviewed on her radio and said I might mention her name on the radio next time I had a chance, as that would surely be the closest she would ever get to being famous. She only gave me her first name, which is Linda. I did as she asked.

In the town of DeValls, a black police chief sat me down in his office and talked about the youth problems of the little town. He wanted to know if I had any suggestions on how he could get them involved in projects that would interest them. Bob Waters and Jason stayed behind to brainstorm with him. I hope they were able to help. There are so many little places where a few extra dollars for a summer program might go a long way. I saw one town in that area that was so depressed that even its pawnshop was boarded up.

The Boys

Nick Palumbo, my young carpenter friend from Chicago who had walked with me in New Mexico, arrived as I approached Memphis. He had worked carpentry jobs to earn his road money and now was ready to join me for the rest of the way. He and Jason hit it off very nicely. They would take turns driving the vehicle and walking with me, and were both full of joyful observations as we moved through this interesting landscape. They would sleep in the vehicle or where a bed was offered, and they lived on a mixture of offered home-cooked meals and junk food.

Serious John Anthony was with us too, living in the same way out of the vehicle, and often wrestling with the laptop computer or making phone calls ahead. In the Delta we were unknown vagabonds; it was great fun to be traveling together toward Washington, a stranger destination than any Oz. We talked to the people along the way to explain the purpose of the walk and to ask their opinions.

So you can tell all these medium-build, dark-haired, twenty-somethings apart if you ever meet them: Nick is the ill-shaven, sleepy-eyed, cool customer who looks a bit like James Dean on his day off; Jason is the bright-eyed, tweedy, collegiate type you might think just hatched a great practical joke or started a computer company; John is the serious fellow with the well-trimmed, beatnik beard. He might be a record producer or, in a tux, a classical musician.

Sometimes, when we were far from anyone who might hear us and laugh, we sang as we walked. Nick's father had belonged to a barbershop quartet, so Nick knows all the old songs. His brother, unfortunately, inherited the family voice. No matter: These were the songs I knew and danced to as a young girl, and they gave me great energy as we walked and walked. The summer heat was moderating—thank goodness for that.

Just ahead was the Mississippi River. Having lived my life east of that great divide, I was somewhat taken aback by the thought that I had much of the walk still before me. That thought pressed down upon me as I neared Memphis. Perhaps I had the Memphis blues. My brilliant psychologist daughter, Betty, heard that low something in my voice over the phone. She packed up with her friend Betty Foster to come walk across the Mississippi with me. The two of them had come out before, back in El Paso. It is interesting that her friend has the same name as my late best friend.

Betty's visit was the medicine I needed. She was in need of comfort herself, as she was closing her counseling office and saying farewell to her clients, as her health was failing her. The hardest thing for her to give up was a weekly group of terminal cancer patients who had become her old friends. But her sense of responsibility to them required her to say good-bye.

Our visit started poorly, thanks to my clumsiness. When I first saw my Betty's two, large suitcases, I said it looked like she would be staying a month. I think she had been a little envious of all the time I had been spending with her brother on this project, and my comment about her luggage just made her feel that she was not a fellow vagabond. Oh, my! It is just as hard to be a good parent when you are ninety and your children are nearly seventy as when all of us were brand new! My own hearing seemed to take a sharp downturn at this time, so it seemed we were just a falling-apart old family. But we were all much closer than we had been for many years, and I loved having my little daughter with me again.

Well, now, whenever you are blue and out of steam, go out and buy a *George* magazine and see if it has a nice story about you. It worked for me. Betty also got a charge out of seeing her old mother written up so nicely. The only sad part, of course, was that John Kennedy, Jr., had been killed during the time when the article was being prepared. The people from his staff who had interviewed and photographed me on the road, and who had conveyed his friendly messages to me, were quite heartbroken. He had indeed been a prince, they said.

I Am a Person

As we approached Memphis, I did all I could to connect with civil rights leaders and learn more about their present goals. The writer and activist Dick Gregory, who had himself run, not walked, across America in 1972, opened many doors for me in the civil rights community. As I approached Memphis, he was walking with me. He is a good-looking man with a gray-and-white beard and a staccato speaking style that was punctuated with the phrase "You see how it works, Granny D?"

I asked him if there was really a chance of joining the campaign reform movement with civil rights. He walked in silence for a while.

"Oh, Granny D, you've got to understand how it works. For so many black people, the problem is the poverty right now—the poverty tonight. If there are roaches in the kitchen and rats in the kid's bedroom, you can't think much past that. People in poverty need to solve those kinds of problems before they can worry about the big, political issues. You see how it works?"

I said that I understood that, but I thought civil rights leaders should help to clean up the political system so that social justice reforms might be possible. If all our tax dollars are being diverted to corporate welfare through the campaign finance system, people who truly need help cannot get it. Dick said that the leaders understand all that very well, but many of them need a second wind before they can do much about it. "A lot of them are just tired," he said.

As he spoke, I watched him with such earnestness that I stumbled on a stone. He sweetly took my hand and did not let go of it the rest of the day.

"But not all of them are tired," he added. "And all you have to worry about, Granny D, is to just keep walking and let your feet do the talking. Just do that. You are planting seeds that will grow here. You see how it works? You are helping change the way people think about all this. So just be patient and keep walking. You have no idea the difference you are making."

He argued that all the news articles about my walk were having a cumulative effect. I argued back, but not too hard, as I needed the encouragement. He told me that he first heard about me when Diane Rehm was interviewing me on NPR; he had pulled his car over to listen. He said the way I was connecting campaign reform with basic patriotic values would do something. He also thought I was encouraging elders to not give up on living their lives. That statement seemed more realistic to me. I do hope the walk will encourage older people to talk to themselves and to each other about keeping at it. They'll say, "Well, maybe we can do this or that, if that ninety-year-old lady can walk across the United States." You see how it works.

But I knew the civil rights thing was going to be hard for me to really tackle. It is impossible for a white person to really know what it is like to be a black person in America. Imagination—the essential tool of empathy, brotherhood, and justice—simply fails us.

As I walked with Dick, I tried to imagine what it must be like to be black. What experience in my own life could help me connect?

When I was a young servant girl on Nantucket Island, after Ida and I had had our big conversation about segregation following the beach incident, I told her that I just didn't understand what she must feel like. She said I would understand something of it someday, when an unfair thing hurt me deeply. "That'll be your chance to understand," she said.

She was proved right later that year. A customer at the hotel heard that I would be studying at Emerson the coming fall and that I needed a job and lodging. She suggested that I interview with her sister, who had a very large mansion at Marblehead and was always looking for good domestic help. I interviewed with Mrs. P in Boston, and she instantly hired me. She offered to drive me to the house right then. As I had no lodging for the night, I accepted.

I opened the door of her great automobile to slide into the front seat beside her. She stopped me: "You'll sit in back, Doris." And so I did. The rope across her beach was a very clear one, as I would learn.

We drove in complete silence to Marblehead, where she and her husband lived in a newly built summer home perched on a hill above the harbor. She took me through the servants' entrance and introduced me to the cook.

Mary, the white cook, about twenty-six, was as big around as she was tall. When the coast was clear, Mary grinned at me with badly rotted teeth. She slapped me on the back and showed me to my room. She was voluble and profane—and a fast ally.

After arranging my clothes, I asked her for the lowdown on our employers.

"Well, Mr. P is very handsome with black, curly hair, but he's really a forty-year-old baby, and Mrs. P tells him what to do. She's the daughter of an innkeeper where Mr. P stayed one summer, and she copped him. She ain't up to the high society she travels in. She keeps trying to forget she is the daughter of an innkeeper, but it shows through. She never sends her things to the cleaner, for instance. Saves money by using gasoline to clean her own clothes. She went to a big wedding this summer stinking to high heaven of gasoline—she even dipped her girdle. You could smell her a mile away!" She broke into a gale of laughter as she thought about it.

"You want to watch out for her temper, though. You'll see when you cross her, and you can't help that."

I was to wait on Mr. and Mrs. P and their dinner guests, when they had them. Even for just the two of them, dinner was always set on a very long and beautiful refectory table, the polished wood gleaming in the candlelight. Mrs. P sat at one end, Mr. P a mile away at the other. The fresh flower centerpiece was so tall they couldn't see each other, which was probably on purpose.

After I had served them and was standing aside in the dining room, Mrs. P addressed me, to my surprise.

"Mr. P will take you into town tomorrow morning on the train and show you what el car to take and where to get off for Emerson," she said. I nodded.

Mr. P was quite a different person away from Mrs. P's gravity. We chatted gaily all the way into Boston. He was interested in where I came from and why I wanted to go to school. I told him that I was interested in acting, and he thought that was a marvelously interesting career. The second morning, as I waited to walk with him again down the hill to the Marblehead station, Mrs. P came into the kitchen to announce crisply, "Now you know your way into Boston, don't you Doris? Mr. P will be going on a later train today."

"She's afraid to let him go with you again," Mary said when she left. "She's afraid you'll take him away from her. She's jealous. She ain't taking any chances! She'll never get another one like that, and she knows it."

The next Saturday I broke a lamp, and Ida's prediction came home to me. I was changing the sheets on Mrs. P's twin beds when my foot caught the electric cord. The fancy ceramic lamp exploded onto the floor. I was panic-stricken. Mr. and Mrs. P were out playing golf. Mary was in the kitchen getting ready for a dinner party, when she heard the crash and my howl. She came panting up the stairs and stared at the mess. "Oh Jee-sus," she said.

"Will she fire me?"

"No, you come too cheap. She loves a bargain. But she sure as hell ain't going to like it. That lamp cost a hundred and twenty-five dollars. You're going to get to see that temper I been telling you about. And she's always in a foul mood when she comes off the golf course anyway. She ain't no good at golf. She's been warned that if she don't stop cutting up the greens, she's going to be put out of the club, and that would be some scandal. When she makes a poor shot, she stands there and beats the turf with her club."

"Oh, Jee-sus," I said, catching on to her English.

I let Mrs. P have the news straight away when she entered the house. Mr. P cringed, knowing his wife as he did. She turned white and thin-lipped and she visibly quivered. Mr. P excused himself. "Come with me," Mrs. P said like an executioner.

She went to the telephone alcove and dialed Shrieve Crump & Lowe and asked for her lamp decorator.

"Frank, one of my servants has broken my lamp—the one by my bedside. Please send me a duplicate. Yes, it's hard to get decent help nowadays. She's a clumsy oaf. I would discharge her, but probably the next one would be just as bad."

She sat facing me as she spoke. I stood braced against the wall, her words lashing deep. I am not a servant, I repeated to myself. Not a servant. I am a student working part-time. I felt real hatred.

"Yes. Well, the expense can't be helped. Yes. A total idiot." She wore a smirk of satisfied triumph. Her steel-gray shark eyes narrowed as she watched me, my hands clenching and unclenching. She hung up and walked away. I felt scar tissue forming deep in me. It would stay there for all my years, the source of a certain amount of social insecurity and class consciousness.

I stood there and took it, rather than defending my human dignity. I was too wrapped up in my need for tuition money and housing to consider doing the right thing, which would have been to tell her off and suffer the consequences. If you are not open about such things, the anger stays inside you.

I later wished I had been more like my grandmother Charlotta Tucker. She had moved to Laconia from Canada with her eight children after the death of her husband. She found work in the Laconia hosiery mill with two of her oldest girls, leaving the next oldest to take care of the younger children. The very first night after work in the factory, she found herself and two daughters jammed together with some four hundred workers all waiting at the locked mill gate for the manager of the mill to let them out. She set a few workers in the crowd to baying like sheep in protest of their inhuman treatment. Every night the baying increased until all four hundred were doing it. The manager asked who had started it. Grandmother raised her hand proudly and was fired, along with her daughters. She did the right thing. The right thing comes at a price, but it leaves you free of anger in your soul.

I was not ready for that kind of courage.

At the end of September we moved to their Chestnut Hill winter estate. The long living room was paneled with books, more than I had ever seen in a home. I began devouring sets of books: Dostoyevsky, de Maupassant, and my old friend, Dickens. I'd start at one end of a shelf and read to the other end of it, then move to the next row. I was up half the night reading, after my homework.

Mary told me that a woman named Effie was coming to help us for a big dinner party.

"Mrs. P brings her in for parties. All her friends think she has three servants that way. Like as not, Effie will get drunk before the evening is out, and you'll have to go it alone in the dining room."

Effie was a thin, dried-up little dust ball of a woman with faded blue eyes and white scraggly hair in a coming-apart bun. The party was to be given in honor of a Norwegian sea captain who supplied Mr. P's company with imports. The captain had sent a beautiful bird from the ship for the main course, but Mary wasn't quite sure what to do with it.

"I ain't much of a cook, at best," she said. "I sure don't know what to do with this f—n' duck."

Effie and I got through the soup course and the fish course without mishap. I could see what Mary meant—Effie had two quick highballs after we served the drinks in the living room. She downed them like water. She had a glass of the wine when we served the fish course—a tumbler glass full. She was beginning to giggle inappropriately and walk with a decided list.

The duck came out of the oven perfectly browned. Mary put it on a platter, decorated it with paper ruffles and sprigs of fresh parsley.

"Isn't that beautiful!" she said as she passed it to Effie.

"Ain't never seen another thing so purty!" Effie said, holding the platter above her head and mincing along with a little dance step. The platter tilted and the bird took an unexpected last flight, crashing with a long skid along the kitchen linoleum to a dark space under the soapstone set-tubs.

Mary muffled her own wail.

Effie got down on her hands and knees and fished out the skinned-up bird. Mrs. P was pressing the buzzer under the Oriental rug at her place. Mary put the bird back on the platter, brushed off the dirt, plastered the skin back into place, and gave it to me to present.

Mr. P stood up to carve. When his first cut dislodged most of the skin, he looked at me with puzzlement, then went on carving, his eyebrows high.

I went out to the kitchen to get the vegetables and the gravy. As I served Dr. Downes, he said, "Could I have a piece of bread to go with my gravy? I'm just a country boy at heart, and I do love to have some bread to sop up my gravy."

Mrs. P asked me to bring out some bread.

"She knows damned well there ain't a piece of bread in this whole stinkin' house," Mary fumed. "They don't eat it, and she only buys it for me sometimes. I already told her this morning we ain't got none!"

"What do we do now?" I pleaded, wringing my apron.

"You'll have to run next door and borrow a piece from the cook."

"Next door? It'll take me at least five minutes each way, even if I run!" Next door was another huge estate, with large lawns and a thick stand of trees between. I had never actually seen the house, let alone been there.

"Here's a flashlight. Just run over and knock at the back door. The cook's helped me out before. Her name is Ruth. Just tell her to give you a couple of pieces of bread—she'll know what's happened."

Effie was stretched out like a rag doll on the floor, her legs parted in a wide V, her arms flung wide, and her thin hair completely on the loose from its bun. Terrible snores were coming from her open mouth. I had a strong temptation to kick her as I passed.

I ran through the freezing night. I got the bread from the grinning cook and ran back.

"Has she been buzzing me?" I asked Mary.

"She knows damn well she better not. She knows f—n' well that Effie's out like a light, or she, instead of you, would have brought in the vegetables. She knows, too, where that bread had to come from. Anyway, the bread will save my neck. She won't give me hell for the way the bird looked after saving her from not having bread in the house."

I adapted. I survived. But it was the business of this family to humiliate me and anyone who worked for them, and the scars from that mild mistreatment are welts I still feel. I learned that it is possible to hate people and to celebrate their misfortunes.

Many years later, I was having dinner in a house quite like and quite near the mansion where I had run to borrow the bread. The hostess wanted to know all about my recent trip to Alaska and our effort to save the Eskimo village from Edward Teller's nuclear tests. She served dinner herself with the help of her cook and seemed a little awkward about it.

"There was a time, you know, when we had a footman behind each of these chairs. But that was another day. No one keeps that kind of help these days."

"I know. It's so true," I said.

"Of course, it was never easy back then, either," she added. "We had, for a very short time, a tiny, old woman server who ended up drunk on our kitchen floor, if you can believe the picture of that!"

I could have said, "Old Effie worked here, too?" but I just smiled at her story. My son, Jim, across the table, gave me a wink of thanks for holding my tongue. After all, it wouldn't have done at all to say how I knew of her—that I had been one of *them*.

I offered to help her clear the dishes for dessert. "Oh, are you sure you wouldn't mind?" She sounded like a Russian aristocrat after the Revolution, so unsure of life in a world not dripping with servants.

"I wouldn't mind in the least," I said like a chipper ex-duchess.

We visited in the kitchen and talked again about the wonderful wedding—when my Jim married her beautiful daughter, Libby. After dessert I enjoyed my tea and looked through the windows to the dark trees in the distance. I imagined I could make out a flickering light through them. God is not limited as we are to only seeing the present moment, and so He sees everything at once: The light was not the distant mansion, but the flashlight of a young girl running this way. To live a long life attentively is to finally see it all in one connected view. And, heavens, you have to smile.

Perhaps because I am white, the story has that storybook but true ending. But if that brief and mild experience working as a house servant changed me, as indeed it did, what on earth would I be like if I had instead suffered a lifetime of real abuse and humiliation? Certainly, I would have a hard time caring much about other people, for abuse is the thing that hardens us until we are finally beyond human caring. These issues trace far deeper than we can touch with campaign finance reform, I realized, squeezing Mr. Gregory's hand. That's all right. We will do what we can.

We walked across the bridge over the Mississippi and into Memphis, continuing to Clayborne Temple, where Dr. King gave his last speech, the "I have seen the mountain top" speech.

That speech was a cloudsplitter—probably the most clearly prophetic speech in modern American history. King planned to be in Memphis on March 22, 1968, to deliver the speech and march with the striking sanitation workers. The day before his trip, as King no doubt went over the coming speech in his mind, the weather changed in Memphis. It was too cold to rain, so it began snowing on the afternoon of the twenty-first. Snow is unusual in Memphis, especially in March. It continued all night, piling up seventeen inches. The local organizers asked King to delay his trip, as the streets were impassible. He would come instead on the twenty-eighth. It was between those two dates that James Earl Ray purchased a rifle.

Thanks to the brilliant organizing of Bob Waters, the Reverend Billy Kyles, who had brought King to Memphis, and many of the same sanitation union men who walked with King were standing there to meet me at the temple. They gave me an I AM A MAN protest sign from the 1968 march. I was glad for the big lettering of it, as my eyes were full of tears.

Together, we traced King's last march, with Reverend Kyles and the others remembering what had happened at each point along the way. At Beale and Main, we made a great circle and the Reverend said a prayer for peace and justice. We ended our walk at the Lorraine Motel, where Dr. King was killed. It is now a civil rights museum. We made a few speeches and shook hands on a promise to work together for reforms. Reverend Kyles said he had taken a backseat in recent years, thinking that he had done his service, but that he felt like getting back into it now. It was the best thing anyone had said in a thousand miles.

Speech at the Lorraine Motel
September 7, 1999

Thank you.

We are on hallowed ground. The petty affairs of the day fade away at this place, where, in 1968, the courage and pain of a righteous life suddenly transcended to the eternal. And with that transcendence, the light from above that shows us the way to justice and love became, for all time, one soul brighter. Did King die here? The part of him we love, his soul, will never die. And so his voice still rings in our ears, and he still implores us to make brotherhood, love, and self-sacrifice our only tools for change. We hear you, Dr. King.

In this place, it is easy to remember that our brothers and sisters of every color have sacrificed their lives to advance our shared dream of a land of equality and plenty. We have *not* made these sacrifices in order to separate our people into rich and poor, privileged and oppressed. Dr. King was in this very place because he believed that equal economic opportunity is the essential partner of political equality.

Our people are more economically divided now than they were when King walked this way. The tax and labor and business laws of this nation drive that division, and those policies are held hostage by a corrupt Congress and its system of campaign finance bribery and billion-dollar political favors. These favors are paid at the expense of programs that could make our society more fair and less troubled.

Whole parts of our society, stripped of other opportunities, have fallen into illegal markets to survive. A young generation of urban poor is in jail or in the justice system. Our families are working too many jobs and too many hours to be able to raise their families properly.

It is the duty of leaders to shape opportunities so that the great masses of its people can work to provide decently for their families and their futures. Our leaders, distracted by the corruption of the campaign finance system, are failing that duty.

They pass laws that destroy the jobs and lower the protections for workers, that segregate the people into rich communities and ghettos of despair, and that provide jails instead of education, shelters instead of decent housing, toxic pollution instead of healthy environments. They do it to favor the wealthy elite who keep them in power through campaign contributions.

We must replace this bribery with the full public financing of our elections, so that candidates may speak as freely to the community as they did in the days of the Fourth of July candidate's picnic in the park. We must get big money out of politics before it destroys us utterly.

Our democracy is sacred ground. It is red with the sacrifices of our people. We are here today to honor those sacrifices, not with our words, but with our deeds.

To the apologists of corruption in Congress, like Mr. Mc-
Connell of Kentucky, understand, sir, that, just like those who
stood atop the school steps to block the historic arrival of deseg-
regation, you cannot stand forever atop the Capitol steps, your
arms folded against the American people's longing for a democracy worthy of our national sacrifices.

I thank Mr. Dick Gregory, Reverend Kyles, and the Memphis
sanitation workers who have walked here with me today. I hope
some of you will walk with me again in January in Washington.
By then I might need a hand up the Capitol steps, and I hope that
we, as American brothers and sisters, might go into that great
temple of freedom together, with the spirit of Dr. King beside us,
and in our hearts.

Thank you.

I went to Sunday church at Reverend Kyles's Monumental
Baptist Church: dramatic drums that rattled the stained glass;
jazz piano and organ keyboard; choirs of men, choirs of women,
choirs of children; a great, rejoicing movement of sound and
swaying, exploding from hundreds of clapping, singing, beautifully dressed people. Communion came amid the swirl of white
linen and red satin fabrics. The Reverend's sermon was about
how African-Americans are survivors—how they endure. It was
delivered with the meter, resonance, and energy that has not only
transformed American music but American public speaking.

It was inspiring, to say the least. But you have to keep at that
sort of thing: A week later I was in a strip club having a drink.

Growing Up

Coming out of Memphis, I had an idea of what needed to be said
and what needed to be done. You sit back most of your life, and
you assume that there are grown-ups somewhere running the
show. If you really get out there, if you look behind the curtain,

you see it is just a bunch of tired people like yourself, needing help, trying their best and not doing half as well as they would like. That is the moment when you have an opportunity to grow up and to take your part. I was feeling that now, at my late age. Yes, I had been involved in civic work through my younger years, but it was always with the feeling that there were responsible leaders somewhere to be appealed to—parents, almost. Now I was starting to get it. What a late bloomer!

Jean Higgs, again walking with me in the miles east of Memphis, motioned me into a seedy strip joint. "C'mon, let's get a Coke." I couldn't imagine what she was thinking. Well, we sat in there and had a soft drink. The gentlemen around the bar gave us a quick but thorough stare and went back to their drinks. One of them said, "Oh, it's that Granny D. I seen her on TV." Another man craned around a little and reckoned that it was, because "she's got a yellow flag." The owner came out and said that he had called the local newspaper, and we should sit tight. When Jean got the drift of things—or when, I should say, the facts began to reveal themselves, we beat a hasty retreat. Outside, I pointed to the big neon sign we had walked under. She, in her thirst, simply hadn't noticed. We marched briskly on, singing the hymns of the Monumental Baptist Church.

I hadn't felt so naughty since I was expelled from Emerson College in my junior year.

Here's what happened. Jim Haddock, my lifeguard from Nantucket who had become my steady boyfriend, had graduated from Amherst. The Great Depression was on, and because he didn't have any better prospect for a job, he came to Boston to be near me while he looked there. Our romance went to another level. It was what we called "heavy petting," which meant that I had not gone over the edge with him, but was having more fun than a proper girl was entitled to have. The stresses of the times were extreme, and some of that found its way into our relationship. It was clear that Jim needed a female partner, and I came to the conclusion that if I wanted to keep this warm and brilliant fellow, I would have to make a big decision. I decided to do it: to go down the aisle with him.

I knew that I would be breaking my mother's heart. As a married woman, I would have little or no chance to be the little actress she now wanted me to be, and that I had wanted for myself since early childhood. Her fantasy, I believe, was that I would become a star and they would all live forevermore on easy street. As the Depression hit, and as I had leading roles in more and more Emerson plays, she became pushy about this. Marriage would end it all, for married starlets were an oxymoron, and Jim told me that he would not want me in a business where any success would be assumed to have been earned on the casting couch. So, the man of my dreams, or the career of my dreams: Choose one.

At Amherst, Jim had worked for Bishop "Tuey" Kingsolving, who had become the rector at Boston's historic Trinity Church in Copley Square. Jim and I met with him and asked him to marry us. He was used to society weddings, but he agreed to slip us into his holiday schedule as a favor to Jim. But we must do two things: First, we must have the permission of our parents, as he thought that in the hard times already upon us, family support was essential to a good marriage. Second, he said we must solemnly promise to never get divorced, as he had a perfect record and didn't want us to spoil it.

My mother was beside herself. I had stabbed the whole family in the back. She calmed down over the space of several days and finally agreed that there was nothing she could do about it, stubborn as she knew I was. She did not come to the wedding, however, nor did Papa. An aunt came to witness for the family.

It was a secret ceremony. We could not invite our friends, except one each. By good fortune, a ladies' guild was meeting in the church, preparing to decorate the altar for the New Year's eve service. When they saw we were getting married with no one to celebrate with us, they found some rice and gave us a festive send-off—a sweet kindness remembered now for seventy years.

It was a secret ceremony because, in 1930, married girls did not attend college. Period. It was strictly against the rules of Emerson and, I suppose, most other colleges. Marriage would be a distraction from one's studies, and there was no thought that a woman might be married and not be pregnant or have children in tow—inconceivable.

After the ceremony, we took a taxi to Cambridge and spent the night in a hotel. Jim bought me a box of chocolates in the lobby, and we spent all that night and the next day in bed eating chocolates and working on consummating our marriage. If you are a virgin woman and looking for a reason to stay awhile longer in that sweet condition, let me tell you that it hurt like hell.

But we became, over the days and years, good and uninhibited lovers, and Jim remembered to buy me a big, sampler box of chocolates every December 30 for each of the next sixty-two years of our marriage, even when he could remember very little else.

I shouldn't keep mentioning chocolates or I might weaken Dear Reader's resolve to be good. If it helps, these weren't expensive, chocolate-shop chocolates, but simply the drugstore variety—waxy by comparison. I would not like Jim's spirit to think I am ungrateful, however; for I did love them—particularly the nut fudges and the cashew clusters. Each box, which provided at no extra charge that happiest of all Earth's atmospheres as you pulled it open, also had its Vermont fudges and chocolate whips, almond nougats and molasses chews. The brown paper cups with pecan and walnut clusters swimming in the dark were not to be missed, nor the hard, flat, toffee chips or those solid chocolate ingots that melted smooth against your tongue. There were, for dessert, chocolate-dipped almonds, coconut creams, and butter cream caramels—all in that box for us to share.

So it was a fine honeymoon. We saved the delicious cherry-filled for last.

I don't know if Bishop Kingsolving thought I was just about to graduate, or what. He evidently did not understand the secret nature of our wedding service. A few days later he was officiating at Emerson's morning chapel. He said something in his sermon that changed my life: that he felt comfortable at Emerson as we were all neighbors on the square and he had just, that weekend, married a fine, young man who had been fortunate enough to catch an Emerson girl. Well, the FBI and the KGB, Sam Spade and Charlie Chan were soon hot on my trail. In class, I received a note to report to the dean's office at the end of the day. After the rush of rumors all morning, I knew what it must be, yet I tried to concentrate and enjoy the day's classes. They would very likely be my last.

Emerson was an intimate college of about 159 girls and one very lucky and pampered young man. We were all schooled on the second floor of an old building on Copley Square. Mrs. Southwick, who had an ownership interest in the school, taught a peculiar but brilliant class called "The Evolution of Expression," in which unsuspecting works of literature were dissected like hapless biology frogs.

Mrs. Southwick was very old and very beautiful. She wore long, white kid gloves at all times. The story was that she had lost all the tips of her fingers, up to the first knuckles, in a scalding accident in a railway compartment. She supposedly had little corks in the tips of her gloves. I never knew if this was true, but I thought I detected a peculiar bending at her finger tips when she wrote on the chalkboard. She wore very old Victorian dresses, with pinched waists and high-boned lace neckpieces—which we suspected had the job of holding her wrinkled neck at bay. She was ethereal in the extreme, and though we poked a little fun behind her back, we loved her very much. Just seeing her was a revelation of the fact, quite new to us, that no matter how long we lived or how wrinkled and abbreviated by railway mishaps we might become, we could yet be elegant, respected, and loved in the world.

She sailed smoothly into the classroom, posture-perfect, with a lavender-scented, white lace handkerchief in her left hand. The handkerchief danced a hypnotizing rhythm in the vicinity of her left shoulder while her right hand inscribed the chalkboard with the unraveled mysteries of art. When she turned away from the board to address us, she stood like an Aladdin's lamp—her hanky at rest in a loose fist upon her hip, and her right hand elevating the always-new piece of chalk like the bright filament of her wisdom. Such a person seen standing in the front of a room otherwise filled with golden streams of morning sun and the lavender scent of civilization itself was a nearly rapturous vision for us all.

We were a fairly close group, though there were divisions. The one sorority on campus would not have a domestic servant like me as a member, which smarted a bit. Nevertheless, I had three wonderful friends: a Spanish Gypsy girl, Ramona, whose family had moved to a dilapidated Boston tenement house because they could not bear to be apart during her schooling; a beautiful Irish girl, Vera, who drove to school in her very own convertible sports car and who had nothing but amused contempt for the "whole f—g scene," as she called school and life. Bobbie was my third friend: a tomboy who was tall, thin, and probably too much taken with me. We four bohemians were, I suppose, the goths of our day. I landed many of the leading roles in the drama productions, which only made the sorority types further shun me as an unworthy usurper.

But I needn't worry about their opinions: I was indeed out, the dean said—just like that. Marriage was a clear violation of the rules. Raising myself to perfect posture and speaking with Emersonian precision, I made a clear and calm case for myself, citing the fact that I was responsible for all the costumes for the Children's Theatre production held every Saturday—a job that, by the way, had paid for my tuition. This was no small job, as I was responsible for making and fitting hundreds of costumes and I had become the apprentice of Miss Bailey, the head of the drama department. Together, we combed through the city's garment district each Saturday, looking for all the necessary fabrics. I spent long nights designing and sewing—knowledge that would prove useful in my later working life. The school officials softened when they realized they would be leaving the drama department in a difficult position. They agreed to let me stay through the rest of my junior term. After all, I couldn't get too pregnant-looking in the five months remaining.

Into the Hard World

After the school term, Jim and I headed back to reclaim our happy memories of Nantucket and to see if we could begin a new life there.

Miss Farrington and Miss Crosby were delighted to have me back at Old Parliament House for the season, and they let Jim, whom they instantly loved, stay in the little attic space with me. Jim got back his old lifeguard job. I hoped that Ida, Dilsey, and Jimmy would show up, but they never did. By the end of the summer, we had determined that there were no winter jobs to be had on the island. Jim came close to getting a job at a local high school, but the position went to a local fellow.

"You do understand, don't you Jim, that island people feel they have to take care of their own people first," Miss Farrington said. He understood, but I was mad: Jim had higher qualifications by far than the other fellow. But I had a new problem of my own: morning sickness. The two great ladies were in a fit of excitement about "their" coming child, and they turned the island upside down, looking for a job that could keep us through the winter. But the Depression had settled upon Nantucket as it had everywhere else.

We sheepishly headed to our hometown of Laconia, where I asked mother if we could move in with them for a time. She stared at me and said that I had made my bed and I could now sleep in it, meaning "get lost." Well, this did not make me feel very wanted, to say the least. I remembered that old piece of grit in my heart: that I was so unlike her other children, she had said; that I was like someone found in a basket. She was to allow no more baskets on her doorstep, I gathered.

Jim's parents, who were financially in worse shape than mine, took us in. This was despite the fact that Jim's mother was certain that this early marriage, and me in particular, were cutting short Jim's great promise. She and my mother had shouted at each other regarding whose child was ruining the other child's life. But she did not turn us away. I was three months pregnant with Betty, who would be a year old and walking when we left.

When false labor pains sent me to the hospital, my own mother changed her tune instantly. She brought me home from the hospital to my old room, where I spent the last few days of my pregnancy. Mama was full of comfort and reassurance, walking the floor with me, her arms wrapped around me. When Papa once said, "Oh, my poor little Dotty!" mother shooed him away:

"Look, you! I had five children, and I never remember you saying, oh, my poor Ethel. You just go away."

After Betty's birth, we moved back with Jim's family. Everyone, including Jim's two brothers and his sister, loved to watch over baby Betty. She was the happy distraction from hard times. She was our television set and our movies—something to watch and talk about every spare minute. All the early stimulation we gave her contributed to her great intellect, I am sure.

During this time, I earned a few dollars conducting readings at libraries and putting on one-woman shows for ladies' clubs. A typical show might include three one-act plays, or one three-act play, in which I took all the parts, changing my voice and manner for each. I was finally using my training to put some food on the table. The most popular was *The Twelve-Pound Look,* which J. M. Barrie wrote in 1914. It regards a working woman, and therefore was quite a political statement in those times. Another favorite was *Mr. Pimm Passes By,* by A. A. Milne.

I quickly warmed to Jim's parents. His mother, Aggie, was a handsome woman—a teacher—who would live to be one hundred years old. Aggie and Joe met each other growing up in Millenocket, Maine, where Aggie's father was a papermaker. He met Aggie at the skating rink, and they fell in love. She was Catholic, and there was no chance they could ever marry unless they eloped, which they did. Her mother disowned her until Jim, my late husband, was born. Aggie's mother, of course, had to go to see her first grandson, and all was forgiven. Biology and time are the great peacemakers.

During the Depression, people looked to old skills to scare up a few dollars. Joe's hockey experience gave him an idea: Maybe he and Jim could make a skating rink in Laconia and another in Lakeport. They worked like dogs, clearing space, pumping water, clearing snow late at night. They came home stiff with layers of ice and nearly frostbitten. But they were able to eke out a living through that winter. When the ice melted, my Jim found a small job reading meters for the New Hampshire power company.

He would, over the years, rise to the position of that company's operations director. He was constantly reading textbooks and attending technical courses to turn himself into a top engi-

neer, which he did. He would invent the concept of selling excess
generating capacity to power grids in other states, which is now
commonplace throughout the world.

Much later, when Betty and then Jimmy were in school, I
would go to work in the office of a Manchester shoe factory,
working my way up to the position of production cost estimator.
I retired in 1972.

Meaningful Things

Those long factory years gave me a great interest in machinery,
and as Jean and I escaped the strip joint outside Memphis and
headed into cotton fields, a great harvesting machine beckoned
from the top of an earthen bank.

Two young, fine-looking men were firing up the big cotton
harvester. Jean and I scrambled atop the bank, and the younger
man was happy to describe how the thing worked. Like a fourfold
lawn mower, the machine had four large prongs mounted on its
front, each holding a propellerlike device that rotated facing the
ground. The edges of these propellers were covered with lethal-
looking nails along their edges. As the arms rotated, these nails
snagged the cotton bolls. Inside the machine, opposite-revolving
arms pulled the cotton from the nails. The loose cotton was then
sucked into a chute and into a great box on the machine's aft. It
was an amazing machine to see, and if it had been invented a bit
earlier, it might have prevented the Civil War.

A woman of about fifty had parked her car behind us and was
trying to catch up to us on foot. When I saw she was struggling
and not going to make it, I stopped and walked back to her. She
spread her arms out; her eyes were streaming tears. She gave me
a great hug and tried to speak, but just shook her head back and
forth as she looked at me, trying to make a word come. I could
only smile at her and say that it was all right and this was a good

place for me to take a rest, so there was no hurry. She finally got her voice and said breathlessly that she was just coming back from the doctor in the city and had seen me walking. It seemed clear to me that she had received some hard news. "Are you all right?" I asked her. "Well, not as well as you are, I guess" is all she would say through a sardonic smile. She gave me another hug and turned away to walk back to her car.

I do not know what she was thinking about or how her life had turned to make this moment so intense for her. But, after scores of little moments like this, I had come to understand that people have a great, unmet need to live a life that expresses their passions and values and that they think they are being cheated out of that life—that they will die and it will have passed them by. They see an old woman doing something she believes in, and she somehow carries this ineffable something for them. Our shallow culture makes us people of great longing, for we are not always provided with opportunities to live out our most meaningful beliefs.

What, indeed, would the community look like if it were the perfect expression of our best instincts and deepest beliefs? The difference between that ideal and our actual lives is the gap that, like a stretched elastic, energizes both our political emotions and our sense of personal longing. Politics, in this sense, is a much more personal thing than we give it credit for.

Now, to prove to you beyond any reasonable doubt that I am not a perfect bearer of meaning into people's lives, let me inform you that I do not remember the name of the profoundly touched woman who embraced me along the road, but just a few miles further, the man who owns the barbecue rib joint and who invited me in for a free lunch is Mr. John McKenzie.

Pretty Old for a Damsel

People through western Tennessee were well informed of my walk through newspaper stories. A postmistress stood outside her post office to shake my hand and tell me she agreed that campaign reform was needed. A man teaching his little boy to walk in their front yard came to the fence to say hello and to tell his son that this was the lady they had talked about at breakfast. A waitress where we stopped for a chocolate fudge sundae said she heard about the reform bill passing in the House, and wasn't it great.

We came across a small community where the few houses were completely covered with vines. One particular house could have been mistaken for a large clump of bushes had it not been for the glint of reflected morning sun from a solitary window hole cut through the thick. Nick said it made him think of the story where a princess sleeps for a hundred years and her palace becomes covered with vines. A handsome prince on a great white horse travels by and awakens her with a kiss. I told him he had hit upon one of the central fantasies of my life, the defect of which is the fact that I was always too short and chunky, and now too old, to ever make the grade in a sparkling white gown. But the idea that a prince might come save me from the mundane tortures of everyday life—that I might belong to someone and, I suppose, not have to be responsible for my own life, was an immature longing that, I'm afraid, lurks yet. The worst kind of belonging, of course, is to belong to someone else to the extent that you are not your own person. So this longing is not very feminist or humanist of me, but I allow myself some layered complexity, as we must so allow for each other.

Indeed, here I was, setting myself out in the middle of the wilds of America, an intentional damsel in distress, expecting and getting all these men, and some women, to come to my defense and to awaken that little girl in me with their hugs and kisses. As

I mentioned before, the subconscious is quite relentless in arranging our lives according to our childhood blueprints, and the only way to take command over these processes is to be able to see them. You don't end them, but you can bend them to good purposes.

My husband had been the great prince of my life. But once you get in the prince habit, it takes more than a lifetime to stop hoping for another arrival.

We were followed by dogs all across Tennessee, and I didn't think much of it. But in Cedar Groves a huge mutt started following us, and we thought he looked sad and lost. We ducked into a body shop to ask if anyone knew whose dog it was. One of the men kept working while the other raised up and greeted us. Here, out in the middle of this green place, was this fellow in his early middle years with a well-trimmed mustache, a golden tan, and well-developed muscles. He took off his work cap and beautiful curls fell loose. He commenced to tell us about all the dogs he had ever owned, while Jean and I listened in rapt nonattention. It is so easy to forget your age on this beautiful planet. Fortunately, he did not offer us a place to stay. We might be there yet.

Get Up and Walk

A Tennessee woman in a red pantsuit came mincing across the highway one day with a pocket camera to take my picture for her mother, who, she told me, was eighty-four and bedridden. After the snapshot, I asked where her mother was living, and it was quite near our stopping point ahead. I told her I would come visit, if she thought that would be a good idea. She did indeed.

Her mother was a dear, but she was hooked up to a breathing machine and was cared for by a granddaughter who had dropped out of college to do so. I encouraged her to figure a way to start walking a few steps at a time. She said she would try. I think if everyone will just do what they can to get in more walking, we can save boatloads of money and enjoy life a great deal more—and impose less upon our children. Often, it is a touch of depression that makes us feel sick, and a walking cure works pretty well.

I hope I didn't send her to her death by encouraging her to walk. If the tables were turned, I would appreciate the advice, even if such activity risked finishing me off. By the way, the old woman knew her senator personally and agreed to call him for me. I hope she did that before she attempted to walk.

We were hiking now through rolling hills and rainy green pastures set off by rail fences. Horses clopped over through the mud to see what was going on as we walked by. At one little farm, a dog and a goat, obviously old friends, came out together to take a look at us. They were joined a few minutes later by a pig. I had the feeling that their spider friend was back in the barn, spelling out something.

In Hollow Rock, an auto mechanic named Joe Green stepped out to the street and offered me a drink. Inside his garage was a row of five chairs, each filled with a good old boy there to watch work being done. Joe hunted through his pockets for a few coins for his soft drink machine. The first of the men said, "We fellas come and sit here in this garage where it's nice and cool. We look out at what's going on out there and tell each other the biggest tales you wouldn't believe. This is Lem next to me, and he's got him a cork leg but you'd never know it by the way he walks." Lem obligingly thumped his left leg. The next chair held an old school-teacher, much beloved by the kids of the town, unless that was one of the tall tales. He said he was kicked out for being too old. That's a silly thing to do, indeed.

Joe Green later took me across the creek to see the hollow rock itself, which was worth seeing. Nick climbed into its cavity and somehow popped out up top.

I stopped at schools whenever I could. Closer to Nashville, I spoke to a gymnasium full of 350 children. They were very sweet and mostly interested in how my water backpack worked. On the way out, one little girl asked for a hug and said she loved me. This unleashed a torrent of hugs and expressions of love, and I was there another half hour making sure everyone got their fair share. It was quite remarkable, really. I hoped it did not mean that they do not have grannies and grandpas to hug and to love them at home.

By the end of September, I was in Nashville with my new friends, Phil and Dikkie Schoggen. Dikkie would fill me with raw vegetables and other goodies, making her own breads and soups, and walking one hundred miles with me. Phil was always on the phone setting things up ahead of us. We walked through Nashville with Senator Russ Feingold, who is a hero of mine because he refuses to take soft money laundered through his party. He had won his last election without it—by a hair's breadth. I admire that kind of principled courage. There's no reason to be martyrs for our cause if we can possibly win.

He made a very fine speech on the statehouse steps, as did Congressman Zach Wamp. And yes, the rain started down. By the time we walked out of Nashville, we were doing so in a downpour, walking under our plastic sheets.

Sneaking into Washington

Senator Feingold told me that the House version of the soft money ban was getting ready to move toward a vote. The bill was being pushed by Chris Shays of Connecticut and Marty Meehan of Massachusetts, as they had successfully done the previous year, only to see it die in the Senate.

I thought it was time to take some action. I used the laptop computer to send e-mail messages to everyone who had sent me a message of support, asking them to call their congressmen and vote for the bill. I sent out about five thousand messages, and asked all the recipients to send the message to their friends. One of these people sent me a note to tell me that AOL had temporarily blocked his mail, thinking this was some kind of chain-letter thing—I guess there was quite a flurry of messages on the system. Other reformers were busy, too, especially Common Cause lobbyists on the Hill. Mr. Meehan and Mr. Shays were the busiest, masterfully rounding up enough support for victory. This was a soft money ban, just as Teddy Roosevelt would have written it, and it was the fraternal twin of McCain and Feingold's bill in the Senate, which would go nowhere against the stonewall antireformism of the Republican leaders Mitch McConnell and Trent Lott.

After the Shays-Meehan victory, I got messages from both men who said they would walk with me when I got to Washington, or sooner on the road if they could get away. The spotlight then moved to the Senate, where John McCain knew he was in for another beating. McCain called and asked if I wanted to come watch it unfold. I knew I should just keep walking, but I couldn't resist taking an extra rest day to see the show. I took off my hiking gear and jumped on a plane to Washington.

On October 13, I sat down in McCain's office, waiting for him. He came in and sat down and groaned. He had just come back from voting on Trent Lott's pork barrel bill that would build a new ship—not needed or wanted by the Navy—in Lott's state, Mississippi. Then Mr. Shays, Mr. Meehan, and Mr. Feingold came in. To break the ice, Mr. Shays embarrassed me by kissing my hand and bending down on one knee. I leaned forward and kissed the bald spot on the top of his head. We all laughed and then walked across the street to a podium in the Senate swamp. "Swamp" is just an old name for a grassy area outside the Senate wing of the Capitol. Senator McCain there presented me with a new pair of walking shoes and told me that I had some walking to do before this thing was over. After some comments by everyone, Mr. Feingold took one of my hands and Mr. McCain took the other and they led me up the steps. I was ensconced in the Senate gallery as the debate began on the McCain-Feingold bill. My hearing aids weren't letting me hear a thing, but at one point I saw Mr. McCain pointing to me in the middle of his speech and so I smiled and waved back.

I sneaked out after a while and, with John Anthony and Matt Keller of Common Cause, delivered letters to all the senators, asking them to please support the bill. Most of them did, but they were blocked by the filibuster by McConnell and the other antireformers. Passage would have cost them too much money.

Naturally, I stopped by the offices of my two New Hampshire senators. Bob Smith said he couldn't support the bill and that he wasn't too worried that the folks back home would even care. He said the general public is too dumb to understand about money and politics. I have witnesses that he said that. At the end of the brief meeting, he stood and shook my hand. He said he had a great deal of respect for what I was doing. I said I wished I could say the same.

Kentucky

In a few days I was back on the road. On October 19, I walked into Kentucky, the home state of Mitch McConnell himself, the fellow who had been orchestrating the defeat of campaign reform for several years. I'm sure I would like him if I knew him, despite his politics. He certainly comes from a friendly state.

Here is a typical Kentucky moment: I was resting on a bit of grass in Smith's Grove after a hard ten miles. A car pulled over. It was Sharon Davis, who lives nearby. She just wanted to know if I was all right, as I looked like an old lady in distress. After hearing about what we were doing, she asked if we had a place to spend the night. We happened not to, so she invited us to her home. Over the next few days, she and her husband, Tim, and daughter, Amy, walked with us, fed us, and entertained us as we walked through the region.

I don't know other countries of the world well enough to know if the spontaneous kindness I was shown is an American thing, or a human thing, but it was always amazing to me that my morning leaps of faith came out so well each evening: tonight in someone's home; tomorrow night in a convent, surrounded by nuns; the next night in a former gambling house.

Nick and Jason had become very good navigators and roadside ambassadors, so John was free to do organizing far ahead. I didn't see him again until I got almost to Washington. More and more, we seemed to attract college girls who would come walk with us for a day or two. They kept their eyes on Nick and Jason, who, as far as I ever knew, were strictly business.

Nick is the kind of person who has his eyes wide open. He would constantly be dragging me through a doorway or along a side path to see some fine old building or a beautiful pond just a little out of our way. He was unflappable, driving the falling-apart van, organizing roadside volunteers, and returning cell phone calls to set up walking press interviews—always with cool deliberation.

He was a master of constructive criticism: "You were wonderful with the children at the school today," he would say. "You might have been talking a little over their heads, but they enjoyed it." Isn't that a nice way to tell me to stop being so pedantic? He was educated in a Waldorf school and had spent time in India, studying under one of Gandhi's spiritual successors. It all had worked.

You have heard of people who would give you the shirt off their backs. Well, Nick did that once when I was short of clothes. He just took off his sweatshirt—"Only worn one day," he said. He found an old dirty shirt in back of the vehicle to wear instead. That night, he slept in the van while I was in the cozy home of a host who had said that she had not been told there would be others. Nick said it was not a problem at all, that he would sleep in the vehicle in the driveway. "Gee. In our driveway?" Not a problem, Nick said; he would find a place to park somewhere else. Now, I am not making the case that Nick is a saint; it's just that I have never seen any evidence against it.

Up ahead was Louisville. I was to give a speech right on Senator Mitch McConnell's office steps. I was trying to remember my Gandhi: Attack the ideas, not the man. But I thought I might fall short. The closer I walked, and the more abuse McConnell was presently heaping upon McCain for daring to suggest that there might be corruption in Washington, the less I felt like obeying what I knew to be the proper way laid down for us.

For once in my life, I did not feel in awe of a senator. I felt we were co-citizens with a bone to pick between us, and it would be all right for me to speak the truth as I saw it.

As I walked closer to Louisville, my lips moved, practicing my speech as I walked.

In Bardstown, I talked to five hundred children in a gym and answered their questions. The last question was "Would you like to come home with me and stay at our house?" Which sent my spirits high. The next day, walking now in the cold, an entire school lined the street to chant "Go, Granny, go!" as I walked past and ran my hand against theirs.

Thinking too much of the coming speech, I had my closest call in traffic. A pickup truck stopped and a fellow yelled out the window, "I want to shake Granny D's hand!" But he had stopped short in traffic, forcing the car behind him to a swerve onto the rain-slick shoulder. I should have jumped back, but I was frozen like a deer as the thing skidded toward me. It stopped inches away.

The Louisville rally and speech was in the rain, but was a fine event. Afterward, I thought I had gone too far in personally attacking the senator. If Gandhi had been at the back of the crowd, he would have shook a finger at me. But I am still learning.

Liz White, vice president of the League of Women Voters of Kentucky, had applied for a permit for the outdoor gathering a week before the Saturday event. Permits normally require a day or two to process. By Thursday, it seemed that something was up: Every time White called about the permit, she was given the runaround. By Friday at 3 P.M., it still hadn't been issued. One of the secretaries told White they were waiting for a phone call from McConnell. White then immediately called the newspapers, who called to ask the permit office and Senator McConnell's office what was going on. The permit was immediately issued. I would have spoken anyway, of course. Our Constitution is our permit.

Around 160 enthusiastic people, including Ellen Miller of Public Campaign, joined me there. *People* magazine, three television crews, and the Louisville *Courier-Journal* covered it. The newspaper, in fact, ran my speech in its entirety on the front page of its political section. It would never be enough to change Senator McConnell's opinion of campaign reform, but it was at least making him have to explain his vote back home, and that would do some good over time. Not the beginning of the end of the struggle, as Churchill said, but certainly the end of the beginning.

From the Speech outside Mitch McConnell's Office in Louisville, Kentucky
November 6, 1999

In the recent campaign finance reform debate in the Senate, he rather sharply attacked Senator McCain, when Mr. McCain had the audacity to suggest that the hundreds of millions of dollars being spent by special interests to influence the passage of laws in Congress might indeed be influencing the passage of laws in Congress. Mr. McConnell thought that was an outrageous assumption, and asked for the names of any members of Congress so low as to bend their votes toward the interests of contributors, like flowers toward the sun. Specifically, he said this:

"I ask the Senator from Arizona, how can it be corruption if no one is corrupt? That is like saying the gang is corrupt but none of the gangsters are. If there is corruption, someone must be corrupt."

He also said:

"It is astonishing. We have here rampant charges of corruption and yet no names are named."

Mr. McConnell demanded the names of those who were corrupt. Mr. McCain, for reasons of friendship, courtesy, and the dignity of the Senate—such as it is—did not name names.

But Mr. McConnell persisted, demanding that Senator McCain give a name. Mr. McConnell was like a reverse-Diogenes, searching the dark corners of the Senate chamber with his lantern, looking for one dishonest man.

I have come here today to answer the question asked by Mr. McConnell, and to end his long search.

See the appendix for more of this speech.

I am sure that Senator McConnell has the respect of Kentuckians, but he would not have liked to see how people honked and gave me thumbs up for days after the speech was printed in the Louisville paper.

In an elementary school near Skylight, a little girl brought me a tiny lion doll, saying she thought I was brave as a lion. She had the Sunday newspaper story about my speech pasted to a cardboard poster for me to sign. After I signed it, she tried to hand me a $20 bill to help me get to Washington. Nick said, "No, sweetheart," but her eyes bulged and she leaned forward on the tips of her toes, looked at us through her eyebrows and said, "Yes!" as she pressed it into my hand and just walked away. I don't know her name, but I know you will hear it someday.

In thoroughbred country, I walked by a great property where a woman, Mary Reagan, was tending her horse. She called me over and asked if I would like to feed Tiger a peppermint. I placed the mint in my hand and Tiger's soft lips lopped it up. The woman said she and her friends had been following my story but she had never expected to meet me, and said she must have a hug. This was often the salutation of beautifully dressed, heavenly smelling ladies of means, and I often wondered how they felt as they smelled me—all sweaty and grimy after a long walk.

I suppose I was like them once, though I was never quite a lady of means. I ran a modest home, and was not much for the Martha Stewart brand of housekeeping.

But I loved being a young mother. I would help Jimmy and Betty build forts in the living room with tables and sheets, and I would provision them with peanut butter and jelly sandwiches and come tell them made-up stories.

On a hot, summer Saturday, I would take them and several town children down to the old quarry, where I would teach them to swim. I can still hear our splashing and laughter echoing in that secret, walled paradise of ours.

When both children were in school, I was beside myself with cabin fever. I volunteered at church, but that was not enough. I took a little bookkeeping job. Jim was furious, but it was just what I needed. Despite Jim's dislike of the whole idea of a wife taking a job, the money was helpful for the kids' educations. From there, I took a job as an executive secretary at the Beebee Shoe Company. I became the person who figured out how much a new shoe would really cost to manufacture. I was paid $50 a week less than the man I replaced. The owner said, "Well, Doris, you don't need to work. Your husband has a good job, doesn't he?"

I did change his attitude over the years. I was eventually the second-highest-paid woman in New Hampshire, second only to the treasurer of the same electric utility where Jim worked. I loved my work.

At home, Jim made a point of not helping with housework or cooking, as he thought that would only encourage my weakness toward careerism. I kept smiling about that, as I loved him so. His attitude would not cut it these days, of course. He would have changed with the times.

In fairness, I must mention that he did sometimes cook one dish, which was a wonderful oyster stew he had picked up when he was a boy traveling with his father. They went to country fairs to race their string of trotters and pacers in sulky races. He always regretted not staying with that life, but his mother drove him out of it, dreaming a white-collar dream for him.

Perhaps if I had not taken a job, I could have spared my son, Jim, the horrors of school. He had a devil of a time with reading, and none of us at that time knew anything about dyslexia, which was his problem. He was branded as lazy by those who did not know better. A wise teacher finally was brilliant enough to slip him a dirty book, and he showed how bright he indeed was. He learned to read quite overnight.

Jim and Betty, when they were young adults, worked together on a Columbia University oceanographic project. Jim served as a diver on a three-masted sailing ship, taking core samples from the ocean floor. Betty, ashore, analyzed the core samples. If I would ever have only enough memory to hold but one picture of them, I would choose that happy time in their lives.

I was not an ideal parent, but I would like to let you in on a little secret: Parents have always been pretty bad. Either they are too young or too old, too inexperienced or too burned-out, too busy and distant, or too hovering and overprotective. It is the larger family and the good town that provides the best part of parenting. The morality hucksters on the loose today who tell us that better parenting will solve our problems don't say anything about the destruction of human-scaled cities and towns by developers' suburbias, or the destruction of family farms and family units by corporate policies. Oh, I know—I have already ranted about that. *For heaven's sake, Doris: Shut up and walk!*

As we walked through the last miles of Kentucky, the horse farms and fine houses gave way to tobacco farms and old barns and modest homes. It was tobacco stripping time, and the farmers were hard at work. The six-foot stalks had been cut and hanging for a month, and all were now dry and ready to strip. The bottom leaves are called "spong," the middle leaves are "lugs," and the top ones "tips." Tobacco will be a hard crop to replace as people stop smoking, for it provides a good income even on a small farm. Of course, the tobacco companies are trying to get the rest of the world hooked, and they receive subsidies from Congress for that purpose.

Please Come to Boston

Ellen Miller, then the head of the group Public Campaign, called and asked if I would take a day off my walk and go up to Boston to help some people who were trying to save the clean elections law that had been approved by the voters, but was now in danger of being killed by the legislature and the governor. The bill to provide the needed funds had been passed and sent to the governor, but legislators had added some new provisions which would make the whole program a sham, if signed into law by the governor. Specifically, incumbents would have been able to raise and spend private contributions in any amount until six months before the election, at which time they would stop raising and spending special interest money and receive public money. A paid vacation from prostitution, in other words—but their honor would already have been sold away.

The governor had always taken a position against the clean elections reform program, and this new complication by the legislature might just give him the cover he needed to veto the funding. Could he really be persuaded to save a program he did not personally care for, and to go against his own party? Ellen said it was worth a try, and she added that Massachusetts reformers were hard at work to build public pressure on the governor and the legislature.

I sent a letter to the governor on a fax machine and then headed to Boston, thanks to an airplane ticket from Ellen.

I was not prepared for the welcome at Logan Airport in Boston. Cheering people with signs joyfully overwhelmed me and escorted me to the capitol. Television, radio, and newspaper reporters were crowding around me. It was quite ridiculous, as I had absolutely no idea what I was doing or how I might help. The local reformers had obviously ballyhooed me to the press and the public, and so here I came like the great savior but feeling quite fraudulent. I am just an old lady, for heaven's sake, whose chief ability is that she can put one foot in front of the other.

But if qualifications ruled politics, I guess things would be different all over.

Hours later, when we were standing our vigil in the main hall of the capitol, Governor Cellucci came out and gave me a warm welcome. He had signed the bill and vetoed the silly parts. I declared him a national hero, which was exactly what I was feeling. It is not easy to support the people's will over your own opinions, and it is very difficult to go against your party. But he did it.

Now the concern was with the legislature. They had until midnight the next night to override the sections he had vetoed. I perched in the House gallery all the next evening and glared down at them, barely able to prop my eyes open. I don't know if the spotlight kept them on their best behavior, or if they were through with it anyway. But the midnight hour finally struck, they adjourned for the season, and Massachusetts was safely the fourth state to have public funding of its campaigns.

A young friend from home, Heidi Becker, was in Boston for this drama. She is a good diplomat, so I confided in her that I was very concerned that I had made an enemy out of Ken Hechler. She thought for a bit, then brightened: "He gave me a KEN HECHLER FOR CONGRESS T-shirt. What if I send it out to you, and you wear it when you walk into West Virginia?" I thought it would be worth a try.

Across the Ohio

On November 22, always a day to remember, I walked alone across the Ohio River. I was leaving the American South, which I had finally come to know and love very dearly. Ray Caldwaller, Ohio's Common Cause reform leader, met me on the bridge. The water of the great Ohio was sparkling in the sun.

The mornings were now quite chilly, and the towns were decorated for the holiday season. People were stringing lights on their eaves and bushes, and they waved from atop their ladders.

If it isn't for putting up decorations, Americans, I discovered, will find other reasons to be up on ladders. Everywhere I went, people were working on their homes, building them from scratch or restoring them to glory. If I were just starting a career, it would be in the lumber and hardware business. That seems to be where every spare American dollar goes.

Nick and I were invited for Thanksgiving dinner by new friends met along the road, Susan Conley and her husband, Paul Thomas. After a beautiful meal we played Scrabble, which is my great weakness.

As I was walking the next day though Owensville, an eighty-six-year-old man stopped his car square across my walking path. He opened his door, stepped out, and said he would now take a picture and make a short tape recording. He spoke with pure confidence and authority. This was very clearly his world, and I saw that we were all in good hands. He held the recorder toward me and said, "Now, dear, state your name and where you are

from and what you are doing here, and then just stand there for a
minute while I add my remarks." I did as I was told, and then he
added his comments, which were about the most thoughtful and
eloquent I had heard in a great while. Somewhere near
Owensville, there is a man with what must be a very wonderful
collection of tape recordings.

After all my walking, the territory was beginning to look a little bit like home. All the crops had been harvested, and the fields
had been put to bed for the season. Two-story farmhouses with
wraparound porches and red barns and whirring windmills were
suggesting that New England must be somewhere ahead. I was
homesick for it, and yet there was a high mountain range ahead,
now being layered in snow and ice. I put it out of my mind and
was led on by a constant sprinkling of corn kernels along the side
of the road, left by Gretel or some leaky farm truck.

As we walked through central Ohio, Nick saw a little barbershop and decided we both were a little shaggy. I had never had a
man haircutter, but he seemed nice enough. As he cut and cut, he
told me the story of a fellow he knew whose hair was so long that
it got caught in some machinery. As he told me the gory details, I
realized that he was making the world safer through shorter hair.
He was making it as safe as he could.

"Don't worry," Nick said as we walked down the road, "it
grows back fast."

In Chillicothe, the smokestack of the old paper mill was
standing like a big cigarette to remind me of my smoking days
and why I was coughing as I walked up these green hills. In fact,
I was coming down with something, though a good pharmacist
would soon fix me up.

Chillicothe was once the capital city of Ohio, and its streets
are lined with beautiful houses from that era. On the edge of
town, an amphitheater holds a community pageant called Tecumseh, which recounts the history of the region, going back to the
days when the great Native American leader brought the tribes of
North America together for one last effort to expel the invaders.
Tecumseh traveled North America, telling the tribes to gather
when they felt the great sign. When he finished his rounds, a great

earthquake, centered near St. Louis, shook the entire continent. It was so powerful that the Mississippi River reversed course for a short time. The quake was taken as the sign, and the tribes gathered for the great but unsuccessful war.

The fact that this story is retold by the children and adults of Chillicothe, who regularly play out this story under the stars for their visitors, means that they respect their history and their diversity. Every community should do this. It is so much fun, and is so good for civic spirit and for mutual understanding.

Down from Columbus, a group of five women who call themselves the Granny Gears and who normally go on great bicycle treks, came to walk with me. We sang as we hiked along, having a wonderful time. They didn't expect that they would be able to walk too far, but their bike riding had put them in better shape than they imagined, and they went the distance. They were doing better than I was, as my left leg kept cramping up badly for some unknown reason.

The hills were getting steeper as we walked ever closer to West Virginia's great mountains.

In the next days, the weather was bitter cold and rainy. We were sprayed by passing trucks one after another, jumping aside in our yellow panchos. Nick was feeling blue, he said, and the vehicle was acting up constantly. It needed a catalytic converter at one point, and the men at Charlie's Speedy Muffler back in Chillicothe stayed up late one night to put us back on the road for free. When *it* stopped sputtering, *I* started, as I had run out of my medicine and the cost of the refill was so outrageous that I thought I would rather cough. Besides, I could well do without the side effects from the horrid pills, which had me constantly on the search for rest stops. I was able to clear myself up with lots of good breathing, water, and the magic elixir of walking itself.

Alaska

The only time my bronchitis had ever really laid me low, other than my collapse in Arizona a year earlier, was in 1960, on the way back from Alaska. I recovered at Theodore Roosevelt's ranch in North Dakota before coming back to fight that fight for the Alaskans.

My husband and I, along with five other people and a dog, drove a very cramped Volkswagen minibus to Alaska from New Hampshire, sleeping and driving in continuous shifts. I will tell you a little about it, just for a change of scenery.

Our mission was to stop Edward Teller from exploding six thermonuclear bombs near an Eskimo fishing village. He wanted to demonstrate how America might build a new canal in Central America, and the only place defenseless enough for a test of his idea was the far, northwest coast of Alaska.

In 1958, Operation Plowshare, under Teller's direction, was created to develop peaceful uses for nuclear explosions. Within that program, the Atomic Energy Commission launched Project Chariot, which was a plan to create a new harbor on the unsuspecting northwest coast of Alaska using hydrogen bombs. They picked the mouth of the Ogotoruk Creek near Cape Thompson, about thirty miles down the coast from Point Hope. I doubt that the gulls and seals and corals would have considered it a peaceful use, nor did the villagers of Point Hope.

The questions asked of the government by the panicked villagers went unanswered for two years. In March 1960, Teller and officials of the Atomic Energy Commission went to the village to tell some great lies. They said the fish around the blasted area would not become radioactive and would be fine to eat. They said that nuclear weapons testing never injured any people, anywhere. They said that the people of Hiroshima and Nagasaki, once they recovered from radiation sickness, suffered no side effects. They said that the villagers would feel no seismic shock—after all, it was only 600 times more powerful than Hiroshima, and they were all living well within the shock-wave zone! I speak with confidence about the meeting because the Eskimo people wisely taped the meeting, and I have listened to the tapes.

I will not go on and on. I will not include all the details about how they had, a few years earlier, injected 102 unknowing Eskimos with cancer-causing radioactive elements in a health clinic as a secret test, or how they had spilled radioactive materials on the hillsides to see how the stuff would migrate into the water supply, which it did.

The purposefully spilled elements were mostly cleaned up in 1994, thanks to the advocacy of the author and activist Dan O'Neill, who wrote a wonderful book called *The Firecracker Boys* about our adventure.

At our church in New Hampshire, sometime in 1960, Jim and I met a minister from the Point Hope Eskimo village. He was swapping summer congregations with our minister, Bradford Young, who was always getting into political trouble and needed to cool off for a while—and where better than Alaska? The Point Hope minister was not just looking for a vacation: He wanted to get to the East Coast to see what he could do to stir up opposition to Teller's tests.

We thereby learned about Point Hope and how the Eskimos, two of whom had come along to New England, were desperate to save their village. Alone, they had no way to stop the insanely discourteous plan. Jim and I were outraged and ready to help.

When the Alaska minister, Keith Lawton, was ready to return to the village, and our Bradford was ready to be fetched back, Jim and I, and Pete Foster (a recent Yale graduate and the son of our best friends, Max and Elizabeth Foster) went with him. Jim and Pete and I traveled in an old VW minibus—already with 100,000 miles on it! Also in the van were the minister, a woman church worker, the two returning Eskimos, and a huge Samoyed dog—to be taken to Alaska by the minister to improve the strain of dogs in the little village. Samoyeds are very smart and therefore very disobedient.

The Eskimo woman was Teenavick, and the gentleman was Narkook. They would remain my close friends for the rest of their lives. I wrote to them every week and sent them Christmas boxes. Narkook died before my Jim, and Teenavick died a few years later. I was always able to talk to Teenavick, though she was terribly shy. Somehow we patched English and Inuit words together with lots of hand waving and exasperated laughter.

Adding to our van load, everyone in New Hampshire had thought it a good idea to send gifts back to the Eskimos. The minister's wife looked at our stuffed van and, with her two children, wisely flew instead.

Before we left, Narkook asked Jim to take him to the Sears store in Manchester to buy a new radio for his house in Alaska. Narkook was a man of few words, but he did know enough English to get by. He took a valuable, handcrafted baleen basket to the Sears for trade for a new radio. It would have been a very good deal for Sears. While store management was conferring about how to deal with this Eskimo's offer, Narkook took the radio to a counter and quickly and completely disassembled it from its cabinet. He looked at the flimsy parts, quite unlike the surplus military equipment he was used to. "No good," he said to Jim, and they left.

Taking four-hour turns at the wheel, we drove continuously across Canada, eating the most gawdawful health food the church worker had purchased for the trip, instead of the hearty food Jim and I, avid campers, had recommended and funded for the journey.

We took turns sleeping and driving all the way to Fairbanks, so that we never stopped except for ghastly cooking, gasoline, restrooms, and dog romping. Jim taught Narkook how to drive, which was a thrill for us all.

From Fairbanks we flew to Nome. Then we squeezed into a series of ever smaller airplanes, to Kotzebue, then to the little village of Tigara at Point Hope. Our plane skidded up to the village on the snowpacked runway. Point Hope sticks out toward Russia on the far northern stretch of Alaska's western coastline, 1,600 miles up Alkan Highway and 125 miles north of the Arctic Circle.

My friends Narkook and Teenavick of Point Hope, Alaska. With my husband, Jim, and I, they were successful in stopping the destruction of Point Hope with hydrogen bombs in the early 1960s.

We were greeted with the enthusiasm you might expect in such a remote place.

We stayed for a week. The houses were igloos cut of tundra, with whalebone bracing, as there were no trees for construction. Jim loved working with the men of the village on their electric station. These people worked half the year in Fairbanks and half the year in their ancestral fishing waters. One or two whales would last them the season.

Because Jim worked for a big utility in New Hampshire, the villagers thought we could fight the Atomic Energy Commission. It was the energy business, after all. We tried to downplay our value to them, but we were all they had. Before we returned to New Hampshire, Narkook said to us, "You will stop these bombs, won't you?" Jim shook his hand and said, by God, we would try.

On the way home, I took ill and we stopped long enough for me to get my breath back and for us to consider what we had gotten ourselves into. We would just have to charge ahead and do what we could.

Back home, Jim, Pete, and I organized ourselves to stop Project Chariot. That sort of thing was not done back then. The government was trusted, and the environment was not a major concern. We enlisted Pete's politically connected father, my dear friend Max Foster, to open doors in the Kennedy White House and in the Senate. Max was an old Yale man who knew half of the Kennedy administration and was related to the other half, including cousin Robert McNamara—then secretary of defense. He also contacted a researcher named Barry Commoner at Washington University in St. Louis who was practically inventing the field of environmental science. Barry sent investigators to Alaska. Their report proved decisive in the battle, as was the courageous testimony of two University of Alaska scientists, who were fired for telling the truth.

I held tea parties all over New England to tell women what was happening in Alaska and what they could do to help stop it. We saw to it that every member of the Senate was briefed on the project and the harm that it would do—and on its clear unfairness, which did bother the senators deeply. They were not like many of today's senators.

Officials at the Atomic Energy Commission, until that moment unchallenged in their godlike power and wisdom, found themselves in defensive territory for the first time. I spoke at more teas and put out more mailings, and Jim organized more scientists and political operatives. He finagled information out of Lawrence Livermore Laboratory—Teller's stronghold—that indeed verified that the village would be ruined forevermore. Jim even taught himself the programming language, FORTRAN, so that he could understand the science of the proposed project. His career as an electric utility executive was certainly threatened, and we and all our friends were investigated up and down by several agencies, including the FBI, who imagined that we were Communists. We were Episcopalians.

All we needed to do was delay the project. There was a great effort being led by Linus Pauling and others to stop all atmospheric nuclear blasts because they caused cancer worldwide. Their efforts proved successful in 1962, when President John Kennedy and Premier Nikita Khrushchev signed the Test Ban Treaty. Project Chariot was promptly canceled.

Jim, Elizabeth, young Pete, Max, and I enjoyed some considerable champagne and lobster when Kennedy signed the pact. And the people of Point Hope became our friends for life.

Max was certainly the man behind the scenes, telling us what to do next. Stopping Project Chariot was the high point of his life and was the accomplishment most remembered at his death. He was slow to help us, but when his son Pete wrote a book about the situation, Max came aboard with his awesome connections and his poet's soul. Access is the soul of politics, and that is why it should never be sold for cash.

The Alaska campaign marked midlife for me: I was fifty. My children were raised, I was in the shank of my career, and I had learned to not worry too much about the consequences of doing what looked to be the right thing. It is always nice, too, when you win, which we surely did.

Never a day went by during my walk across America, that I did not think of the old gang stuffed into that minibus, driving endlessly across the continent for a good and urgent cause. I know that was the memory that had called me back to the road.

A Familiar Old Face Returns

On December 18, I again crossed the Ohio River, this time into West Virginia at Parkersburg. I walked across the bridge with about seventy-five people. Among them were Governor Cecil Underwood, Mayor Jimmy Columbo, and the wonderful secretary of state, Mr. Ken Hechler. I was wearing his campaign shirt, and he had a great, happy smile for me, and a kiss. I had sent him a long letter, and Dennis and my son had talked to him to tell him how much we missed him. The family was back together.

Then the dreaded hills! I had worried about them from the very beginning. I was right to do so. The steep grades and icy shoulders were murder. One step at a time, Doris. With caution and constant internal encouragement, I climbed and walked and climbed. The miles took much longer, but at least I didn't have to worry about overheating. It often snowed or blew ice as I walked. My sipping tube would freeze, but I could get a sip of moisture by opening my mouth and sticking out my tongue.

One evening, in a warm kitchen, I received a call from a woman named Lisa who identified herself as a producer from *60 Minutes*. I learned the most extraordinary thing. She said that she had come to West Virginia to do a story that Mike Wallace wanted to have her set up with Ken Hechler. The story was about how the coal companies were slicing off the tops of the green mountains, extracting the coal, and dumping the earth into the valleys, completely flattening the land and choking off the streams. These companies had been making huge political contributions to the governor and other officials who might otherwise have stopped the practice. Ken, as secretary of state, was the only one railing against this environmental rape.

Now, Ken is a lifelong political man, and the idea that Mike Wallace and the *60 minutes* crew had called him and wanted to hold him up as the spokesman of righteousness was the kind of thing that such a fellow would only fantasize about. But what Ken did was to tell them that there was a better story in West Virginia, and it was the old lady walking across the country. So she was calling me to get more information. I was too amazed at the gallantry of my old friend to even try to hear much of what she was saying after that. He was, after all, in the middle of a political campaign for Congress and such exposure would be priceless for him.

As it happened, I was tired and couldn't hear her very well, so I'm sure I made a terrible impression on her. And I don't know if I tried too hard. After a time, she seemed to cool to the idea of a story. She said she would run it by Mr. Wallace, but I sensed that she would not sell too hard. It didn't seem like a *60 Minutes* story to me either, as they are more into busting villains. But, bless them, they went ahead with the story about Ken's fight against the coal lobby. He was marvelous on the air, talking energetically with Mike Wallace, laying out the problem with great authority and dignity. I have never seen Mr. Wallace treat someone with greater respect.

Ken finally got what many consider to be the holy grail of political publicity, and he got it by giving it away, with love, to someone else. That is often the way it is with the truly important prizes we long for.

In the towns of West Virginia, Ken warmed up audiences of schoolchildren and adults with the real brilliance one might expect from a noted historian, author, congressman, and presidential speechwriter. He was shining at his full wattage. I had to remind him to mention his campaign when introducing me.

(NICK PALUMBO)

Followed closely by Ken Hechler with friends along a West Virginia road.

The long grades up wooded hills were as beautiful and darkly forbidding as they were difficult. One day, I saw four dead owls near the road, with no signs of what had killed them—just as if they had fallen out of the trees. I am not superstitious, but these symbols of wisdom, present in that balanced number of completion, gave me pause. My long walk was nearing its end, and the lessons it had brought into my life were poised now at the end of my own life. It was possible, I thought, that these hills would be too much for me. I worried about my cough a little bit, and the worsening cold air. On December 21, I saw the biggest and brightest moon in 133 years—according to the newspaper. I could see a distant flock of sheep in the moonlight. The world was looking unworldly to me, its mysteries beyond the reach of my curiosity but not my interested gaze.

Twenty degrees cold, I was walking now with Maureen McKeough of Chicago, who had been following my website reports, and with my friend Mary Howe, who had been walking with me for two weeks. We all took a Christmas break for a few days to get warm.

On December 28, the margins of the road were caked in oily ice, so every step had to be deliberately calculated. Ken walked with me, and we took care to keep each other upright on the slippery road. We passed snow-covered farms and dear cows looking most dejected.

For some days after that, I walked alone up long and icy hills. Nick was driving the vehicle ahead—where I could warm up every mile or so. Jason was back in Little Rock with his business but would soon be rejoining us.

It was steep hill after steep hill, with more ups than downs as I approached the crest of the range. I would never have told Ken, but the coal companies' plans to flatten West Virginia had a certain new appeal to me. Ken was off on his campaign trail in his trademark red Jeep.

Finally, it was the last day of a long year. I could have used a good-looking fellow like Ken on New Year's Eve, but I turned in early instead, waking up to the year 2000 and walking into beautiful Clarksburg. It made me heartsick for my own, beautiful hometown.

It is so easy to ruin a town—it can be done in one day with a bulldozer and a redevelopment plan. I was always delighted to walk into an old town yet intact. When I retired from my job in 1972, I became active as a volunteer in my town, helping on the planning committee. This sent me into the trenches when an interstate highway was announced for construction through the middle of town. It is a fight that is not yet over, and which I knew I would probably have to face when I got home. But for now, here was Clarksburg: a historic town that had generally saved itself. It always made me genuinely happy to be in a walkable townscape of history and charm.

From the Clarksburg, West Virginia, Speech
January 3, 2000

There is a stage play that I'm sure you know about, entitled *Our Town,* by Mr. Thornton Wilder. It is about life and death in a small New Hampshire town. More exactly, it is about all the beauty we miss because we are not fully awake to the brief magic of life. Mr. Wilder wrote the play while residing in the New Hampshire community where I live, and where my children have raised their children. We take his play as a correct description of the heartbreaking beauty of life in a caring community of decent people.

See the appendix for more of this speech.

Out of the blue in Clarksburg, Ken arrived to present me with a one-year-walking medal of his own design. With a guitar-playing friend dressed as Uncle Sam, Ken sang a corny but charming song he wrote for the occasion.

From Clarksburg to Fairmont, four of us walked in heavy rain and were occasionally drenched by dark shells of water from passing trucks. Reporters were starting to crop up, and the poor dears had a hard time of it.

On January 5, the rain turned to snow with such ferocity that Nick, driving behind me up the grades, had a hard time seeing me, even when I was but a few yards ahead. Laura Mellor Wellor and Mary Roebuck, two students from Oberlin College, arrived to walk with us, as did Ken and a Japanese TV crew. The fellow walkers were welcome, as they kept me from being afraid of wandering off in the snow in the wrong direction. We single-filed through the whiteout like a bunch of good, frozen scouts, with the young eyes in front.

Several days later, after conquering the six-mile hill we had been warned about, our slipping and sliding little parade made it into Morgantown.

From there, through mid-January, the road curved into Pennsylvania at Markleysburg, just below Pittsburgh, and the weather turned remarkably worse. Nick nervously drove the van several feet behind me—it was the first time I had seen him so anxious. If he lagged too far back, he could not see me in the snow—too close, and he feared rolling right over me. So it was hard going. On top of the blizzard, the grades were steep and slippery, and my breathing sounded inside my head like an old tea kettle. It was impossible to go the full ten miles each day. Six was a good day in a blizzard. I had the walking company of Jason, now returned, and the girls from Oberlin.

This was the mountain I had dreaded for three thousand miles. I knew for all of those miles that the long year would either have me in shape for this climb, or I would be too worn out to even think about it. One foot in front of the other, Doris.

The whiteout of a blizzard is a remarkable environment to experience for long hours. The world is a blank screen all around you, save for the glow of headlights and the faint, pastel shapes of your walking companions. It is a most private space where one cannot help but review the hard facts of a life. As in the desert, there are no distractions.

My life did seem greatly condensed in my thoughts. It goes so fast, you know. One minute you are noticing odd changes in your young body, and the next thing children are popping out, running into the house with their high school and college friends and their husbands and wives and children, and you are suddenly wrinkled—your friends and family are falling dead around you. Remarkable! Beautiful! And so horribly sad to be quickly gone forever.

Of course, it isn't really gone. I was born five years after Einstein concocted our present view of reality, and it was all the rage as I was growing up. We still haven't really caught on to much of it. But we understand enough to know that once an event happens—a glance across a dance floor or a smile between infant and mother—it exists forever, as does every person and thing. Our position relative to it changes, and we lose sight of it. But it is comforting to know that everything we ever saw still exists outside the flow of time. The people we loved and the moments of loving them are preserved in a profound reality that exceeds our grasp and sweeping gaze. Remarkably, we are back there too, preserved in those moments with those we love—we just don't understand it while we are yet alive. Old Einstein did, of course; and when a good friend died, he wrote to a physicist friend to say that, of course, death is an illusion to those who understand the world at its deepest level.

I suppose this means that all the bad things are preserved, too. Projected on the white screen of snow before me, I relived some of the bad moments. The deaths of my parents and my husband, and of my brother and two of my sisters. There comes a time in late midlife when it seems like all the people you love are falling away on either side of you like soldiers at battle. You see your dwindling friends more at funerals than at parties. I am not much for funerals because of all the baloney you hear there, but I go when it is proper.

I saw in the white blizzard the image of that poor girl in the snow sixty-five years before, crushed under the runner of a great sleigh that was filled with singing girls and bales of harvest hay. It is an image that never leaves me for long.

I had organized a girls' activity group for my daughter, Betty, when she was thirteen—and for the other girls her age in town. I kept hoping that a pair of spinster scout leaders would materialize for Betty as they had for me, but I had to give up on that and get involved. We started a Girls Friendly group. We would learn to design and sew party dresses and then have a dance and invite boys to it. This was a very popular plan, and I soon had more girls showing up than I could handle. I didn't want to draw lots, so I cranked up the program and got other adults involved, and we were soon hosting monthly dances and sewing up a storm. Kids from other churches were attending, which caused some friction with the priest of the Catholic church. He called up a radio program where I was trying to get more help for the sewing program. He said he thought I was trying to attract kids away from his church. Well, I lit into him for not having any activities for the children of his church, and it did some good. The Catholics bought an old house and turned it into a social center for kids.

My life as a volunteer was going very well until an accident.

A girl, who was not part of the group and who had jumped on the back of the sleigh without my knowing it, fell off to the side and under the rear runner. So silent are the seconds after something like that! You run toward horror and can hear nothing or think nothing. She survived, though she was terribly injured and I took it as my responsibility. It sent me into a depression, and it discolored the middle years of my life.

But you know, when you take on some leadership responsibility in the world, you must accept the fact that you will change lives. Your intention is to do good for everyone. But you will change lives in ways you cannot fully control, and sometimes things will go terribly wrong. The hard part is to stay at it and not give up trying to do good in the world. But my, it is hard when tragedy and defeat come visiting, as they do. If love is your motivation, and if you respect the people you serve as your moral equals, you will do more good than harm over a lifetime—by far. But you will do some harm, and it may haunt you when you take a walk in your old age.

Walking in the blizzard toward Cumberland, Maryland, up that endless grade to the top of the range that kept the colonists from moving westward for a hundred years, I occasionally checked my fingers and toes as I walked to see if they were movable without the feeling of pins and needles. Frostbite would put a fast end to this little stroll, and the circulation in an old body is not always strong enough to fight the elements. But I have known the snow all my life, and I respect it well enough to bundle myself against it. I was doing all right, though cold is not good for arthritis and moisture is not good for emphysema, so I was not enjoying myself as much as I could. There were many minutes and hours when I thought I might just refuse to put my foot forward. I might just stand there until someone gave me a ride home. Had I not invested a year in this thing, I certainly would have quit that mountain.

When one of my companions asked through the howl of the snow if I was singing, I said that I was not. I then realized I was crying aloud. But the crest of the range was not far. Another few days, old girl! So many people were counting on me now.

Still, the blank screen of the snowstorms showed me everything. Mother was rather a tall woman, with long, awkward legs and arms, and big hands. She had very black hair and brown eyes and a sweet face. She was a presence and a great flirt who adored harmless, verbal fencing with men. I enjoyed watching her operate. After Papa died of an enlarged heart, she lost her edge.

When Sybil died, Mother was absolutely bereft. Sybil had always protected her. Mother went to Maine to live with Vivian for six months of the year, then to South Carolina for five months with my brother, Rex. His wife, Grace, did not like sharing Rex, and my mother was a houseful—a real takeover artist. When she needed a hip replacement, she stayed with Jim and me in New Hampshire, but my husband was impatient with her. When it was time for her to return to Rex's, she clung to me hard and I had a feeling it was the last time I would see her. She died on the way to South Carolina. She just slumped over in her wheelchair and was gone.

I don't think I was kind to her. I think I took on some of Jim's impatience with her, and it makes me ashamed to think about it. She had worked hard all of her life, and she deserved more respect than I gave her. I took care of her and gave her the kind of foods she liked. I would hope I didn't let her see that she was a burden, but she was an intelligent woman and I probably didn't fool her a bit.

My sister Merle, after a long marriage and a career with the phone company, and many camping trips with Vivian and their husbands, went shopping one fine day in 1992, came home, sat down, and died. A lovely way to go—before the bills arrive.

My brother, Rex, my only brother, died too. It is now just Vivian and me left from the old days.

The Maryland–West Virginia notch in the Appalachians that permitted the migration of ancient hunters and migrating pioneers, and that still facilitates the passage of autos and trains and an occasional walker, occurs at Cumberland, Maryland. It is not the famed Cumberland Gap, which is located in Kentucky and Tennessee, but it is a gap and it is at Cumberland and it was a lifesaver to me in the winter of 2000, as it was to the pioneers before me.

The town of Cumberland is remarkable in many ways. It is full of churches with beautiful steeples, all of which are beautifully lighted at night. A little creek that flows from the town becomes the great Potomac River. A log cabin stands across the way from the beautifully restored train station. The cabin was the headquarters for George Washington during the Whiskey Rebellion. Most important, the people of the town are marvelous, as I always found to be the case in our American towns.

I arrived on my ninetieth birthday, which the townspeople of Cumberland knew all about, thanks to the organizing of Ed Mullaney and Bob Taft. A large crowd walked with me through town, carrying flags and singing "This Land Is Your Land," and we stopped at the train station, where I climbed on the back of a red caboose and made a small birthday speech.

From the Cumberland, Maryland, Speech
January 24, 2000

I am not trying to make anyone feel sorry for what happens in a long life. All things end. But I want to say something important about it, and that is why I bring it up. I stand here on the tail end of a caboose. And so it was when Jim and Elizabeth were gone. Life seemed very much over—all the picnics, all the hikes, all the frosty ski trips. I was deeply depressed, and I know that many people today are in that same place. And what I want to say to them, and to all of you to remember for that day ahead when you think you are standing at the end of your life, is, damn it, don't give up the ship.

See the appendix for more of this speech.

GrannyD.com

Dear Granny, I am British, not an American, but your addresses have made me an American in spirit. What is happening in America is happening everywhere, but unfortunately most people feel powerless to change it. Your optimism is wonderful, and I sincerely hope that you can help to change America, because America was founded on the hope of creating a New World. We are all waiting for that New World. May your dream sow the seed of regeneration in the garden of our minds.

Peter Preston, Zielona Góra, Poland—
Wednesday, January 26, 2000

Dear Ms. Haddock, "Let's adjourn to make our plans for Washington, and have some cake together." Happy, happy birthday! We will bake a cake in our house to celebrate your birthday and your march, which excites all of us to action. Thank you for every step. I can't tell you how much strength it gives me to carry on.

Jennifer (and girls, Heather, Sarah and Megan
and husband, Michael)—Friday, January 28, 2000

It was quite cold in Cumberland, and it had snowed a great deal on my walk toward town, but it cleared to a sparkling, snow-capped morning for my arrival and speech. Afterward, the worst winter storm in four years swept through the mountains between Cumberland and Washington, D.C.

If you are wondering whether or not I think I make it rain and snow by making a speech, I certainly do not. That is not the way it works. When you are doing the right thing, it just so happens that you arrive just when certain things are happening anyway. Moses had wonderful timing, is what I mean. We all have a little bit of that when we are in our soul's right groove. And, when praying for such help, it is less rude, I think, to pray for some special help in fitting in, rather than to ask God to scrap and revise all His plans for the day—He, of course, knew you were going to ask anyway and would have already made adjustments if that was proper.

Now, why would I think it was good timing to have a big winter storm? It just worked out that way. Part of it is to be always on the lookout for the silver lining.

Nick scouted the roads ahead. Lanes were cleared for traffic, but the snow plows had heaped the margins high with icy snow—impossible for walking. Washington was now less than two hundred miles, and a number of the people I had met along the way had made travel plans to meet me there. Claudia Malloy of Common Cause, John Anthony, Matt Keller, Nick Penniman, George Ripley, and others had been working to organize local Washington supporters and to obtain permits to march though the K Street lobbyist row and down Pennsylvania Avenue to the steps of the Capitol, which also required a permit.

I do not think it is necessary or even a good idea to apply for a permit to peaceably assemble to petition our government for a redress of grievances, but there were several elderly people who were planning to go the last miles with me, some in wheelchairs, and I had no business risking their arrest.

If I had to wait the week or two for this heavy snowpack to melt, however, permits would expire, airline tickets would be no good, and my appointments with press and with congressmen would all be in disarray. So I had a problem.

Miraculously for me, there is an historic canal that runs 184 miles from Cumberland right into the Georgetown section of Washington. This canal, the C&O (for Chesapeake and Ohio), was a barge canal opened a hundred and fifty years ago. The original idea for the canal had come much earlier from surveyor George Washington, who saw the Potomac as a possible route to the Ohio Valley. There is a towpath alongside the canal where the horses and mules walked to pull the large barges. The towpath is still intact, under the protection of the National Park Service.

It begins right at the Cumberland railroad station, about one hundred yards from where I made my birthday speech—right under my nose! I sent the boys out to check the snow conditions on the towpath. It was, as I hoped, just right for cross-country skiing.

My son, Jim, rushed my old skis to me, and we found skis for Nick and Jason.

In this way, I finished my trek to Washington.

Along the C&O

The trail was cold and parts of it were quite remote. Every five miles or so, Nick would find a snowy road where he could intercept the towpath with the vehicle, so I could warm up and rest. We considered packing a tent for that purpose, but Nick was such a genius at finding me that we could ski without that burden.

Taking to the wilderness meant that I wouldn't be able to talk my reform talk to too many reporters. They had been walking with me almost constantly up to that point. Dorinda McCann, a reporter from *The Sunday Times* of London and Paul, her photographer, would not be deterred and trudged behind in our tracks for a good way. My friend Jean Higgs, who had come back for more punishment, trudged with them.

There was a strong sun and magnificent blue sky, and those of better hearing said they could hear the Potomac River rushing by on one side and the ice cracking in the canal on the other. I imagined I could, too. We spotted beautiful red cardinals, herds of running deer with their white flags up, rabbits, a beaver lodge, and other kinds of wildlife whose own ancestors entertained and sustained Indians and pioneers of old.

Coolfont, Berkeley Springs, Sleepy Creek, Harpers Ferry—I was closing in on my great destination. There was a fellow cheer-

Cross-country skiing down the towpath of the C&O Canal in Maryland. Despite the area's biggest snowstorm in four years, I kept on schedule by skiing more than 100 miles.

ing me along the path at about Berkeley Springs. He was bundled like an Eskimo, but the red cheeks were unmistakable—Ken, of course, taking time off from his campaign to see how I was doing in the snow.

Skiing was hard work. I was much more worn down after ten miles of it than I ever was by walking. Nick started to worry about me, as I think I did not look too well. Cold gets to your bones, and you lose your energy and color. But I was close enough that I thought I should push on. We were right on schedule. The people from towns along the way gave me great welcomes and warm beds.

Like an emissary from the strange land ahead, John Anthony, who had been organizing people in Washington, came out to welcome me into the home stretch. It was so good to all be together again.

It's interesting to me that I kept accidentally thinking that, when I finished this walk, I would be expected to give a full report to my husband and to Elizabeth. Habits of sixty years die hard. Elizabeth would angrily say, "Doris! Where have you been?" That is what she would say when I visited her in her last days after her stroke, in the big house at Dundee.

As her mind deteriorated, she spoke more and more French, which she had learned traveling the world with her father. I do not speak French, but I could usually guess what she was saying. I believe her nurses, who lived with her for four years, must now include French on their résumés.

Elizabeth and I visited and remembered our adventures together, which were many. We laughed about the time we escaped our men to go visit the 1967 Expo in Montreal, and saw the Shah of Iran and his wife—he in white military splendor and she in a flowing, white gown. We thought they looked ridiculous, as if they were looking for a cake to go stand atop.

We remembered the countless summer evenings at Dundee around the great dinner table and in the little theater. We remembered the evenings when Elizabeth painted her lovely watercolors as I hooked my rugs and Max would read us something interesting by a writer we probably knew.

It was just odd to think I would not be able to celebrate with them and tell them all my stories. I would have to wait for that.

Ann Bennett, Elizabeth's beloved Dundee caretaker, stood at the bedside with me when Elizabeth took her last, struggling breaths. The three of us held hands until Elizabeth was gone. Ann and I set her hands gently down, and we wept. After a time I went out to the barn and took her gardening hat off its nail. It would be too sad to just leave it hanging there, getting dusty. I resolved to wear it when I could, remembering her as she was when we were two good friends, chatting and weeding in the garden near the kitchen. In my memory, the time is always late afternoon, and Elizabeth, quick to laugh, is always wearing that wide, straw hat with the colorful band. I thoroughly ruined it in the Mojave Desert. But I had used it up for a good cause, which is, of course, what we must do with ourselves.

While I would not be able to share the stories of my journey with my husband and Elizabeth, I had my other Jim, my son, and the trip together had been a great time for us as mother and son. I got to see him at his best, quickly handling emergencies, asking for help when necessary with no concern for his own ego—only his mother's well-being. I got to see both my children through new and more deeply loving eyes. To have had Betty walking beside me again as my little girl was worth the trip. And I grew closer to my grandchildren and great-grandchildren, as I was no longer the old woman in the house back home, but a living person of some interest to them.

The snow became spotty as I got closer to Washington. Finally, I was walking again, but I stayed on the towpath most of the way because I had fallen in love with the deep nature of the place. It was so like the treks of my early life with Jim and the children. What a joyful place and time to think of my whole life! It spread before my thoughts. All my mistakes and shortcomings and worries seemed fine now. My children had turned out brilliantly and, more important, full of humanity and creativity. My husband had enjoyed a good and fulfilled life and was cared for well in his final years. I had come to look to my own beliefs and passions and had done something about them while there was yet time. In this, I had discovered what so many already know: that the art of your passion, embraced fully, redeems you from all the sins and shortcomings of a life.

I stopped from time to time for quick trips off the towpath to speak at nearby colleges, and I began to communicate more and more with the people waiting for me in Washington, including several members of Congress who wanted to walk with me when I got to town.

From the College Speech in Maryland
February 2000

We would do well to install our new senators and representatives in the same way that we Americans did when we were the Five Nations [of the Iroquois]. Here is a part of the ceremony, addressed to any new representative arriving at council:

Your heart shall be filled with peace and good will and your mind filled with a yearning for the welfare of the people. With endless patience you shall carry out your duty, and your firmness shall be tempered with tenderness for your people. Neither anger nor fury shall find lodgement in your mind, and all your words and actions shall be marked with calm deliberation. In all of your deliberations in Council, and in your efforts at law making, in all your official acts, self-interest shall be cast into oblivion."

. . . Let us remember who we are. Let us remember that a good government can fall away unless we forever give ourselves to its defense, and unless, in all our official acts, we cast self-interest forever into oblivion. . . .

Let me say finally that you are being raised in a culture that ever tries to trivialize your life. Your life is not trivial. It is not designer labeled. It is not on-line or virtual. It is real. You are a free man or woman in a land of free people who have served each other with dignity and sacrifice for many centuries. Do your duty to those who came before you. Do your duty to your own freedom and to the freedom of Americans to come. Cast your self-interest into oblivion and see, through the progress of the soul, what a magical world this is!

See the appendix for more of this speech.

A Few Days to Washington

A few days yet from Washington, I saw Great Falls on the Potomac. It is well worth seeing if you get a chance. Here the Potomac is still wild and beautiful, before it becomes an inconvenience between Capitol Hill and the airport.

As I walked along on February 28, the houses within my view became larger and older. My God, I thought, that is Georgetown!

John Anthony, Nick Palumbo, and me on the final miles in Washington, D.C.

The towpath suddenly ended at the Francis Scott Key Bridge. There, waiting for me, were a good fifty or so people who then walked with me across the bridge to Arlington National Cemetery. From there, we would begin the final miles to the Capitol the next morning, leap year's day.

Well, indeed, there I was amid the countless graves of Arlington. I can't tell you how moving that was for me and for most people who go there. But after so many conversations about America and democracy with so many thousands of people over the previous fourteen months and nearly thirty-two hundred miles, and after such a very long walk, it was a great and watery moment. Things come to an end; the endless rows of gravestones made the point—so many lives lived in service to one another, so many endings found and loving hearts becalmed. In the grass and the trees, life continues, as those beneath are atomized for recomposition by that irresistible force of life—God Himself, I believe.

Tuesday morning, February 29, 2000, was a brisk and clear morning. I arrived on the sidewalk near the entrance to Arlington. The news trucks from the network morning shows were there, and one by one, I gave my last happy talk interviews with people whom I had come almost to know.

When they were finished with their interviews, I looked around to see that there were a good fifty or sixty people gathered for the walk. They had banners and were in a festive mood. I saw a number of old friends from the road, and I met some whom I did not know, but who had come from as far as Alaska to support the cause.

There is a subway stop under the sidewalk at that point, and you could tell when the train must have stopped because a new batch of a few people would come up the escalator with signs. Then they started to come in larger clusters. Soon, a half hour before we said we would begin, a steady stream began to arrive. More than twenty-two hundred people had come, and I knew more of them than I could have imagined, because I had slept in their homes and eaten at their tables.

Here comes Jim Hightower in his white cowboy hat. Here comes Senator Carl Levin. Here comes the singer David Crosby. Here come Golda Velez from Tucson, Herb Weinberg from Phoenix, Todd Jennings from Greenwich Village, the Granny Gears bicycle club from Ohio, friends from Maine, Alaska, Texas, Kentucky, and Arkansas! Here come all the gang from Common Cause, the Raging Grannies, women in wheelchairs from nursing homes, all the gang from Public Campaign, Alliance for Democracy, the League of Women Voters, the Public Interest Research Group, and on and on, many of them wearing the pretty shirts my friend, Francie Von Merton, designed for the occasion. You know, it was like I hope heaven might be: meeting all our old friends again with great laughter and hugs. My God, we made it to heaven after all! Who would have thought!

Hightower rounded the group into a great circle and used a bullhorn to welcome everybody and get the crowd cheering and ready to go. We triple-filed across the Memorial Bridge and stopped at the Lincoln Memorial for a tiny speech. Then down alongside the reflecting pool to the Washington Monument,

With Jim Hightower (center), making the turn by the Reflecting Pool on our way to the Capitol.

where we turned left to go find K Street. Two Scottish bagpipers had joined us and helped lead the way. At Decatur Square on K Street, Jim Hightower and I used the bullhorn to say a few choice words about Lobbyist Row, where we now stood.

I looked up to the office towers and saw what I never expected to see: a number of windows were open and banners hung down: GO GRANNY GO! Some women were cheering from the open windows. We were singing and making a happy racket—a moving party through the streets.

Most Washington marches go down the great mall, but I thought we would be lost there. Besides, I hoped we would be loud enough to cost the K Street lobbyists at least a few minutes of bribe time.

We turned down to Freedom Square on Pennsylvania Avenue for the final leg to the Capitol. There we were joined by about a

Two fans high above K Street, Washington's Lobbyist Row, as I pass on my way to the Capitol with 2,200 supporters.

dozen members of Congress and more local supporters. When we got to the edge of the Capitol grounds, we were told that too many had come, that the permit was only for two hundred people.

Well, we went anyway.

We curved around the side of the building to the main steps. I couldn't believe what I saw when I rounded the corner to the great steps and the beautiful columns of this, the world's headquarters for democracy: hundreds more people, a good many members of Congress, banners galore, and great cheers from all. It was electric, and I was twenty years old as I walked up the steps.

There were a good number of speeches welcoming me, and they were all quite wonderful and heartfelt. I made my speech, directing my eyes to this group over here and that group over there—the Capitol police had rudely and almost abusively broken up the crowd into smaller units. Did they think we would storm our own building? Twenty-two hundred people stood with me from all over America—we had disproven the lie that people do not care about the corruption of our elections.

Speech at the Lincoln Memorial
February 29, 2000

The beauty of this memorial we take from the ancient Greeks. Inside this temple of democracy, however, is no god of Olympus, but a man of Illinois—a country lawyer with a talent for self-government which we all must share if a government of the people and by the people and for the people is not to perish from the earth.

We all have our own religions to guide us, but we share a common civic belief, and this is a temple of that shared belief—the belief in our ability and our responsibility to manage our own government as a great people.

It is our belief in the proper human scale of things. We have sculpted Mr. Lincoln large in stone, but only so that this solitary man might not be dwarfed by the columns of our institutions, and only so that we might remind ourselves that those who would overwhelm any of our individual voices in matters of our self-governance with their money or with power we have granted them, are the enemies of all good things represented in this place.

If our experiment in self-government is to survive in reality as well as in name, we must defend the position of the individual. That is what we march for today, and Mr. Lincoln's great smile of enduring optimism for his people encourages us onward. So let us now go to our own Capitol, just up the hill from here.

Speech on the East Steps of the U.S. Capitol
February 29, 2000

Thank you.

Before the days of the civil rights movement, a senator might have said that the millions of oppressed people were happy in their condition. But now, after so much history, after so much painful growth, we see the insensitivity and ignorance of such a statement. How did anyone dare think that the oppressed and abused were happy in their condition?

Before the rise of the environmental movement, a senator might have looked upon a polluted Hudson River and said that the old river is simply paying the inevitable price for progress. But now, after so much sickness endured, so much new understanding gained of our fragile network of life, and after so much effort by so many, we see the insensitivity and ignorance of such a statement. How did anyone dare think that our beautiful land stretches itself out for companies to ravage for their profit and our misery?

Before the campaign finance reform movement, which grows every day now with such power that it shakes the political parties to their foundations, a senator might have advised his fellow member to not worry about voting down campaign reforms, because the people don't care. That is, in fact, what Senators McConnell and Lott did say—and that is what precipitated my walk. I have come to tell them that they are wildly mistaken, and I am glad to have you along to add your voices to mine.

This morning we began our walk among the graves of Arlington—so that those spirits, some of whom may be old friends, might join us today and that we might ask of them now, Did you, brave spirits, give your lives for a government where we might stand together as free and equal citizens, or did you give your lives so that laws might be sold to the highest bidder, turning this temple of our fair republic into a bawdy house where anything and everything is done for a price?

We hear your answers in the wind.

What might we call the selling of our government from under us? What might we call a change of government—from a government of, by, and for the people, to a government by and for the wealthy elite? I will not call such a change of government a treason, but those more courageous shadows standing among us, whose blood runs through our flag and our history and whose accomplishments are more solid beneath us than these stone steps, might use such a word in angry whispers—whispers that trace through the polluted corridors of this once great Capitol and slip despairingly through the files of correspondence and receipts in this city of corruption.

Senators, we speak for these spirits and for ourselves: Of course you may not have our democratic republic to sell. What our family members died for, we do not forget. They died for our freedom and equality, not for a government of the rich alone.

Along my three thousand miles through the heart of America, which I made to disprove your lie, did I meet anyone who thought that their voice as an equal citizen now counts for much in the corrupt halls of Washington? No, I did not. Did I meet anyone who felt anger or pain over this? I did indeed, and I watched them shake with rage sometimes when they spoke, and I saw tears well up in their eyes.

The people I met along my way have given me messages to deliver here. The messages are many, written with old and young hands of every color, and yet the messages are the same. They are this: Shame on you, senators and congressmen, who have turned this headquarters of a great and self-governing people into a bawdy house.

The time for this shame is ending. The American people see it and have decided against it. Our brooms are ballots, and we come a-sweeping.

While we are here to speak frankly to our representatives, let us also speak frankly to ourselves: Along my walk I have seen an America that is losing the time and the energy for self-governance. The problems we see in Washington are problems that have been sucked into a vacuum of our own making. It is not enough for us to elect someone, give them a slim list of ideas, and send them off to represent us. If we do not keep these boys and girls busy they will always get into trouble. We must energize our communities to better see our problems, better plan their happy futures, and these plans must form the basis of our instructions to our elected representatives. This is the responsibility of every adult American, from native to newcomer, and from young worker to the long retired. If we are hypnotized by television and

Speaking on the steps of the U.S. Capitol. Behind me are Senator Russ Feingold, David Crosby, U.S. Representative Christopher Shays, Rabbi David Saperstein, and U.S. Representative Marty Meehan.

overwrought by life on a corporate-consumer treadmill, let us snap out of it and regain our lives as a free, calm, fearlessly outspoken people who have time for each other and our communities.

Let us pass election reforms and anticorruption measures in our towns and cities and states, winning the reform wars where they are winnable, changing the national weather on this subject until the winds blow even through these columns.

Now, senators, back to you. If I have offended you speaking this way on your front steps, that is as it should be; you have offended America and you have dishonored the best things it stands for. Take your wounded pride, get off your backs and onto your feet, and go across the street to clean your rooms. You have somewhere on your desks, under the love letters from your

greedy friends and co-conspirators against representative democracy, a modest bill against soft money. Pass it. Then show
that you are clever lads by devising new ways for a great people to
talk to one another again without the necessity of great wealth. If
you cannot do that, then get out of the way—go home to some
other corruption, less harmful to a great nation. We have millions
of people more worthy of these fine offices.

So here we are, senators, at your doorstep: We the people.

How did you dare think we do not care about our country?
How did you dare think that we would not come here to these
steps to denounce your corruptions in the name of all who have
given their lives to our country's defense and improvement? How
did you dare think we were so unpatriotic as to have forgotten all
those rows upon rows of graves that mark how much we, as a
people, care for our freedom and our equality?

The people of our nation do care. They have told me. They
laugh with disgust about you on the beaches of California. They
shake their heads about you in the native village of Hashan Kehk
in Arizona. In Toyah, Texas, they pray for deliverance from your
corruption. In Little Rock, they understand in anger how you un-
dermine their best dreams for our society. And in Memphis and
in Louisville and in Chillicothe and Clarksburg, through Pennsylvania and Maryland and into this city today, the people see you
for what you have become and they are prepared to see you another way: boarding the trains at the great station down the
street. They are ready for real leaders, unselfish and principled
leaders who will prove their worth by voting for meaningful reform.

The time has come, senators, for reform or for some new
senators. Tell us which it will be, and then we will go vote.

In the name of the people who have sent me along to you,
and in the name of the generations before who have sacrificed so
much for the sanctity of our free institutions and who stand with
us in spirit today, I make this demand.

The Evening and Next Day

After the speeches, a number of people from the Alliance for Democracy went into the Rotunda and unfurled a campaign finance reform banner. That is enough to get you arrested in the free speech center of the world, and they were. While they were being hauled away, I met with as many members of Congress as I could, until it was time for us to finally relax and celebrate the completion of the walk at St. Mark's Church, right behind the Supreme Court.

Lasagna was served by a catering company that trains people from a homeless shelter. There were more speeches all evening, all of them wonderful, funny, and full of memories and tears—especially those by my grandchildren. The high point of the evening was when the young people who had been arrested were released and came to the church. I gave each of them a big kiss.

I went to get a big plate of lasagna for Ken, but I could not find him. He had quietly faded away, off in his inconspicuous red Jeep. Someone told me he had to get back to his battle in West Virginia.

The next day, after a long visit with NPR's Diane Rehm on her show, I met with more members of Congress, as many as would meet with me. It was not many, despite written requests to each of them. I sat in the rain at a tea table under the trees across from the Senate office building, waiting for them to respond to my request for meetings. Silence. Refusals.

Of course, the reform advocates in the Senate were warm and full of high spirits, and they promised that they would keep at it. But the old "no" votes had no interest in talking—even my own senators.

And so it ended.

Ken called to say he had arrived home all right. He would be terribly outspent by a candidate who took money from the coal mines. Ken would lose the election, but he stayed in good spirits and, at this writing, has invited me to West Virginia to visit for a while. I have, of course, agreed.

Nick headed home to Chicago to resume carpentry work and to get involved in campaign reform in Illinois.

Jason returned to Little Rock and to his restaurant, Grass Roots Pasta. He framed some magazine articles about the walk and now serves a little campaign finance reform on the side to anyone who will listen.

John continued his work as a reform organizer in Washington, and Dennis returned to Arizona and to a political reform project he had started there.

The walk, I must say, improved my health. My son-in-law, Dr. David Lawrenz, said that, in terms of physical condition and mental attitude, I finished the walk twenty years younger than when I started. It was good for my arthritis and my emphysema. It didn't do much for my back, but what are we ever going to do with our backs! I will have to talk to the Creator about that someday, or maybe we must just wait for Mr. Nader to get to heaven.

Was it worth it otherwise? Well, for myself, yes. It was a great adventure and an opportunity to think about my life and to connect the dots of it. I made friends. I think I was a useful sounding board and counsel to people along the way, who were always quick to share their personal problems with me for some reason—I was always flattered by their instant trust. I got to meet many of the great leaders of our day and talk with them about the great issue of our day, and I met and discussed politics with thousands of my fellow citizens.

Did the walk do any good politically? Well, I think it gave many people some hope and energy, and it served to connect them with others who care. I think the walk helped bring the issue forward, and even gave some presidential candidates assurance that the issue was emotionally potent. Quite a few different reform organizations came together for the first time during my arrival in Washington, which Claudia Malloy of Common Cause coordinated with great skill.

For myself, I learned how deeply we Americans love our country and how discouraged people are by big money politics. The greatest lie of our time—used by politicians and by big business media—was that the people did not care about campaign finance reform. People in early 1999 were not fully conversant with that term, but they knew their government had been sold out from under them, they knew it is wrong, and they were dying to see something done about it. From my thousands of conversations along the way, I would guess that over ninety percent of Americans felt that way, so the Big Lie was pretty big, indeed. But it is no longer believed.

I also learned that there is an answer to big money politics, and it is the public financing of campaigns, which is now happening in the states.

That was an area where I thought I might next get involved. I would go home to put my feet up for a spell. But then I would poke around and find out what I might do to encourage public financing programs in the states. That would be worthwhile and full of adventures for my later years.

Finally, let me say that while I was nearly always treated with love and courtesy, I did have the opportunity to see the difference between the politics of love and the politics of hate. You may think of good and evil as relative things, and I agree that the words are often used that way. But I think I see uses for those words that have an objective aspect. I believe goodness is the attractive force of friendly and cooperative gathering—not gathering to the point of melding, for that, too, is destructive, as the merger of hydrogen atoms into a hydrogen bomb demonstrates perfectly. I mean that goodness is the attractive force that joins as much as possible without damage to independence, liberty, and diversity. This force shows itself in our best politics and our happiest towns, families, and marriages.

There is also a repulsive force—the force that separates people and groups, emphasizing and energizing their differences, desensitizing the groups to each others' needs, and trampling diversity. If evil is too harsh a word for it, then perhaps this repulsive force can be described as deathlike, for it describes the process of decomposition, just as the attractive force describes the assembly process of new life. Both are necessary in the soil of a garden, but not in the higher reaches of human aspirations, where our politics should reside.

We have both kinds of political leaders, and I do not see too much gray area between them. Either you lead with love, or with hate. Take your pick, leaders. Take your pick, followers.

Back Home and Onward

I spent the weekend with my daughter, Betty, and her family in Chevy Chase. Then Jim and I, at long last, got in the vehicle and drove home to Dublin, New Hampshire. My, it was delicious to see the miles fly by and not have to even think about walking them! And then my town ahead, and there it is! And the old house! My old chair! Bathtub! Books! Ahh, my tired bones!

On Tuesday morning I made my way back to my old friends—our Tuesday Morning Academy. They were happy to see me, but it was rather as if I had been ill for a time or off on a cruise. Within a few minutes, I was one of the girls again—except for one difference. One of my friends, after a few minutes of conversation about my walk, said she didn't see what was so important about campaign finance reform.

It is reported that I took her rather sharply to task with a presentation of memorable ferocity. Well, was that me? Old Doris? It was not the Doris who had sat meekly among them a year and a quarter earlier. Even at my age, I had changed quite a bit.

For the first time in my long life, I was clearly not afraid of what someone might think of me—I cared more about the issue than my vain self. That transition was worth the walk, though I must keep working on it.

Several weeks later I received a call. A group of campaign finance reformers from the Alliance for Democracy were going into the Capitol Rotunda to petition for the redress of our grievance against campaign corruption. Yes, I said—I would go with them this time. I could care less anymore if people thought I was crazy. This was a way to push the issue forward—to demonstrate the depth of our concern and to take the pain of social change upon ourselves.

So I returned to Washington. On the evening of April 20, 2000, I walked from a train at Union Station to a church building near the Supreme Court. There I was to meet thirty-one others who would risk arrest. I was a bit late, as the streets of Washington can be confusing. I entered a room where the thirty-one were seated in chairs gathered in a great circle, and my perilous seat waited empty for me.

In the few steps across the room, I reminded myself that my whole life had been spent worrying too much about what others thought about me. Go ahead, old girl, have a seat.

It was a comfortably well-worn chair, and I looked around with wonder at the smiling people around me, bathed as they were in the golden light of the old room. Many had lost themselves to their causes many years ago. Some, like me, were young beginners.

I was arrested the next morning for reading the Declaration of Independence in a calm voice in the Rotunda. I did so to make the point that we must declare our independence from campaign corruption. My wrists were pulled behind me and cuffed. I was taken away to jail along with the others. When you jump fully into the river of your values, every moment glows with a blissful joy, even when your arms hurt behind you.

But, oh, dear husband, Jim! Are you up there looking down, laughing at me in the pokey? Get used to it, dear.

The fear of not being liked—of not belonging—has been central to my life. "She's not like the others. She's different. Sometimes I wonder if she's mine at all, like I found her in a basket on my front doorstep," I overheard my mother say when I was seven.

Not knowing how else to proceed, I embraced the idea that I was different. I was a princess in disguise. The pink granite Laconia Public Library, complete with turret, became my castle, and I read every adventure book in it. At home, my nose was always in a book until Mama scolded me to do my chores.

That overheard conversation, and that uncertainty, helped

me to become well read and adventurous, which has made me a connoisseur of life and of people. It has sent me on a lifetime of adventures—I can't imagine how boring I might have otherwise become to others and to myself.

It does help now to know that I was, in fact, loved. At Sybil's wake, when a priest asked Mama who would be taking care of her now that Sybil was gone, Mama's eyes brightened with joy when I said, "Why, she will be coming to live with me, won't you, Mama?" It may have been only the sparkle of an extinguished worry, but I have clung to it.

Do we see who we are, finally? Do we see, behind the curtain, the scars and insecurities that have controlled us? And when we see them and look them squarely in the eye, do they lose their power over us, backing down from their bullying bluster? Indeed they do. We become free to take our life in whatever shape it has become, and find a good and enjoyable use for it, serving others and ourselves.

Interesting! After all this chattering, I have not told you five minute's worth about my long career in the shoe industry. For so many years, that was all I could think about, and now it hardly seems worth bringing up. I think the lesson there is that a career, in the end, is a much smaller part of our lives than we can possibly imagine at the time. Our career distracts us from our real work, so we must learn to see past the limits of that blinkered world. All those years condense now in my mind to a chuckle.

The aftermath of my arrest was that I was later brought before the judge in Washington for my crime of being a troublesome person. While I hoped he would not put an old woman in jail for six months for reading the Declaration of Independence in the Capitol, as well he could, I yet worried that perhaps all of this, all of me, had been silly and he would now send me away to contemplate my silliness for a few months. As he sat expressionless in his great robe, I wondered what this wise-looking old man thought.

Judge Hamilton finally spoke, and most mercifully. He sentenced me, and the others, to the time we had already served, and he added these words of heavenly grace:

As you know, the strength of our great country lies in its Constitution and her laws and in her courts. But more fundamentally, the strength of our great country lies in the resolve of her citizens to stand up for what is right when the masses are silent. And, unfortunately, sometimes it becomes the lot of the few, sometimes like yourselves, to stand up for what's right when the masses are silent.

His honor gave me a fine hug in his chambers afterward. His staff members were tearful and I was tearful, and America felt like my own country again.

So I am happy for how my walk has turned out, and for how my life has turned out. I am thankful for the troubles that have shaped me. If you and I were having a cup of tea and you were telling me your stories, as I have told you mine, I would see that it was your hard times that made you so interesting, so wise and able to laugh at life. Aren't we lucky, friend, to be the creatures of such a genius Creator that even our darkest troubles graciously serve to deepen and widen our hearts? And all our memories, like days cast in amber, glow more beautifully through the years as the happy endings finally reveal themselves and flow slowly into the bright and mysterious river of the Divine.

Well, I am finished with this book, but I am not finished with my life or with my passion for campaign finance reform. There is almost always time to find another victory, another happy ending. I hope that is your feeling about life, too.

I thank you for the time you have spent with me between these covers. I apologize for preaching far more than I intended, but I'm sure you skipped through the worst of it.

If we have not already met, I hope we shall do so while there is yet an opportunity in this brief life. Or some other time, most certainly.

Epilogue
by Dennis Burke

In the spring of 2000, Doris Haddock was awarded her college degree at Emerson College.

On August 10, 2000, her name was placed in nomination for vice president of the United States at the Reform Party convention in Long Beach, California. She respectfully declined.

She spoke at the "shadow conventions" during the Philadelphia Republican Convention and the Los Angeles Democratic Convention. After her speech in Los Angeles, Ellen Miller of Public Campaign sat down to have a cup of coffee with her in the lobby of the old Figueroa Hotel. Doris had tea.

Just outside the door, thousands of people were protesting, and a common theme moving into many of the protest messages was campaign finance reform. Al Gore, the Democratic Party's nominee for president, in his acceptance speech the next night, would say that campaign finance reform would be his first legislative priority, if elected. When he first brought up that subject on the campaign trail, he cited Bill Bradley, John McCain, and Granny D Haddock.

Ellen told Doris that regardless of the outcome of the elections, campaign reform's time had come, and much of the new energy was the result of her walk across the United States.

In that walk, presidential candidates had been watching over Doris's shoulder, reading her speeches, and watching how she made campaign reform an emotional issue with many Americans. She purposefully brought together right and left, white and black, old and young.

"Well, that's very nice of you to say," Doris told Ellen. Doris asked if it would be helpful if she walked through some of the states where public campaign financing reforms are being planned.

"That would be lovely," Ellen said.

When Doris arrived home in New Hampshire, she began walking ten miles a day to get back in shape.

GrannyD.com

I have just read this account that my mother forwarded to me. I am a French citizen, but I was moved. It feels like a Capra movie. That is the America that the world wants to love, the America we French went bankrupt helping win the War of Independence.

Years ago, when I was serving my 12-month tour as a conscript in the French army, I was posted in a mid-18th-century building that once housed the Ministry of the Navy. It is on Rue de l'Indépendance Americaine—American Independence Street—right across the street from the great Palace of Versailles. History has its addresses, and sooner or later they will whisper in your ear.

God bless Doris Haddock and the true ideals of America.

Philippe Dambournet, Paris—Saturday, March 11, 2000

Granny's walk and her stories taught me not to be afraid. No matter how alone I am now as an activist, I can be assured that I will find support and friendship along the way. She also taught me not to be afraid of being vulnerable. Being vulnerable opens others' hearts to hear what you have to say.

Diana McCourt—Thursday, March 16, 2000

The last time I marched for a cause was as a teenager in my native Switzerland—a candlelight procession through the dark streets of Zurich to protest against the Russian invasion of Hungary. Yes, 1956! I've long since become a U.S. citizen, and can't remember having felt so joyous and hopeful about being able to affect a public issue as when I was walking last Tuesday through the sunny streets of Washington, banging a Brazilian carnival noisemaker to the rhythm of "Go, Granny, go!" Let's continue the good fight at her side!

Regina Bringolf, Hancock, NH (a new member of the Tuesday Morning Academy)—Monday, March 20, 2000

It's a good thing that I didn't go to work the day following the march, because it took me a long time to come down from the emotional high and overflow of energy flooding through my entire being from that walk, and I'm not over it yet. The last time I marched for anything was the March for Women's Rights on Fifth Avenue in 1970. I think that was also the last time I believed that a demonstration could have any impact on getting the average person to fight for changes needed in our democratic system. I have spent the better part of the last twenty years feeling shut out of the opportunities and prosperity America is supposed to offer all its citizens, and helpless to do anything about it, until now.

I will never forget walking those five miles and standing on the Capitol steps cheering Doris Haddock. . . . I, for one, have been reawakened by her spirit.

C. J. Gelfand, New York City—Monday, March 20, 2000

I walked with my nine-year-old daughter behind Granny D from Arlington to the steps of the Capitol. While I am a longtime campaign finance reform advocate, the personal value of this march was not standing on the steps of the Capitol roaring with approval as Doris issued her challenge to Congress. It was the challenge she issued to all of us by taking that first step in California. Her actions sent a message that resonated deeply with my daughter. If Doris Haddock can take that long grueling trek across this country at the age of 90 to fight the scandal of special interest money in our political system, each one of us must take our own steps to combat injustice. It is that image that will continue to inspire my daughter Jane, and that makes Doris a hero for all of us.

Michael and Jane Caudell-Feagan—Thursday, March 23, 2000

Appendix:
Selected Speeches of Doris Haddock

The Center of the World
Speech at the Buck Jackson Rodeo Arena, May 14, 1999

Thank you. I am honored to be here in Pecos.

On January 1, I began my walk to Washington, D.C., from Los Angeles, some twelve hundred miles ago, and all of those miles have been walked in a place that is best described as the land west of the Pecos. On Sunday, I will wade across the Pecos and enter the other half of creation. But tonight I am here at the center of the world and am so proud to meet all of you who live here, and I am pleased that we can share such a perfect evening.

Life is a beautiful experience, and here we all are together, alive at this moment, breathing the same, cool air. The issue that brings us here tonight is a terrible disease, and we fight it because we naturally rise to the fight against any evil that threatens us and those we love.

Deep inside, we can be joyful to remember that nobody really dies in this great drama of the soul we live in eternally. Some of us move on faster than others, and we so deeply miss those who have left this little world before us. Tonight we see that there is something we can do with that loneliness and pain.

When my husband died several years ago, and when my best friend, Elizabeth, died last year, I looked at my life and my lifelong beliefs and said to myself, what shall I do now? What useful thing can I do to honor the memory of the people I have loved? How can I turn my pain into something beautiful in the world?

Something beautiful? Let me tell you that great art and great writing often are the transformation of suffering to beauty. Life is full of suffering, and when we have more of it than we can bear, we must try to trick it into beauty through a medium of exchange such as art, or handiwork, or a written story or poem, or good parenting, or good friendship, or the creation of good work in the community, or the pursuit of some work we may find unfinished among our lifelong interests and concerns—some of which we put away in the attic for too long. What work can I do that may be done now as a memorial to those I miss? What can I do to amaze them and fill their angel eyes with tears and laughter as they watch me lovingly from the other side?

And so, if you are here because you are remembering someone lost, you are turning that loss into the art of this special evening we share together. And if you are here to pursue your own battle with a dangerous disease, or to give emotional support to someone you love who is doing that, then you are a part of that creative transformation of pain to beauty. What is more beautiful than people warmly sharing an evening together in the glow of candles? What is more healing?

The issue that I decided to do something about as a memorial to the people I loved and still love is political reform of our elections. It is, of course, a fool's errand. It is just an old woman walking across the land, wearing her friend's gardening hat and talking to whomever will listen about the kind of political reforms most people don't believe can really happen.

But there are two things I would like you to understand about impossible missions. One is the fact that, sometimes, all you can do is put your body in front of a problem and stand there as a witness to it. That is part of healing because it is not denial of the problem, and our individual conscious mind is part of the larger conscious mind of society. Your thoughts affect the world, and your actions matter.

Never be discouraged from being an activist because people tell you that you'll not succeed. You have already succeeded if you're out there representing truth or justice or compassion or fairness or love. You already have your victory because you have changed the world; you have changed the status quo by you; you have changed the chemistry of things. And changes will spread from you, will be easier to happen again in others because of you, because, believe it or not, you are the center of the world.

There is a second thing you need to know about impossible causes and it is this: There are no impossible causes on this earth if they are good causes. We can do anything together, and we really do remarkable things. We will cure cancer most certainly because people like you walk through the night to make it so. We have nearly eradicated polio worldwide; we have actually cured smallpox; we are curing many of the diseases—the cures for which were thought impossible dreams a short time ago.

My dream of political reform will come true. I may live to see it from this side of life, or I will smile to see it from the other side. But it will happen. It will happen because people love this country so, and this democracy so, and because they have given their sons and daughters and the best years of their own lives to defend it. They will not let it be destroyed before their eyes. I know we will again be able to run our communities and our nation in ways that look after the interests of the common people, for that is what a democracy is all about.

I walk this road for my late, dear friend Elizabeth, and for my darling husband, Jim, so that they will be surprised and proud of me and we will have something new to talk about when next we meet. And I do it for myself, and for the thousands of people I have met along my path who love this country and who are deeply worried about it.

I wish all of you good health. I wish for all of you the courage to live out your emotions and your beliefs in your daily lives, as you are doing tonight. I admire you all, and I will remember this evening at the great center of our beautiful world.

On the Road So Far

Reform Party Convention, Dearborn, Michigan, July 23, 1999
(excerpt)

Ladies and Gentlemen,

It is said that democracy is not something we have, but something we do. But right now, we cannot do it because we cannot speak. We are shouted down by the bullhorns of big money. It is money with no manners for democracy, and it must be escorted from the room.

While wealth has always influenced our politics, what is new is the increasing concentration of wealth and the widening divide between the political interests of the common people and the political interests of the very wealthy who are now able to buy our willing leaders wholesale. . . .

What villainy allows this political condition? The twin viral ideas that money is speech and that corporations are people. If money is speech, then those with more money have more speech, and that idea is antithetical to democracy. It makes us no longer equal citizens. This perverse notion, and the general, unrestricted participation of corporate and—yes—union money in our elections, must be and will be stopped if democracy is to survive. . . .

It is all quite enough to make us mad, but let me advise you, on the eve of your meetings, that we cannot afford to act out of anger. . . .

If you have true enemies in politics, pray that their lives are filled with anger, for no one so filled can win for long. Anger drains your energy and makes you incapable of endurance or of creative leadership. If you win, your victory will be short-lived. Negativity is negativity, and it has no place at the helm of a democracy. It doesn't know what to do with power when it gets it. Only joy and optimism—and love, really—can win in the long term.

General Eisenhower said, "Pessimism never won any battle." He was right. Pessimism visualizes defeat. What we visualize, we bring forth. Carl Sandburg wrote: "Nothing happens unless first a dream."

To the reformers, then: Learn optimism if you would have the endurance to succeed, and endurance is required.

Where to find optimism? Well, I have found it for you out on the road, and I give it to you now. It is this:

I give you the Americans I have met. Without exception, they deeply love the idea of America. It is an image they carry in their hearts. It is a dream they are willing to sacrifice their lives for. Many of them do. There is no separating this image of democracy from their longing for personal freedom for themselves, their family, their friends. To the extent that our government is not our own, we are not free people. We feel a heavy oppression in our lives because we have lost hold of this thing, this self-governance, that is rightfully ours because it is our dream and our history. But the spirit of freedom is strong in the American soul, and it is the source of our optimism and joy, because it will always overcome its oppressors.

On the road so far, these Americans have taken me into their homes and fed me at their tables—shown me the children for whom they sacrifice their working lives and for whom they pray for a free and gentle democracy. And I will tell you that I am with them. I am with their dream, and I know you are, too. We are all on this road, and we must stay on it together, forgetting our minor differences until, together, we achieve the necessary objective of restoring democracy for individuals and allowing each individual an equal voice in the civil discussions we have as a self-governing people. . . .

It is a long road ahead. But what nation can look at their neighbors and friends with such pride as can we? Who thinks they can stand in the way of our need to be free, to manage our own government, to be a force for good in the world, to protect our children and our land, to sweep away before us anyone who tries to turn our sacred institutions of civic freedom to their greedy purposes?

On the road so far, I have seen a great nation. I have felt it hugging my shoulders, shaking my hand, cheering from across the way. I am so in love with it. I know you are, too.

Thank you.

The Five Steps

First Missionary Baptist Church, Little Rock, Arkansas, September 22, 1999 (condensed)

Dear friends, it is a great honor to stand here in your midst, to stand here speaking where Dr. Martin Luther King, Jr., once stood and spoke. Here was a man—and we feel his presence in this place—who came into this world to speak the truth. Some people listened and understood, and some did not.

And the truth was this and remains this: that we are brothers and sisters; that our struggles to overcome injustice and unfairness, cruelty and oppression are only successful in the long run where our method is love—love of one another, love of our enemies.

When we hate our enemies, we stop praying for them. And when we stop praying for them, how can we ever hope to turn them around?

We all have known family members who were on the wrong path and who created turmoil and pain in our families. We pray for them, in love, to turn them around. Well, America is a family, too. And our struggles are family struggles, where love is the greatest power and, in the long run of history, the only real power. Look at the best things, the enduring things, that America has done for itself and for the world in the centuries of our history: they are changes motivated by love, by a dream of equality, by a dream of peace and justice. The changes wrought by hatred fall away, while the changes wrought by love endure.

The use of love and truth to bring forth justice nonviolently was brought to this nation by Dr. King, and we thank him for it. He studied it and learned it from the writings of Mr. Gandhi. Mr. Gandhi learned it from the writings of John Ruskin and Leo Tolstoy, who learned it from the American Quaker abolitionist, William Lloyd Garrison, who learned about it from the Sermon on the Mount. Thus, the great need for justice and freedom in America, the need to end slavery, resulted in a ripple of thought and love that spread across the world, and came back to us in our time of need—thanks to Dr. King. He brought that teaching here, to this place, this room. Such is the enduring power of the Sermon on the Mount and of love itself in the world.

The teaching of nonviolent political action is a five-fold technique that we must always remember. It must be taught in our schools. It must be remembered wherever people gather with the intention of improving their community or their world. Here are the five steps:

First: Determine the truth of a situation before taking a strong position. If it is an injustice, can it be clearly documented? Bring in the experts if you can. Be sure what you are advocating is actually and demonstrably the truth.

Second: Communicate your findings, your position, and your request for change in a respectful and achievable way to the people who have the direct power to correct the situation. Don't ask someone for something they don't have the power to give. Don't shout on the sidewalks if you have not yet communicated respectfully with the parties in authority and have respectfully waited for a reply.

Third: If the response does not come, or is insufficient, bring public attention to the issue. Work openly so the thinking process of the entire community can be engaged. Gandhi and King were accused of staging events for the media. Of course they did. Social change is a public process, and it does not happen for the good when it happens in the dark. Engage the community openly so that they can be a part of the debate and the decision. Openness works easiest in a democracy, but it also works in authoritarian regimes, so long as there is visibility between the action and the public. Few governments, no matter how authoritarian, are immune from public sentiment.

Fourth: If those in authority will not correct a very serious situation that must be resolved, despite an open airing of the issue, then the advocates must be willing to make sacrifices to demonstrate the seriousness of the matter. When King marched forward toward batoned policemen in Selma, he showed that the issue was important. When Gandhi led marches and gave speeches that he knew would lead to his imprisonment that day, and when his followers stood in long lines to be clubbed by security forces standing in the way of their rightful path, the world stopped its daily routine to inquire: "What injustice motivates the self-sacrifices of these people? What, in fairness, should be done?" And here is the difficult key to success: The endless willingness of the advocates to make a continuing sacrifice guarantees their victory. No injustice is powerful enough, or has enough supporters, to stand against the flow of such generosity.

"You have been the veterans of creative suffering," Dr. King told his followers in the "I Have a Dream" speech. Well, creative suffering is something we all have the power to do. It happens to be the most powerful force for change in the world. It is always in our pocket, ready for the call of our conscience.

There is a fifth step, made necessary by the fact that the nonviolence technique, when properly practiced, always wins. The fifth step, as developed by Mr. Gandhi and as practiced by Dr. King, is to be gracious in victory—to remember that your enemy is your brother, and that you should therefore settle the dispute kindly, accepting some compromises and granting as much face-saving courtesy as possible to the other side. You will meet again, after all, and why not as friends? Gandhi said on many occasions that we have to love and respect our adversaries because they are our brothers and sisters and also that they are parts of ourselves and of our God. He meant it.

Here is a passage from his autobiography:

> Man and his deed are two distinct things. It is quite proper to resist and attack a system, but to resist and attack its author is tantamount to resisting and attacking oneself. For we are all tarred with the same brush, and are children of one and the same Creator, and as such the divine powers within us are infinite. To slight a single human being is to slight those divine powers, and thus to harm not only that being but with him the whole world.

Dr. King believed much the same, and you can hear it clearly in the "I Have a Dream" speech, where he calls us together as "all of God's children."

These are the five steps that gave India its freedom and which gave America its second revolution of independence at a moment when it could have devolved into a full race war. The moment King left this world, the violence that could have been ours all along showed itself in Watts and Detroit and a hundred other cities and towns. There is no courage in a thrown bottle of gasoline. Courage is what we saw in the buses arriving at Little Rock's Central High School and in the Selma march, not the riots of so many cities. Good changes, like the Voting Rights Act and the opening of universities and public facilities, came from King's work. Poor changes, temporary changes, came from the anger of riots.

Love works. Love wins. Love endures. It is our religion, and it must also be our politics.

In my walk across the country, I speak against the idea that those individuals and those corporations with the greatest wealth should be able to buy our elections and our candidates and our representatives, diverting their attention from the needs of the people and preventing honest candidates from winning.

That we have a problem, that money has become more important than ideas in our political debate, is a proven fact. That this huge, national influence-peddling scheme results in a mass diversion of the public wealth from where it is needed to where privileged people would have it for their own use, is no longer a debatable point. When I walk with this message, I have the advantage of speaking the simple truth, proven by every major research institution and news organization, on both the right and left of political life, who have taken the time to investigate the issue.

We have asked those in power to remedy the situation, and they have refused. We have asked them again, and again they have refused.

We have engaged the press of the nation to shine a great light on this cancer, and still there is no movement by the leaders.

And so we must reveal the depth of our concern. We must make a sacrifice of ourselves to demonstrate the serious nature of this problem and this injustice. All great political change requires pain. Mr. Gandhi and Dr. King advised us to take that pain upon ourselves, not to inflict it upon others. And that is what we must do: to sacrifice, and to stand more and more forcefully in the way of this injustice.

There can be no true equality in America so long as only the rich are represented at the table of power. That is no democracy. There can be no true justice in America so long as only the privileged make the rules and build the jails for those outside the rooms of power. That is no democracy.

Only when we sit together at the table of power can we do the right things by our communities. . . .

For when we are in the same room, looking eye-to-eye, speaking heart-to-heart, it is hard for us to deny each other justice and equality as Americans. If I tell you what my children need, you will help me provide for them. If you tell me what your children need, I will help you provide for them. That is the essence of self-government in a free land. The trick is to get us all in the room, all at the table, and campaign finance reform is one of the keys to making that finally happen. . . .

We are a free and equal people—in theory and in law. But I don't believe we will have real equality, practical equality, and I don't believe we will have democracy, practical democracy, until the influence of money is reduced in the elective process and people can run on the strength of their character, not on the size of their wallet; on the brilliance of their ideas, not on the network of their business connections; on their proven leadership ability, not on their slick powers of influence peddling and political extortion. To take money from those you regulate was bribery a thousand years ago, and it is bribery today. And while our leaders take campaign bribes with one hand—bribes that deprive us of our democracy—with the other hand they falsely pledge allegiance to the great dream of America—the dream so many have died for.

"They promise them freedom, but they themselves are slaves of corruption; for whatever overcomes a man, to that he is enslaved." Second Book of Peter, Chapter 2, verse 19.

And from Psalm 26: "Gather not my soul with sinners, nor my life with bloody men in whose hands is mischief, and their right hand is full of bribes. But as for me, I will walk in mine integrity: redeem me, and be merciful unto me. My foot standeth in an even place: in the congregations will I bless the Lord."

I ask the Lord to bless this congregation and I thank Him for bringing me safely to this place. I thank you for the honor of being able to address you here, under the Lord's roof and in the presence of Dr. King's spirit. I pray for those in this country who have the burden of responsibility for leading us. I pray that they shake off the chains of unrighteous obligation that tighten around them through the present campaign finance system. I pray that they will have the courage to do the right thing for themselves and for their fellow Americans. I know they are not happy with the present situation, nor are we, the people.

I tell you this: From this day forward, from this church forward, the campaign finance reform movement and the civil rights movement must join hands and sing a song of democracy together. Either the common people will rule this land, or they will be ruled. . . .

We are walking together on the high road of history. We are on even ground, now, because so many sacrifices have been made behind us. We have nothing to lose that we care about and our shared freedom to gain. We are walking in love, our successes sparkling behind us. We cannot be stopped so long as our souls are alive, and our souls live forever.

Thank you.

I Have Come to Answer Your Question, Mr. McConnell

Outside Mitch McConnell's office in Louisville, Kentucky, November 6, 1999

Thank you for this welcome.

I have so enjoyed walking through Kentucky—the beauty is nearly overwhelming. This is a wonderful state, filled with great people.

I want to speak about one great Kentuckian in particular, Senator Mitch McConnell, whose office I have come to after 2,400 miles of walking.

He is on the other side of the battle lines in our effort to return the American democracy to the human scale—our effort to get the $100,000 check out of politics. But he is a most worthy opponent. He fiercely represents his beliefs and the interests of Kentucky in Washington. He sits as chairman of the Senate Rules Committee, which has jurisdiction over federal election laws and the administration of the Senate. He is the chairman of the Foreign Operations Subcommittee, a key foreign policy committee, and is a member of the Agriculture and Appropriations committees. These positions of leadership indicate that he is held in high esteem by his fellow senators. He is also the chairman of the National Republican Senatorial Committee, which means he is responsible for supporting the campaigns of Republican Senate candidates in every state.

In 1997, he raised nearly $11 million for these campaigns from corporations and from wealthy contributors. Presently, he is raising even more for the upcoming elections.

When he speaks on the Senate floor, his arguments are well reasoned and a delight to listen to. They make good reading, like the orations of Cicero of ancient Rome. He defends our Constitution—as he sees it—with a vengeance.

You are waiting for me to say something unkind.

In fact, I have come here to do him a favor, and to ask a favor. I will scold a bit, but I am not here to vilify him.

He asked a question on the Senate floor recently, and got no answer. I have, on foot, brought him his answer today.

In the recent campaign finance reform debate in the Senate, he rather sharply attacked Senator McCain, when Mr. McCain had the audacity to suggest that the hundreds of millions of dollars being spent by special interests to influence the passage of laws in Congress might indeed be influencing the passage of laws in Congress. Mr. McConnell thought that was an outrageous assumption, and asked for the names of any members of Congress so low as to bend their votes toward the interests of contributors, like flowers toward the sun. Specifically, he said this:

"I ask the Senator from Arizona, how can it be corruption if no one is corrupt? That is like saying the gang is corrupt but none of the gangsters are. If there is corruption, someone must be corrupt."

He also said:

"It is astonishing. We have here rampant charges of corruption and yet no names are named."

Mr. McConnell demanded the names of those who were corrupt. Mr. McCain, for reasons of friendship, courtesy, and the dignity of the Senate—such as it is—did not name names.

But Mr. McConnell persisted, demanding that Senator McCain give a name. Mr. McConnell was like a reverse-Diogenes, searching the dark corners of the Senate chamber with his lantern, looking for one dishonest man.

I have come here today to answer the question asked by Mr. McConnell, and to end his long search.

Lately, Mr. McCain has been accused of having a temper. But he did not answer Mr. McConnell's question in anger on the Senate floor.

Nor will I answer it in anger here, though it is true I can get a little testy, too. My feet do hurt sometimes, and need to be taped so that I can walk. I wear a steel corset to help my back, and it can sometimes make my words a little sharp toward the end of the day. Torture, even a little of it, does make you testy.

I have come a long way to address great men like Senator McConnell and tell them what Americans are saying about the condition of our democracy, and the role of big money in that democracy. The road wears on me sometimes, and I am tempted to say in anger what all America seems to know except a few sheltered men and women whom we care for in a special room in Washington and who do not seem to notice deterioration when it comes over them slowly, or corruption when it becomes the water they swim in.

The answer to your question, Senator McConnell, is elementary.

You ask, "How can it be corruption if no one is corrupt? If there is corruption, someone must be corrupt." You are right, of course. Your analysis is pure genius. Someone must be corrupt. Who can it be?

Perhaps it is the bagman who shakes down American industries in return for protection in Congress, and in return of special tax breaks in Congress from the party in power, while average, working Americans struggle mightily to make ends meet. Have you seen such a person, Senator McConnell?

In 1997, Senator McConnell, when you took $791,945 from insurance interests who needed protection from patient rights efforts, and $602,885 from oil and gas interests who needed a free flow of tax benefits and protections against pollution laws, and $597,915 from communications interests who wanted free access to the digital spectrum and a free hand to merge into giant monopolies, you might have seen such a bagman in their offices. He's the man you were asking about on the Senate floor.

When you let a Ukraine group host a fund-raiser for you in 1996, and you used your position as chairman of the Appropriations Committee to provide a $225 million appropriation for development programs in Ukraine, did you see another fellow there, trading money for public policy? That's the fellow. He is at such meetings and making such deals almost daily, year in and out.

More to the point, Senator McConnell, though I admire your abilities and your achievements, and the hard work you perform for this state and for all of us, you are the man you asked Senator McCain about. And you are not alone. The House and the Senate are full of some of the best minds and most caring hearts in America, and they are being ethically destroyed by the financial demands of campaigning in the modern age.

We must do something, Senator McConnell, and you must help us. I have poked hard at you in these remarks, but I do so with a grandmother's love and the certain knowledge that we Americans are good people at heart who must be encouraged sometimes, and scolded sometimes.

Senator, we need your help. . . . I do not doubt that you are a great American. I know that you are. Let us drag ourselves from the noxious fumes of this poisoned house and breathe the free and clean air of true democracy again. Let us stand up and measure ourselves against each other, not against the size of our friends' bank accounts. Let us return democracy to the human scale, where it belongs.

Join us, Senator McConnell, in calling for the public funding of campaigns. Join us in demanding that broadcasters who use the public airwaves provide a public benefit at election time. Join us in ending corporate contributions to political campaigns, for corporations are not people, and democracy is.

Thank you all.

On Taking Responsibility

Clarksburg, West Virginia, January 3, 2000

Thank you.

It is a great pleasure to be here. Clarksburg is a beautiful community, and I know how you must love it. Your people have been here for over two centuries, surviving deep snows and wide floods, and you have watched your children grow and your friends grow old. You, yourselves are still looking fine, however.

I know about the magic of being from a good town, and loving it.

There is a stage play that I'm sure you know about, entitled *Our Town,* by Mr. Thornton Wilder. It is about life and death in a small New Hampshire town. More exactly, it is about all the beauty we miss because we are not fully awake to the brief magic of life. Mr. Wilder wrote the play while residing in the New Hampshire community where I live, and where my children have raised their children. We take his play as a correct description of the heartbreaking beauty of life in a caring community of decent people. The area is called Dublin and Peterborough, New Hampshire, just west of Manchester.

Now Mr. Wilder was careful not to start any arguments about where the real Our Town might be, and whether some of the characters might therefore have real counterparts. In the very beginning of the play, he cites the longitude and latitude of the town. If you go to a map, however, you will see that the coordinates he gives describe the middle of Massachusetts Bay, quite a ways out at sea. So, respecting his wishes, we do not claim to be the town of Our Town. We do, however, live and die as he described, and we understand the emotions that stirred within him as he wrote.

He wrote in an area of thirty-two little cabins set up for writers and artists by Edward and Marian MacDowell. At the MacDowell Colony, Mr. Wilder wrote his play, and America's great music composer, Aaron Copeland, wrote much of his masterwork, *Appalachian Spring.* Virgil Thomson wrote *Mother of Us All.* Leonard Bernstein completed his great symphonic *Mass.*

Other artists and writers have taken their turn working in those little cabins, including Edwin Arlington Robinson, Milton Avery, James

Baldwin, Willa Cather, Jules Feiffer, Studs Terkel, Alice Walker, and many others.

I spent most of my weekends for a half century at another such colony, called Dundee, several hours up the mountain, where we spent our leisure hours with great thinkers and artists, and where we prepared our big meal together each evening, and put on plays for each other in the theater built for just us and our children.

This all may be something of a revelation to many people who have grown up in big cities or towns under clouds of oppression. They may not have imagined that humans can form happy and creative communities—that they can make something of a heaven for themselves here on earth. It can be done. I have done it all my life, and I can see that you have, too.

For those not so fortunate, if they would like to find their way to a community of love and courtesy where the purpose of living is to reach one's full potential as a creative human being and help others do the same, I think you and I can give them some helpful advice.

There is a secret to the creation and nurturing of true community. Once people know the secret, they can create community anywhere they choose—any place they happen to find themselves.

The secret is to take the world as your own—and to take full responsibility for it. Once a person steps into the circle of those who take responsibility for the happy operation of the community—once someone decides that they are not a customer of government, but that they are government itself—the magic of community begins.

As long as we are breathing and thinking, and our hearts are beating, the world is ours to shape as we please, according to our values.

There are many people who would like us to believe that the world is theirs, not ours, so that they might steal our world from us—steal our lives from us. They would like us to be their little slaves, mindlessly working for their happiness at the expense of our own, and accepting all the evils of the world as somehow necessary. Nonsense!

If you want to know who has been hypnotized by this lie, look to the role people have adopted for themselves. If they accept the "them versus us" divide between the people and the government, they have bought into the lie that destroys democracy. The hypnotized need to wake up, and frankly, we need to wake each other up from that trance from time to time, don't we?

The violence in our society is a symptom of that hypnosis. A real citizen, a person who takes responsibility for the community, is not someone who returns poison with poison, rudeness with rudeness, violence with violence. When someone can return rudeness with concern, poison with understanding, violence with peace, they are not being ruled by others. They are free. The world is theirs, and it begins to turn their way, toward their higher values, because they are not giving rudeness what it needs to survive, nor violence what it needs to grow. They are spreading their consciousness over the large view, and taking responsibility for the workings of their community.

In our land, the rise of violence is held as a mystery. It is no mystery to me. It is what happens when people, young and old, no longer feel responsible for their communities. There is a great, and now global, corporate-political complex at work to strip people of their feelings of responsibility for their communities—of their connection with its needs.

In my long walk, I am trying to get some new laws passed that will make it easier for people to be responsible for their own communities and their own government. I worry that the influence of very rich companies and very rich people make it difficult for regular people to feel that they are in charge of their own affairs. We need to get the big, special interest contributions out of our elections. Those contributions shout down you and me, and there is no true free speech nor true political equality so long as this condition persists.

I would not be on this path if I did not believe that America is my responsibility; I am responsible for its happy workings, as are you.

Even in the very act of trying to help, I find my happiness and I find a creative community of people. In this way, we have already won.

In this generation, the fate of our natural environment, and of our democratic environment will be decided. Only great leadership, and great love, can get us through the times ahead. We must all take our part in this great drama. It is more than politics; it is a struggle of the soul, and it is exquisitely personal to each of us.

I have talked long enough for someone who is supposed to be out walking. But let me say that I take my little town with me. Our Town always travels with us, not even two steps down the path. The longitude and latitude of it cross upon our hearts. We bring the good community into being with our love and our relentless consciousness. We mustn't fail to appreciate the magical moment of life, and to fully participate in it joyfully and constructively—never giving an inch to injustice, unfairness, or inequality, nor ever forgetting the long line of people we have known and loved in the great circle that extends well into the next life.

Thank you for listening to me today, and thank you for your warm hospitality along a snowy road.

Don't Give Up the Ship

Cumberland, Maryland, on Her Ninetieth Birthday, January 24, 2000

Thank you all very much indeed. What a wonderful birthday this is, here in the exquisite setting of historic Cumberland. It is such a treat to be in a place so much older than myself.

President Washington, I have learned, was here in 1794 to review the federal troops sent here to discourage a little rebellion called the Whiskey Insurrection—a disagreement over the advisability of a tax on distilled spirits, levied by the rather new federal government.

President Washington noted this in his diary:

> After an early breakfast we set out for Cumberland—and about 11 o'clock arrived there. . . . I passed along the line of the Army; & was conducted to a house, the residence of Major Lynn of the Maryland line . . . where I was well lodged, & civilly entertained.

Well, I know how he felt.

That residence, by the way, is just over there, across the way. You see how the past is cherished and respected in Cumberland.

If we cherish these buildings, how much more must we cherish and respect the institutions that provide, after long and bloody years of defense, our freedoms as a self-governing people. I am headed to a city where those institutions are being sold for scrap—a place far downhill from here.

But before we depart from this place, let us look around at the beauty of America. Let us look at a town where there is no other way for public servants to be except honorable. If a mayor or constable or executive of such a town as this should sell out the interests of his townspeople for the sake of a campaign contribution, a career would be over and shame would come to a family. This is the real America. Down the hill is another America, where there is no shame, and where the buying and selling of America's interests are not called bribery, though that is what they are, and where the stealing of real power away from what we founded as a government of, by, and for the people is not called a coup or a treason, though that is what it oozes toward.

So we Americans stand here no longer concerned about the tax on our whiskey. We can bear that; we can drink to that. But we cannot bear the greater damage that is being done to us by far more intoxicating poisons: power, money, and prestige—distractions that blind the vision and poison the souls of those within the Beltway in an epidemic of disdain for the American people, whom they take as a mere market for their political products.

A flood of special interest money has carried away our own representatives, and all that is left of them—at least for those of us who do not write $100,000 checks—are the shadows of their cardboard cutouts. If you doubt it, write a letter to them and see what rubber stamp drivel you get back. For all we know, they might all have died ten years ago and the same letters continue to be sent out.

Now, standing here on the back of this charming caboose, why would I spoil my own birthday party with a bunch of politics? Well, because I love politics and this is my party.

I love it to death and I shall love it to unto death. It was the dinner table meat and potatoes of my wonderful, sixty-two-year marriage. It is what we talk about on Tuesdays in my little town, at a thing we call the Tuesday Morning Academy. It is what self-governing Americans must hold in steady fascination and endless conversation if we are to be free.

My husband, Jim, died several years ago after a ten-year struggle. At the end, he said that he was ready to go and that he did not want any more food or water. It took him eleven days and nights before he was successful. My son, Jim, and my grandson Raphael, sat with him at night, and I held his hand during the eleven heartbreaking days. After ten years of caregiving, it is difficult for an old wife to adjust, especially when the mate was such a sparkler—such a person of light and life and red-blooded activism. He was fun. And how do you wake up each morning in a world where the fellow you would run to with a new thought to share is nowhere to be found? Where he does not answer your call through the house?

My dear friend Elizabeth died too, shortly after Jim, and also after a long period that did wear me out.

I am not trying to make anyone feel sorry for what happens in a long life. All things end. But I want to say something important about it, and that is why I bring it up. I stand here on the tail end of a caboose. And so it was when Jim and Elizabeth were gone. Life seemed very much over—all the picnics, all the hikes, all the frosty ski trips. I was deeply depressed, and I know that many people today are in that same place. And what I want to say to them, and to all of you to remember for that day ahead when you think you are standing at the end of your life, is, damn it, don't give up the ship.

I know I am mixing my transportation metaphors with trains and ships, but it is my ninetieth birthday and I have just walked a bit over three thousand miles and I shall mix metaphors all day long if I please.

For those of you who have lived a long life and think your are finished with it, I tell you that, if you will pray for courage and look to the needs of your community rather than yourself, a great energy and happiness will come to you. Indeed, your community needs your wisdom and your patience. Your family needs you, too, whether or not they believe it. Your country needs you.

Friends, look at this country—our genius republic—this great sailing vessel we have built that we might find our way to the future together as free and equal citizens, as friends and partners in self-governance. Though it is two and a quarter centuries old, the paint still smells new some days, and the flag still snaps in the wind. But what a price we have paid for it! I do not have to remind you of the rows upon rows of marble stones that mark the sacrifices our friends and our children and our fathers and their fathers have made to build this great craft and keep it safe.

But now, in a time when people are so stressed in their lives and are so unaware of what it means to truly live well—to live free, to live with enough leisure and confidence to be the stewards of their own lives and communities—in this time, we strangely find ourselves having to explain why it is a bad thing if multinational corporations control our elections, and why it is a bad thing if our elected leaders no longer represent the interests of the people.

I know that some of these people just need to be awakened. We can do that. We can show them a future they will want. But there are others who know very well what has been lost in this nation over the last few decades, and they have lowered their fists slowly in despair. To them, to my generation and the generation younger and the generation older, I cry to you, please—don't give up the ship! . . .

Thank you for helping me celebrate one of the great days of my life—I know that many of you have come a very long way. Let's adjourn to make our plans for Washington, and have some cake together.

Self-interest Shall Be Cast into Oblivion

At Several Maryland Colleges, February 2000

Thank you.

I am honored to speak to you all today. . . .

I am walking for the issue of campaign finance reform. I speak wherever I go of the need to remove from our elections all money that has unhealthy strings attached. We are a wealthy nation, and we don't need to let our elections and our leaders be sold at auction. The right things for us to do, I believe, includes the outlawing of what is called soft money contributions. . . .

After we close the loophole, I believe we need to take the next step and enact programs to provide public funds to candidates who agree to do no other fund-raising. . . .

There. Now you know what my big issues are. I don't know what your big issues are, but let me tell you that if you are interested in any big thing—from the environment to human rights, farming, business, health policy, science policy—you will sooner or later have to knock on the door of Congress if you are to go very far with it. If you want that doorway to be open, you had better help me first to get that fat cat out of the way, because right now he will not let you in.

Today, your senators and representatives have no time for you, nor interest in your ideas—unless you walk in with a $10,000 check. We simply cannot afford, as a people or as a planet, to let that condition persist.

I do hope you have a vision of your own life that includes a great deal of political involvement in the big issues of our day. We are a free people, and we each have a responsibility to understand and work and provide leadership in important areas. Don't forget that you stand on the same ground as Tom Jefferson, Frederick Douglass, Cesar Chavez, Tecumseh, Susan Anthony, and so many others who cared about the life and freedom of future generations—and that is you.

How long do you think democratic government has been the sacred tradition of the soil that you tread every day—on your way to class, on your way to free meetings, on your way to church services, on your way to wherever you freely choose to go?

You may think I began at the beginning when I listed Tom Jefferson, but Tom and you and I are latecomers to this land of democracy.

The Iroquois Constitution, the memorized document that ruled this very soil hundreds of years before the rest of the world arrived, was the very model of fairness and balance that helped inspire Jefferson and his contemporaries. . . .

We would do well to install our new senators and representatives in the same way that we Americans did when we were the Five Nations. Here is a part of the ceremony, addressed to any new representative arriving at council:

> Your heart shall be filled with peace and good will and your mind filled with a yearning for the welfare of the people. With endless patience you shall carry out your duty, and your firmness shall be tempered with tenderness for your people. Neither anger nor fury shall find lodgement in your mind, and all your words and actions shall be marked with calm deliberation. In all of your deliberations in Council, and in your efforts at law making, in all your official acts, self-interest shall be cast into oblivion.

In all your official acts, self-interest shall be cast into oblivion.

Their rule of law broke down from the pressures of change from abroad, as we know. They were cast into warfare and anarchy. We must ask ourselves: Is our modern rule of law breaking down? I can show you very fine laws against bribery that sit high and dry as an incredible flood of influence-buying money sweeps away our democratic representation and our history as a free people.

Let us remember who we are. Let us remember that a good government can fall away unless we forever give ourselves to its defense, and unless, in all our official acts, we cast self-interest forever into oblivion. Our planet and the people of the world now depend very much on our ability to keep control of our government and rule it with the hand of love and reason, and not greed and profit.

Let me say finally that you are being raised in a culture that ever tries to trivialize your life. Your life is not trivial. It is not designer labeled. It is not on-line or virtual. It is real. You are a free man or woman in a land of free people who have served each other with dignity and sacrifice for many centuries. Do your duty to those who came before you. Do your duty to your own freedom and to the freedom of Americans to come. Cast your self-interest into oblivion and see, through the progress of the soul, what a magical world this is!

Thank you.

An Overscaled Monster

Reform Party Convention, Long Beach, CA, August 8, 2000
(excerpt)

There is an interesting difference in the two main branches of the American populist reform community today. They agree that an over-scaled monster is stalking the land and ruining our lives. But if you set them down with a police sketch artist and ask them to describe the giant, half will describe multinational corporations, and the other half will describe government itself. This division goes back to FDR's administration, when people began to be concerned with the size and power of government.

While the anti-government populists and the anti-corporation progressives are on a long-term collision course, they can today agree on a common enemy: the control and expansion of government as a direct result of corporate campaign donations. If they can join hands just long enough to force corporate money out of politics, they will have a democracy to fight over again, and they can debate the proper role of government in our lives.

But for now, both sides of the reform community are dead in the water, because corporations in fact have bought the key institutions of government.

In my walk across America, I spoke against this involvement of corporate money in politics. I shall continue to do so until we repair the problem. I see no reason why I should not live long enough to see the day when corporations are once again prohibited from making any kind of political contribution. That prohibition was put in place by Theodore Roosevelt in 1907, and it has eroded, simply because he was not here to prevent it. Nor was any other leader of sufficient mettle. So we shall have to repair it somehow ourselves, in the streets.

To Live with Our Hearts Wide Open

A New England High School Graduation, June 2000

Thank you.

I am honored to talk to you all today. I know you have worked hard to get to this moment, and I admire you for that. Life is so much more complex and fast-moving than when I went to school, and things were already hard enough back then.

I would like to try to give you something of value in my brief remarks today—some piece of useful knowledge that perhaps you weren't taught in school or at home, something that perhaps is easier to hear from someone who has lived a long time.

It is the simple fact that the world as it was back when I was your age is still with us, and you live in that world, too. And the world of several hundred years ago is also still with us, as is the world of the misty, prehistoric past. We live in a many-layered world, and we are many-layered people. Each era of our history makes a contribution to the way we live our lives, and each era imposes expectations upon us to this day. Unless we understand that fact, we will have a hard time navigating through the conflicting rules and expectations of life. Think of life as a seven-layer cake and you will do all right.

As an example, I have often overheard young men arguing about how difficult women are to deal with. Are men supposed to open a door for a woman or not, pick up a check at a restaurant or not? Aren't they supposed to now treat a woman as a total equal? They are confused because they don't understand that a person is not one thing. A person is many layered. There is certainly a very old layer where women are princesses and men are princes, and that layer needs to be acknowledged sometimes when the moment is right and a carriage door needs opening. That layer is still with us and it glows under the moon. There is also a modern workplace layer, where men and women are colleagues or employees and where they treat each other in a businesslike way, without reference to gender, and where it is a great sin to open a door for someone instead of an equal opportunity.

And there is, of course, an ancient, biological layer that compels a man to aggressively seek mates and compels a woman to find the resources for a safe and respectable nest. This is just one layer, but it must be acknowledged and given its due. Because it is one of the oldest layers, it is the first one you come across as you approach maturity. Though you may not believe me, there is more to life than that layer.

There are also layers from our own childhood, still there intact, demanding comfort and security and the freedom to creatively explore.

So you must look at a person and see all of this, if you are to see truly—which is to say, wisely.

When we make snap judgments about people, based on some single quality, we dehumanize them, and that is a great crime. I know you have probably had the experience of being in the same activity with someone and getting to know them, even though you never might have talked to that person on your own. But you became good friends or at least you came to respect each other. That happened because you got down a few layers with that person.

Most people are worth knowing, if you will take time to understand them. Unfamiliarity with other people, ignorance of other people, is what makes war possible and violence possible, and it drives all the social divisions in a school or in a town or a nation or a world. When you understand people well enough, you can't help but love them, even if you hate them, too. If you think those are incompatible emotions, I remind you to think about your relationship with almost any close family member.

Understanding people is indeed loving them. If you hate them and if your hate is not balanced by some love for them, it is a sign of your ignorance, for you simply do not understand them well enough yet. Hatred is what we feel when we do not understand.

Are there some people so over the top with their evil deeds that they do not qualify for this sweeping statement? Some people may take more understanding than we are capable of possessing. We must accept our own limitations.

One of the most difficult and important tasks we have as humans is to regularly, and sometimes without cause, forgive each other and move ahead with our lives together. If one layer of someone's personality flares up and causes us harm, we must try to put it in perspective among all the other layers of a life.

A long marriage requires the willingness to do that, time and again. No relationship can long survive on the basis of what happens in just one or just a few of those layers. Understanding and forgiveness requires a view of the whole person.

That whole view can also help us to forgive ourselves. It is a great act of maturity, I think, to not condemn yourself or define yourself by what goes on within just one of these different layers, some of which are intensely biological or set down in cement in early youth. Sometimes we are given to suddenly see with great clarity an amoral and reptilian side of our own motivations, but it is wrong to think we have suddenly discovered our real self. That one layer is no more important than the layers of loving kindness, so long as the negative layer is not given free rein.

Emotional maturity is the ability to stay balanced, not letting any one layer dominate our lives. I do not mean that we should fiercely suppress the darker layers, for to do so causes us to transfer our fear and loathing onto other people. But we must give every layer an opportunity to go for its walk at a time when it will do no harm. And our more positive layers we must encourage and put in the company of like souls, for the most important thing we can do for ourselves is to surround ourselves with people we respect for the best reasons—we simply cannot help but become like the people around us.

After acknowledging and coming to understand the layers of life, a gentleman may finally come to know when to open the door for a lady and when to share a check. A woman may come to know that a fellow is more than the polygamous forest creature he sometimes seems—he is also the artist and the prince, the poet and the friend. It is not easy to negotiate through all the layers laid down through the eons of evolution and the rise of civilization. But if life were easy, it would be a bore. Life is that seven-layer cake, and so are our hearts.

It has a layer of icing, by the way; it is not youth or old age or victory or wealth, but a smiling measure of enlightenment and love that comes as we live with our eyes and our minds and our hearts wide open.

I wish you a happy life. I hope you have a high opinion of yourself, and that you will understand that you are worth the trouble you have invested in yourself so far, and that you are worth a continuing investment in a future that begins always at this moment.

I hope you will look to the people around you—in your family and your community, and your nation and the world—with an open heart and an active curiosity so that you may not condemn but better understand them, and so that your understanding may mature into love.

Thank you very much.

About the Authors

DORIS HADDOCK is a retired shoe-factory worker and great-grandmother of twelve. She lives in Dublin, New Hampshire.

DENNIS BURKE is a writer and government-reform activist who helped Doris Haddock through the deserts of the Southwest. During their time together he agreed to craft her nightly road journals into a narrative. This is his first book.